Land, Indigenous Peoples and Conflict

Land, Indigenous Peoples and Conflict presents an original comparative study of indigenous land and property rights worldwide. The book explores how the ongoing constitutional, legal and political integration of indigenous peoples into contemporary society has impacted on indigenous institutions and structures for managing land and property. This book details some of the common problems experienced by indigenous peoples throughout the world, providing lessons and insights from conflict resolution that may find application in other conflicts, including inter-state and civil and sectarian conflicts.

An interdisciplinary group of contributors present specific case material from indigenous land conflicts from the South Pacific, Australasia, South East Asia, Africa, North and South America, and northern Eurasia. These regional cases discuss issues such as modernization, the evolution of systems and institutions regulating land use, access and management, and the resolution of indigenous land conflicts, drawing out common problems and solutions. The lessons learnt from the book will be of value to students, researchers, legal professionals and policy makers with an interest in land and property rights worldwide.

Alan C. Tidwell is Director of the Center for Australian, New Zealand and Pacific Studies in the Edmund A. Walsh School of Foreign Service at George-town University.

Barry Scott Zellen is a research scholar, editor and author specializing in Arctic, indigenous and strategic issues.

Routledge Complex Real Property Rights Series

Series editor: Professor Spike Boydell

University of Technology, Sydney, Australia

Real Property Rights are central to the global economy and provide a legal framework for how society (be it developed or customary) relates to land and buildings. We need to better understand property rights to ensure sustainable societies, careful use of limited resources and sound ecological stewardship of our land and water. Contemporary property rights theory is dynamic and needs to engage thinkers who are prepared to think outside their disciplinary limitations.

The Routledge Complex Real Property Rights Series strives to take a transdisciplinary approach to understanding property rights and specifically encourages heterodox thinking. Through rich international case studies our goal is to build models to connect theory to observed reality, allowing us to inform potential policy outcomes. This series is both an ideal forum and reference for students and scholars of property rights and land issues.

Land, Indigenous Peoples and Conflict
Edited by Alan C. Tidwell and Barry Scott Zellen

Beyond Communal and Individual Ownership
Indigenous land reform in Australia
Leon Terrill

Land, Indigenous Peoples and Conflict

Edited by Alan C. Tidwell
and Barry Scott Zellen

Routledge
Taylor & Francis Group

LONDON AND NEW YORK

First published 2016
by Routledge

2 Park Square, Milton Park, Abingdon, Oxon OX14 4RN
711 Third Avenue, New York, NY 10017, USA

Routledge is an imprint of the Taylor & Francis Group, an informa business

First issued in paperback 2017

British Library Cataloguing-in-Publication Data
A catalogue record for this book is available from the British Library

Library of Congress Cataloging in Publication Data
Land, indigenous peoples and conflict / edited by Alan Tidwell and
Barry Zellen.
pages cm. — (Routledge complex real property rights series)
Includes bibliographical references and index.
1. Indigenous peoples—Civil rights. 2. Indigenous peoples—Government
relations. 3. Indigenous peoples—Legal status, laws, etc. I. Tidwell, Alan,
1958- editor. II. Zellen, Barry Scott, 1963- editor.
JZ4974.L36 2015
333.2—dc23
2015014366

ISBN: 978-1-138-84763-7 (hbk)
ISBN: 978-1-138-09293-8 (pbk)

Typeset in Sabon
by FiSH Books Ltd.

Contents

Illustrations

Figures

Contributors

Saleem H. Ali, PhD, is the Director of the Centre for Social Responsibility in Mining and Affiliate Professor of Politics and International Relations at the University of Queensland, Australia. His areas of interest include environmental sustainability and conflict resolution.

Arnon Ben-Israel, PhD, is a cultural-humanistic Geographer. His research deals with human/space relationships as articulated by peripheral population's sense of place, landscape interpretations, art and education. He is also Head of Geography Specialization, Kaye Academic College of Education, Beer Sheva, Israel.

Spike Boydell, PhD, is Professor and Director of the University of Technology Sydney's Asia-Pacific Centre for Complex Real Property Rights. His research interests include customary land rights and resource compensation on customary land.

Marjorie Mandelstam Balzer, PhD, Research Professor in the Center for East European and Russian Studies (CERES) and the Department of Anthropology at Georgetown University, has research interests in social theory, inter-ethnic relations, religion, the dynamics of nationalism, and the anthropology of the Russian Federation.

Ken Coates, PhD, is a Professor and Canada Research Chair in Regional Innovation in the Johnson-Shoyama Graduate School of Public Policy. He is also the Macdonald-Laurier Institute's Senior Policy Fellow in Aboriginal and Northern Canadian Issues.

Cheryl Duckworth, PhD, is an Associate Professor of Conflict Resolution at Nova Southeastern University. She is the author of *Land and Dignity in Paraguay* and co-editor of *Conflict Resolution and the Scholarship of Engagement.*

Carl Grundy-Warr, PhD, is a Senior Lecturer in the Department of Geography at the National University of Singapore. He serves on the Editorial Board of the *Singapore Journal of Tropical Geography*, *Journal of Indian Ocean Research* and the International Advisory Board of *Geography Compass*.

Julia Keenan is a PhD candidate in the Center for Social Responsibility in Mining at the University of Queensland, specializing on agreement-making with Indigenous Peoples.

Darren Kew, PhD, is Associate Professor and Chair, Department of Conflict Resolution, Human Security, and Global Governance at the University of Massachusetts, Boston.

Abra Lyman, Esq., is an indigenous Rights Attorney in the Washington, DC area, and has worked on land rights issues in Kenya, Botswana, South Africa, and Mexico. She received her JD/MA in International Law from American University, and an LLM from the Indigenous Peoples Law and Policy Program at the University of Arizona.

Avinoam Meir, PhD, is a Professor in the Department of Geography and Environmental Development, Ben-Gurion University of the Negev, Israel. His research focuses on pastoral nomads and indigenous peoples, the Bedouin in Israel, environmental ethics, and spatial processes.

Greg Poelzer, PhD, is Executive Chair at the International Centre for Northern Governance and Development, as well as an Associate Professor of Political Studies and an Associate Member of the schools of Public Policy and Environment and Sustainability (University of Saskatchewan).

Batya Roded holds a PhD in geography from Ben-Gurion University of the Negev, Israel. She specializes in political, social and cultural geography, studying ethnic frontiers and indigenous peoples in comparative perspective, grey cities and urban informality, and frontier towns within power relations at the global, national and the local levels.

Mak Sithirith, PhD, is a Lecturer and Researcher at the Department of Natural Resource Management and Development, Faculty of Development Studies, Royal University of Phnom Penh. His research interests are in resource politics, environmental geography and water governance.

Alan C. Tidwell, PhD, is Professor and Director of the Center for Australian, New Zealand and Pacific Studies in the Edmund A. Walsh School of Foreign Service at Georgetown University. His research interests include extractive industries, conflict resolution and land rights.

Jon Unruh, PhD, is an Associate Professor in the Department of Geography at McGill University. His area of research includes post-war land tenure and migration.

Debra Wilson, PhD, is a Senior Lecturer in the School of Law at Canterbury University in Christchurch, New Zealand. Her areas of interest include law and medicine, competition law and intellectual property.

Barry Scott Zellen, PhD, is a Research Scholar, Editor and Author specializing in Arctic, indigenous and strategic issues. He is the author of numerous books on the Arctic including *Breaking the Ice: From Land Claims to Tribal Sovereignty in the Arctic*.

Foreword

Real Property Rights are central to the economy and provide a legal framework for how society – be it developed or customary – relates to land and buildings. Property rights are both institutional arrangements and social relations. We need to better understand property rights to ensure sustainable societies, careful use of limited resources and sound ecological stewardship of our land and water.

Land conflict is all around us – from corporate and political corruption over land dealings in the developed world, to land grabs in developing countries, to compromised indigenous property rights, to resource exploitation. At a time where global food security, water security and shelter are paramount, an understanding of property rights is key to sustainability.

Contemporary property rights theory is dynamic and this series strives to engage thinkers who are prepared to step beyond their disciplinary limitations. 'Property Rights' is a broad term that is fundamentally about social relations. Real property rights, obligations and restrictions can be found in and change across the full range of human societies, both in time and space. Property rights research has emerged from a broad range of disciplines including (but not limited to) archaeology, anthropology, ethics, sociology, psychology, law, geography, history, philosophy, economics, planning, and business studies.

Much writing on property rights has, historically, been mono-disciplinary. A disciplinary approach has caused a plurality of understanding about property rights that extends significantly beyond the dominant legal/economic divide. Disciplinary thinking has not minimised or helped to manage/limit land conflict. What makes this series special is that it facilitates a transdisciplinary approach to understanding property rights and will specifically encourage heterodox thinking.

Land, Indigenous Peoples and Conflict is the appropriate title with which to launch the Routledge Complex Real Property Rights series. As the editors of this volume, Alan Tidwell and Barry Scott Zellen have brought together an eclectic collection of expert authors who mutually share a depth of insight into contemporary conflicts over indigenous land.

Land, Indigenous Peoples and Conflict has several distinguishing features. Primarily, it is transdisciplinary in nature. Any discussion of the link between land, indigenous peoples, and conflict necessarily requires drawing on ideas, concepts and principles from such disparate disciplines as cultural anthropology, political science, sociology, and economics, just to name a few. Taking a transdisciplinary approach helps the authors connect theory to observed reality, which in turn gives traction to inform potential policy outcomes.

A second distinguishing feature of *Land, Indigenous Peoples and Conflict* concerns the geographic breadth of coverage of the volume, spanning from the Arctic to the tropics and including mainland Asia as well as the Austro-Pacific islands; both North and South America; northern Eurasia (Siberia), as well as Africa. Touching upon a geographically broad range enables readers to become more generally acquainted with the diverse property rights challenges indigenous peoples face. A third distinguishing feature of *Land, Indigenous Peoples and Conflict* is its emphasis on both land rights as well as identifying the many ways in which conflicts between indigenous peoples and the state are managed or resolved. Uniquely, *Land, Indigenous Peoples and Conflict* provides a breadth and depth to the question of indigenous land conflict not found in other texts.

Spike Boydell, Series Editor
Sydney, Australia
February 2015

Introduction

Alan C. Tidwell and Barry Scott Zellen

Land, Indigenous Peoples and Conflict grows out of our earlier work analyzing indigenous rights, and blending our regions of expertise, the Australia-New Zealand-Pacific region and the Circumpolar Arctic region. For several years, starting as far back as 2008, the editors have corresponded and discussed the merits of a volume that canvassed the comparative experiences of indigenous peoples around the globe. Of particular interest was the intersection of land, indigenous peoples and conflict. From location to location around the globe, persistent patterns emerge showing indigenous peoples engaged in a continuing struggle with the state over access to land rights. All too often those struggles have erupted into sharp social conflict and all too frequently into violence, but in several regions, notably the Arctic, great gains have been made in indigenous land rights resulting in a noted de-escalation of conflict resulting in a new model of sovereignty with the state partnering with its indigenous peoples with the result being a new form of collaborative sovereignty resulting in historic transfers of land title, financial wealth, and political powers (at the local and regional level) benefiting the indigenous peoples. While there were general trends that could be observed, there equally existed a particularity to the indigenous experiences that varied from region to region, with some cases providing much hope and inspiration, and others restraining that hope with more cautionary lessons. In different locations, indigenous peoples have made varying gains, and this volume aims to explore this variance, and to derive insights from it. In examining this interplay between land, indigenous peoples and the state much can be learned that gives greater insight into these gains and their asymmetries as we circle the globe.

Indigenous peoples have struggled to retain their identity and independence since the emergence of the modern nation state. Between disease, dispossession and warfare protecting and maintaining identity has been an existential struggle. Increasingly the state has come to dominate the allocation of resources, as well as access to political rights. In an effort to overcome political marginalization indigenous peoples have sought to negotiate over the allocation of political and property rights. The venue of that negotiation may shift from street protests to the campaign trail to the courthouse but make no mistake, it is a negotiation. Negotiation or interdependent decision-making is required because the state claims a monopoly on the allocation of rights and the means for resolving interest-based and rights-based disputes. Indigenous peoples find themselves having to negotiate with the state over negotiation itself. These meta-negotiations, negotiations about negotiation, concern the 'Who', 'What', 'When', 'Where', 'Why' and 'How' of interdependent decision-making.

As evident in this diverse sweep of chapters, which follow in sequence to a large degree a voyage of circumnavigation, starting in the north and traversing the Pacific Rim from Siberia through Alaska, Canada, and Latin America, across the Pacific to Asia and from there to Africa and the Middle East, this volume brings together experts from around the globe on indigenous land rights and state-tribe conflict, with the goal of sharing our collective expertise and to stimulate comparative insights of indigenous land conflicts with the state, and the historical evolution of indigenous institutions for managing land and property disputes into the contemporary era, with new and emerging structures and institutions being formed to foster the ongoing constitutional, economic, legal and political integration of indigenous peoples into contemporary societies. It presents specific case material from indigenous land conflicts worldwide, including the South Pacific, Australasia, mainland Southeast Asia, Africa, North and South America, and northern Eurasia. It touches upon broad themes of traditional and contemporary indigenous property rights; the evolution from traditional to modern land use, access and management in indigenous homelands; indigenous identity and changing values relating to land and property rights, and their modernization; and land and resource conflict between indigenous peoples and their non-indigenous neighbors and with the modern states which now assert sovereignty over their homelands. We focus on distinct geographical and ethno-cultural regions, with our contributing authors commenting on how their specific regional cases can provide us with insights into the broader problems experienced by indigenous peoples throughout the world as they confront the challenges and embrace the opportunities associated with the modernization of their property rights, and the evolution of indigenous systems and institutions regulating land use, access and management, as well as lessons and insights from the resolution of indigenous land and property conflicts that may find broader application to other conflicts worldwide including inter-state as well as intra-state civil and sectarian conflicts.

Land, Indigenous Peoples and Conflict is an interdisciplinary enterprise in nature, drawing upon ideas, concepts and principles from such disparate disciplines as cultural anthropology, political science, sociology, and economics, just to name a few – providing context for understanding both the historical roots of indigenous land issues as well as the modernization of indigenous institutions relating to property rights. Its presenters focus upon both indigenous land rights as well as the many ways in which land and property conflicts faced by indigenous peoples are managed and resolved.

Uniquely, they provide a breadth and depth to the question of indigenous land and property rights and conflicts not found in other texts.

In Chapter 1, 'Indigeneity, Land and Activism in Siberia', Marjorie Mandelstam Balzer examines the diverse levels and dynamics of indigenous politics in Siberia. Adapting anthropological concepts of 'indigenous cosmopolitans', urban activists and indigenous people living on 'traditional lands' are compared. She argues that the most effective urban indigenous leaders are those whose lives are deeply intertwined with their original homelands. Of course, socio-political conditions make some groups more successful than others in defending their social, ecological and cultural interests. Recent legal constraints on the definition of indigeneity in the Russian Federation are reviewed before discussion of how and why indigenous people have been driven to urban environments, for 'push' (forced migration) as well as 'pull' (urban attraction) reasons. She then turns to the Sakha Republic (Yakutia) in the Far East, a relatively positive case where the author has done fieldwork since 1986. Her analysis focuses on strains of ethnic interaction and contestation created by development, rather than on 'urbanization' alone. Implications for civil society in the 'Federation of Rossiia' are also discussed.

In Chapter 2, 'From Counter-Mapping to Co-Management: The Inuit, the State and the Quest for Collaborative Arctic Sovereignty', co-editor Barry Scott Zellen examines the empowerment of the Inuit of the North American Arctic through the land claims process, and how with formal land settlements from Alaska to Labrador, the Inuit now possess a wide range of officially-recognized and constitutionally-entrenched powers offering them new and historically unprecedented controls over their traditional homelands, with substantial authority to regulate land access and development, to maximize environmental protection, and to protect traditional values and practices including subsistence hunting, fishing and trapping. In addition, the Inuit are now among the largest private land owners in North America, with fee-simple title to millions of acres of resource-rich coastal land as well as limited control over adjacent lands, and their emergence as major land owners has contributed to their enrichment and empowerment. Having asserted extensive claims to much of the Arctic and successfully negotiated their claims with governments in Alaska and Canada, the Inuit now play an important role in the region's evolution and development, rivaling the powers of the modern state in regional importance, and influencing the goals and objectives of state policy over arctic lands, waters and resources. Their gains extend across such a vast domain that while not formally sovereign, the consent and collaboration of the Inuit has become essential for the successful assertion of sovereignty by the state over their homeland.

In Chapter 3, 'Re-Imagining Indigenous Space: The Law, Constitution and the Evolution of Aboriginal Property and Resource Rights in Canada', Ken Coates and Greg Poelzer examine the growing international importance of constitutional provisions and legal processes that indigenous peoples often view as 'the last cannon shot' in their defense of resource rights and interests.

This 'shot' represents the efforts of indigenous populations to use constitutional protection and recourse to the courts to carve out indigenous space within nation-states, thus ensuring themselves the land, resources, and political power necessary to survive in a globalized, multi-cultural world. Where colonial domination once suppressed indigenous rights, courts and legislative actions are now gradually restoring them. Over the past 20 years, Aboriginal people have secured new political and legal powers related to natural resource development. To a degree that few realize, most First Nations and Inuit groups have used these powers to carve out a more extensive and beneficial role for themselves within the natural resource sector. They have used Aboriginal rights to gain influence over approval processes, ensure greater financial and other returns for their communities and provide themselves with a much greater role in environmental assessment, monitoring and reclamation. In short, Aboriginal peoples have not used their rights to stop development – often the sole substantial economic opportunity in their territory – but rather to ensure that it proceeds in a manner consistent with Indigenous values and priorities. In the process, Aboriginal Canadians are revolutionizing the very foundations of the natural resource economy and providing new prospects for economic and political empowerment.

Situation and context challenge political leaders, even when those leaders advocate indigenous interests and rights. In Chapter 4, 'President Lugo and the Indigenous Communities of Paraguay', Cheryl Duckworth considers Paraguayan President Fernando Lugo. Elected in 2008, he was the first opposition party candidate to win the highest office in generations. Even more, significantly, he was elected on a platform of anti-corruption, human rights and economic justice. The indigenous communities of Paraguay featured prominently in his campaigning; they are among the poorest of Paraguay's poor and commonly suffer from hunger and illness related to being displaced from their lands. His accomplishments for indigenous interests and rights have been constrained by others. His ousting returned to power Partido Colorado, the party of Stroessner who for generations oppressed them. How have indigenous communities been responding? With what impact? Have they been able to hold on to gains such as the return of some lands or increased representation of their culture in schooling? This chapter will address those questions.

Indigenous peoples often form alliances with others in an effort to leverage their capacity to negotiate better outcomes. In Chapter 5, 'Awkward Alliances: Is environmentalism a bonding agent between indigenous and rural settler politics in America and Australia?' by Saleem H. Ali and Julia Keenan examine the development of large extractive industries projects has led to alliances between indigenous groups and non-indigenous ranchers – groups which had previously not shared much in common. Their focus on the Keystone XL pipeline in North America and the Coal-Seam-Gas industry development in Queensland Australia probes the resilience of such alliances. The ultimate question, of course, is whether indigenous people gain more secure and long lasting alliances, or whether the exigencies of politics make such alliances short lived. In choosing two specific recent cases of extractive development which have seen a parallel level of indigenous and environmental activism; the authors show that environmental organizations have the potential for providing some measure of knowledge-based connectivity between indigenous and rural-based settler politics in Australia and North America.

While not having the weight of law tribunals can deliver useful and important decisions that help guide property right outcomes. In Chapter 6, 'Satisfying Honour? The Role of the Waitangi Tribunal in Addressing Land-Related Treaty Grievances in New Zealand', Debra Wilson considers the development of the Waitangi Tribunal in addressing Maori grievances. The Treaty of Waitangi was only recognized in the last 30 years as New Zealand's founding document. From its signing in 1840 until the mid-1980s, the Treaty was considered a 'legal nullity' and the promises made to the indigenous Maori people under its Articles largely ignored. As a result, the Maori people were deprived of the majority of their land (and the rights associated with that land) in a manner that was, in most cases, less than equitable. In 1974 the Treaty of Waitangi Bill established the Waitangi Tribunal, and the process of addressing the increasing conflict between the Maori people and the New Zealand Government began.

For some, mention of the South Pacific conjures dreams of idyllic palm strewn beaches and perfect holidays. For others, media images perhaps portray the recent tsunami in Samoa or reminders of coup d'état and political instability in countries like Fiji, Papua New Guinea, Vanuatu and the Solomon Islands. For many, there are perceptions that the prevailing land tenure traditions impact on, and prejudice, business ventures in the South Pacific. In Chapter 7, 'The "Pacific Way": Customary Land Use, Indigenous Values and Globalization in the South Pacific', Spike Boydell challenges this reductionist perception and explains the customary nature of land ownership and control in the Pacific, while acknowledged and respected, does not prevent the optimum use of the land for development (in its many forms). Influences of globalism and modernity are placing greater emphasis on individual economic wealth accumulation and related pressures to derive economic benefits from customary land. This westernization means that at times decisions are made for personal gain rather than in the best interest of the land-owning group as a whole. There is a recognized clash between indigenous values and capitalism; some commentators see this clash as an impediment to business development within the region. However, despite the influences of individualism, most indigenous people see their relationships as coming from the land rather than using it as a commodity.

The Tonle Sap Lake in the interior of Cambodia is a hotly contested space marked by complex issues of resource governance, in particular the political-spatial complexity of the lake and floodplain in addition to institutional arrangements relating to resource governance. In Chapter 8, 'Threats and

Challenges to the 'Floating Lives' of the Tonle Sap', Carl Grundy-Warr and Mak Sithirith explain that to understand the current challenges confronting indigenous people of the Tonle Sap and river systems requires understanding their central place within 'the pulsing heart' of Cambodia and the Mekong Basin as a whole, which is a hotspot for biodiversity, inland fisheries, and unique 'floating communities'. The biggest challenges to human and ecological security for the indigenous river- and water-based people, they find, are primarily exogenous ones relating to long-term land-cover change, water diversions, hydropower dam developments, and climate change that are likely to impact upon the duration, timing and reliability of wet and dry seasons and the regulatory flood-pulse of the Mekong Basin.

Like many countries in Africa, land dispossession of indigenous peoples in Kenya began in the colonial era, but was expanded upon by post-independence governments seeking to solidify their national sovereignty and a state-based model of economic development. Indigenous attempts to seek redress through legal or political means have been systematically stymied by the state, until recently. After the inter-ethnic violence of the 2007 presidential elections, which was largely rooted in land disputes, Kenya adopted a new constitution, its first national land policy, and a series of land laws that provide a solid legal foundation through which indigenous rights could potentially be recognized and protected for the first time in the region. In Chapter 9, 'Long Road to Justice: Addressing Indigenous Land Claims in Kenya', Darren Kew and Abra Lyman examine Maasai and Ogiek case studies to illustrate how the conflict over land has persisted throughout Kenyan history, discuss how the national and regional legal landscapes have changed over the past five years, and consider how this and similar conflicts across the region might thus be resolved in the future.

In Chapter 10, 'Indigenous Land Rights and Conflict in Darfur: The Case of the Fur Tribe', Jon Unruh examines the land rights of the Fur indigenous group in Darfur and how these have interacted with those of other indigenous groups in the region and the state's approach to land rights, to become highly contentious. Subsequent to a description of how the Fur indigenous land tenure system functions in the region and how it came about, the chapter looks at how indigenous land tenure has intersected with formal statutory tenure and Islamic law, and then focuses on the role and functioning of land rights in the conflict itself. This is done by exploring the stress, exclusion and resistance involving the indigenous tenure system; the intrusion and confrontation of the statutory system; and the role of Islamic law regarding land rights.

Indigenous property rights are examined most often through legal lenses. In Chapter 11, 'Indigenous Rights, Grey Spacing and Roads: The Israeli Negev Bedouin and Planning in Road 31', Avinoam Meir, Batya Roded and Arnon Ben-Israel examine indigenous property rights through a case study of planning a regional highway that used to be a local road for the indigenous Bedouin in Israel. This road has constituted a cultural place for them, but the planning and implementation of an upgrade of this road into a high speed highway raises serious questions that tie together informality, grey space, and issues of Bedouin rights. We refer to these rights in terms of planning rights that include right for participation, rights for the road, property rights and due process. The analysis of the interaction between these issues led us to explain why the state has resorted to a grey planning mechanism and how this mechanism contributes to weakening the power of the state manifested in 'under-sovereignty' and strengthening Bedouin status in their struggle for recognition of their indigenous rights.

In the chapters below, we will survey a broad range of case material from around the world, and from these, we hope that themes and patterns emerge to help map the challenges faced by indigenous peoples seeking to protect, maintain and/or recover traditional property rights, and to highlight both their struggles as well as the solutions that have emerged worldwide as indigenous peoples have sought to empower themselves. The conflicts that emerge between tribes and states are often structural in nature, and sometimes, though not always, violent, but with the passage of time, the potential for just and lasting peace between the modern states and the many indigenous peoples that found their homelands in the state's expanding path appears to grow. Efforts to manage, resolve and transform these conflicts have met with varying degrees of success. By taking a comparative approach, we hope to help all involved in managing the relationship between states and indigenous peoples and the continuing effort to empower Native peoples and restore the traditional land rights, to identify viable patterns and trends for success. Equally, by helping to map the full spectrum of indigenous land conflicts, from emergence, to escalation, to de-escalation, and ultimately to peaceful and lasting resolution. We thus hope to foster a global dialogue, not between indigenous peoples and the state, but among indigenous peoples, the state, and all who are engaged in the process of reconciling the interests of these two parties, long viewed as opponents but increasingly partners in the modernization of sovereignty itself – thereby helping indigenous leaders and rights activists, policymakers, and scholars learn from one another, leveraging insights presented in this volume for successfully resolving the conflicts that have long marked their relationships with the state, becoming partners in the management and governance of their homelands, and in the making of peace itself.

1 Indigeneity, land and activism in Siberia

Marjorie Mandelstam Balzer

Introduction

The activism of Siberian Natives in defending land claims, ecology, and civil rights has been supremely tested in the post-Soviet period, particularly in the past decade. Rodion Sulanzandiga, Vice President of RAIPON, the Russian Association of Indigenous Peoples of the North, Siberia and The Far East, reminded me in 2012: 'Russia has the biggest Arctic and the most serious stake in the Arctic. This is bound to influence indigenous peoples, and our politics'. This chapter, based on long-term anthropological fieldwork, expands on his thesis by examining diverse levels and foci of indigenous politics, ranging from cases of community devastation and assimilation to impressive cultural and social revitalization. As elsewhere, Siberia has experienced the precipitous rise of 'indigenous cosmopolitans' (compare Forte, 2010; Simpson and Smith, 2014). However, I argue that the most effective urban indigenous leaders are those whose lives are deeply intertwined with their original forest, tundra and river bank homelands. Conclusions explore the socio-political conditions that make some groups more successful than others in defending their social, ecological and cultural interests. My analysis adapts theories of flexible and negotiated indigeneity, exemplified by de la Cadena (2010), Neizen (2003), and Starn (2011).

In 2013, the first fracking operation, run by Gazpromneft Razvitiye on Yamal peninsula, home of the reindeer-breeding Nenets, was successfully completed. In 2012, transport ships without ice breakers were able to pass through the Northern Sea Route earlier than ever before, and this trend continued the following summers. Particularly disturbing, in late 2012, Russia's 'federal' government suspended RAIPON, the main umbrella organization that defends the rights of indigenous peoples. While it was reinstated in March 2013, this was done with blatant government pressure to change their leadership and direction. These events are all correlated. In the past decade, the pace of Northern land claims and grabs related to the energy and mining industries has accelerated, causing indigenous people increased strife, including illegal expulsions from lands they have considered their use-right family and clan territories for centuries. This in turn has led to an unprecedented pace of indigenous urbanization in Siberia and the Far East, so that by some estimates as many as 45 per cent of self-identifying indigenous individuals are today urban, so called 'asphalt Natives', living in cities or medium sized population centers.[1] Indigenous leaders well understand the connection between increased development, increased pressure against their activism, and increased urbanization.

Many levels of indigenous self-identity and contestation are reflected by the growing numbers of groups (from 26 to over 41) qualifying for membership in RAIPON since the Soviet Union collapsed. RAIPON represents a total of about 300,000 Natives. By definition, its member ethnonational groups must be under 50,000 in population; other more numerous indigenous peoples of Siberia (including the Far East) have 'republics', designated by their names, and are thus not qualified to be part of RAIPON. While RAIPON has had continued troubles with authorities, it remains the most viable and organized group to protect indigenous peoples' rights. Two other somewhat competing organizations also represent indigenous peoples, as recognized in Moscow: the Association of Indigenous Communities, and the Reindeer Breeders' Association.

An urban Moscovite lawyer and government advisor, Shor leader Mikhail Todyshev, explained to me in 2004 that indigenous people dislike, even despise, being called 'minorities': 'We much prefer to be called by our own specific ethnonyms or, if we are to be categorized, we prefer being called 'korennye' (indigenous) or 'aboriginal', like the Australian Native peoples'. This correlates with the importance and prominence of the Canadian term First Nations for its indigenous peoples. It is logical because 'minority' is too slippery to be a general category. It is geographically relative and historically shifting, for example when indigenous groups have been a 'majority' in their self-defined homelands until recently. Thus it is analytically crucial to stress the shifting and situational nature of ethnodemographics and politics over time, and how this has effected changing definitions and perceptions of 'indigeneity'.[2]

Recent legal constraints on the definition of indigeneity in the Russian Federation are reviewed here before discussion of some specific cases. I feature several chilling cases in diverse regions that show a pattern of how and why indigenous people have been driven to urban environments, for 'push' (forced migration) as well as 'pull' (urban attraction) reasons. I then turn to my main field research site since 1986, the Sakha Republic (Yakutia) in the Far East, a relatively positive case with still serious problems. Analysis focuses on strains of ethnic interaction and contestation created by development. Implications of increasingly constrained civil society in nominally federal Russia are also discussed.

Definitional battles: why they matter

In Russia's parliament (*duma*), efforts have been underway since the early 2000s to revise laws that govern indigenous peoples, to make the definitions as narrow as possible so that *lgoty*, legal dispensations, apply to as few as possible in Native access to hunting, fishing, forests, and land. This especially restricts those who have moved to towns and cities of their regions, and who may want to return periodically to their families in their shrinking home-lands. It limits options, literally and psychologically, for returning to indigenous peoples' territories, and becomes an assurance that there will be as few competitors as possible for post-Soviet land ownership claims. In addition, because of shrinking budgets, Soviet-style laws creating the equiva-lent of affirmative action for Native education have all but disappeared. In the Soviet period, the 26 officially recognized 'small-numbered' peoples had a range of privileges that were meant to entice them into 'civilization' and showcase them as self-identifying illustrations of Soviet Progress (Balzer, 1999; Slezkine, 1994).

In addition to the Russian Federation 1993 Constitution, three major Federal level laws have formed the basis for post-Soviet indigenous rights.[3] Especially salient is the logic behind a 2001 law on special rights for those who live in 'territories of traditional land use', influenced by indigenous lawyers such as Julia Yakel' and sociologist Olga Murashko. Legal language did not single out any particular ethnonational groups. If Russians lived in 'territories of traditional land use', and practiced hunting and fishing, theoret-ically they could benefit. However, stress was on Native groups within the under 50,000 population threshold, especially those 'recognizing themselves as independent ethnic communities'. A newer law has far more restricted language, so that an indigenous person must: 1) follow traditional ways of life – hunting/fishing/reindeer breeding; 2) live in the place of one's docu-mented ancestors; and 3) know one's native language.

Each of these points is controversial, and the law was still being debated in Committee in 2013. Several experts confided to me that the law may be one of several factors explaining why increased political pressure has been put on indigenous leaders. Many indigenous people practice more than a stereotyped 'traditional way of life', and some are involved in trading, mining, energy industry and other activities that require continual contact and travel across traditional villages and camps and urban centers. Like many others across the North, they may operate at various levels of a globalizing economy and still consider themselves Native. They also are coping with notorious 'primitive people' image problems, pressures of local authorities to render them into local 'brands' to attract a tourist industry, higher rates of alcoholism and lower life expectancy than country norms (compare Axelsson *et al.*, 2011; Shtyrov *et al.*, 2013).

The language restriction is particularly sensitive, since Native Siberians who are now 'urban', including those living in propagandized Soviet style 'villages of the town type', have fewer opportunities to know their native languages or to study them. Many lost their languages in the Soviet period. Yet contemporary Khanty and other Native groups are perfectly capable of praying in Russian that their 'clan lands' be spared from energy company incursions. Some indigenous language recovery programs have been more effective than others. In a few places, nomadic schools have been revived, where qualified indigenous teachers have 'returned to the forest' after schooling in cities and urban centers.[4]

In sum, newer legal definitions provide little room for self-identity, at a time when an influx of outsiders has already destabilized indigeneity. The laws are supposed to correct abuse of the system, for example too many Russians or people of mixed marriage backgrounds gaining free access to hunting and fishing resources that the state would like to control. Indeed, some Native lawyers are worried about Russians who claim Native identities or buy documents for dispensations [*lgoty*]. A 2010 'Law on Hunting and Protection of Hunting Resources' is unprecedented in its restrictions against Native access and licensing. A 2013 law 'On Changes to the Federal Law Concerning Special Nature Preserves' has gutted Russia's National Parks and Nature Preserves protections, including officially protected Native territories. But much worse has been happening in the North, mostly away from 'civil society' critique or ability to correct abuses. The following cases go far beyond critical issues of language loss, Native alcohol and health problems, and concerns about exploitation ('when will the Natives dance?') in the growing tourist industry.

Cases and voices: driving people off their lands, snowmobiles and mines

'Native homes have been burned in suspicious fires, even arson in whole villages' confided one urban indigenous activist in 2012. When I requested clarification and specifics, s/he explained that in Narym, where Sel'kup and Khanty live, 'a special contingent of arsonists came and burned a village in one night in order to drive indigenous people off their land, so that energy exploration could be continued in the area without indigenous interference...'. This kind of crime must involve collusion with local authorities, and therefore indigenous families have had little safe legal recourse and little chance for muckraking publicity. Instead, they have been forced into housing in the regional center, where authorities hope they will become assimilated and acculturated without turning themselves into a special 'cause célébre'.[5]

In Buriatia, a high profile case involving murder accusations was in the press in 2012–13, and some hope it is resolved in the International Court of Human Rights in Strasbourg. This 'Dylacha' jade mine case has pitted a wealthy Evenki mine collective near the famed Lake Baikal against Russian officials, including intelligence officers. Local Evenki explain that they have long mined jade in the region, and that reindeer breeding was not their sole occupation before Sovietization. Evenki claim that one of their community collectives (*obshina*) managed to get rights to mine jade in the 1990s, although access to subsurface resources by Native people is rare. Their mine director suspiciously went missing in 2012, and the business ombudsman for

Russia, Boris Titov, was brought in to mediate the case. Local competitors accused the Evenki of tapping an illegal jade vein, and of failing to pay taxes. The mining collective was subjected to a hostile take-over by the well-connected head of the local Federal Security Service, who was able to enlist highly placed allies in Moscow against the Evenki. The whole case destroys stereotypes that all Evenki are reindeer breeders, and tests the way Native ownership can potentially be defined, or, ideally, negotiated, to include more than 'traditional land use'.[6]

Julia Yakel', a lawyer who travels often from Khabarovsk to Moscow, has an Amur River community leader Nanai husband. In 2011, she described their shock when a legal case was brought against their community revoking their lucrative fishing rights on clan lands they had long considered undisputedly indigenous. Their local fishermen got into trouble for using snowmobiles from a base village to get to their special, legally designated 'place of traditional land use'. A local judge told the community that they needed to travel there 'on reindeer or by canoe' to maintain their legal status. These particular Nanai (a Tungusic-speaking group related to the widespread Evenki) had never owned or herded reindeer, and thus they were horrified not only by the implicit corruption of the Russian judge, but also by her ignorance. They appealed, but lost the case in a higher court in Moscow, and have no money to take the case further. Members of the community still use their snowmobiles, popular throughout the North, but are nervous that they will be caught and fined on their own clan territories. The lands themselves may be auctioned to the highest bidders, who are unlikely to be Nanai. This kind of pressure adds to the stress on any young person in the community weighing whether to stay in their 'small homeland' [*malaia rodina*] or move to an urban center. By 2013, Yakel' mentioned that officials from a local ecological preservation zone get rides from Nanai snowmobile owners, and that they are still fishing despite their uncertain future.[7] This case and others have created ripple effects of fear across Siberia concerning the instability of 'territories of traditional land use'.

On Yamal peninsula, in the rapidly developing Arctic, two groups in 2011 faced off across a river, Native and non-Native. Someone in the local Nenets group shot into the air, signaling to people perceived to be strangers to get off the land. They were answered with jeers: 'It is not your river any longer....'. And then the non-Natives, who were Russians and others associated with local energy development, called for backup from friends, who happened to be policemen. The police later testified that several in the Native group had aimed and shot directly at the new rightful 'owner' of the land in question. The land was in dispute after an 'auction' that had been held without local consultation or 'ethnological expertise', as technically required by law.

Such interethnic tensions have resulted in court cases that create misery on all sides, and festering resentment well beyond 'normal' strains of consensual, selective modernization. Nenets families themselves may well have a TV in their tents [*chum*], and relatives who work in the energy industry. But they resent that their children are forced to leave their lands and reindeer breeding traditions before they are ready, and that they have had little choice in how, when and where development is planned, for example at the Bovanenkova-Utkha gas trunkline megaproject in Yamal-Nenets. During some of the GAZPROM planning for this project, negotiations with local communities included plans for 'reindeer corridors', enabling reindeer in theory to relatively easily bypass the pipelines. However, according to consultants, these have turned out to 'break up the reindeer routes in very disruptive ways'. One explained: 'the reindeer have eaten everything in parts of Yamal', suggesting overburdened resources with few buffer zones for nomadic groups' flexibility. Land auctions and distortions in customary reindeer tracks have meant unease for future Nentsy well-being.[8]

In 2010, sociologist Olga Murashko conducted a comprehensive 3-4 hour survey on what Nenets reindeer breeders in Yamal are concerned about in areas where energy projects – oil and gas – are well underway and effecting reindeer breeding. The survey results rated Nentsy concerns: 1) increased alcoholism; 2) dogs biting energy workers and sparking interethnic fights; 3) education, including skilled technical training, has been difficult to obtain despite promises of better access; 4) traditional lands access and familiar reindeer paths have been disrupted because of the new urban centers, roads and pipelines; 5) non-local energy workers have been maliciously trespassing or trashing graveyards and other sacred sites; 6) feelings of isolation have increased, as venues for grievance recourse have been shrinking. In many of the respondents' views, their local indigenous association 'Yamal Potemkam' ('Yamal for Our Descendants') and the national level RAIPON have not been doing enough and have been rendered impotent by local and federal-level development politics.[9] In addition, some Nenets consider that their local government (administrative and parliamentary) has not been effective enough, although the head of the local parliament has been Sergei Kharyuchi, the prominent Nenets leader who was until recently the head of RAIPON.

In his comprehensive farewell speech at the RAIPON Congress in March 2013, significantly and symbolically held in Salekhard, the capital of Yamal-Nenets, Kharyuchi (2013: 13) acknowledged that development of northern resources was 'unavoidable' (*neizbezhno*), but that it must be done 'with consideration of ecological demands, specifics of local populations' interests, legal formulas that incorporate local values and compensations, preserving local ability to make a living using traditional means, and enabling the culture and health of indigenous small-numbered peoples of Northern territories to continue'.

Feelings of powerlessness, presumably meant to be calmed at the Congress, instead were exacerbated. While some attendees who I interviewed applauded the election as President of former Nenets reindeer breeder-turned-duma deputy Grigory Ledkov, others worried that his record as an activist for indigenous human rights is secondary to his record as a spokesperson for President Putin's United Russia Party. Relevant for some analysts is the significance of keeping leadership within the Nentsy community, as the largest of the indigenous peoples. The Nenets numbered 44,640 in the 2010 census, an increase over 2002, and may surpass the 50,000 threshold by the next census. One patriotic attendee went so far as to suggest that rival indigenous leaders of the Amur may have too many contacts with China! However, several interlocutors explained that pressure was put on Ledkov's main political rival, Pavel Sulanzandiga, from the Amur River, to withdraw from an election that was far from democratic.[10]

Searching for positive examples: The Sakha Republic?

Has the vast Sakha Republic (the size of India) provided better conditions than other constituent parts of the Russian Federation, as its propaganda claims, for its indigenous peoples? The answer may be affirmative, but they still have a long way to go. As elsewhere in Russia's north, the most vulnerable groups are minorities within minorities. Just as many Sakha feared Russification during the twentieth century, so have smaller indigenous northern groups feared Sakhaization or 'Yakutization'. Salient local proportions (demographic factors) and structural recognition mechanisms (political factors) partially explain indigenous activism: they provide context and some enabling conditions.

In the Sakha Republic, officially recognized indigenous groups are Chukchi, Yukaghir, Even and Evenki, as well as 'old-liver Russians', and the Dolgan, a mixed Sakha-Evenki-Russian group on the Taimyr border. The slim majority 'titular' Sakha (also called Yakut) numbered 466,492 out of a total of 958,528 in the republic in the 2010 census. Of these, 193,251 were listed as 'urban' and '284,834' as 'rural'. Evenki have the next largest number of indigenous representatives (in 2002, 18,232; and in 2010, 21,008), and their 'home community' [*zemliachestvo*] representation in the capital is also relatively substantial. The total Evenki population of Russia was 38,396, of whom 10,141 were urban and 28,255 rural.

Among the key reasons for cautious optimism has been official recognition for certain groups to have their own, legally designated regions at various internal levels (region, state, district – *raion, ulus, nasleg*), with Native-administered regional centers. In addition, renewed efforts at the republic level, after a post-Soviet lag, have been made to teach indigenous languages in the schools and in after-school programs. Most significant, indigenous groups have an activist republic Association of Indigenous Small-Numbered Peoples of the North, with subdivisions for Evenki, Even, Dolgan, Chukchi, Yukaghir and old-liver Russians.[11] This Association lobbies for Native rights with a relevant local parliament committee, with academic institutes, and with official bureaucracies such as the Ministry for the Protection of Nature, and the multiethnic Department of the Peoples of Sakha Republic (Yakutia), downgraded from being a full Ministry during the first Putin administration.[12] The Department's multi-ethnicity is not at the level of the U.S.

Bureau of Indian Affairs, or Canada's Ministry of Indian and Aboriginal Affairs – where most officials are Native. But it is a useful bureaucratic base in an environment where leadership and role models are extremely important. An intellectual center, the independent and influential Institute of the Problems of the Small-Numbered Peoples of the North, led by the late Even linguist Vasily Robbek, was subsumed under the Institute of Humanities in 2009, and many are still mourning its *de facto* demise.

Since 1989, the republic's Association of Indigenous Small-Numbered Peoples of the North, chaired by Even writer and republic parliament (Il Tumen) deputy Andrei Krivoshapkin, has been able to influence local laws on language protection, clan collectives, on reindeer breeding, on hunting, and on sustainable development. The most significant legal framework for protecting indigenous rights is a 2006 republic law: 'On territories of traditional land use and economics for indigenous small-numbered peoples of the Northern Sakha Republic', hard won by Andrei Krivoshapkin, who had become the Il Tumen vice-chair. A newer 2010 law enforcing ethnological expertise applies to more recent resource exploitation projects.[13]

Diverse semi-organized 'home community' associations have provided enabling environments for multicultural growth in the cities and towns of the republic. They are usually poorly financed, however, surviving on volunteer enthusiasm and funding. Using informal networks, they tend to stimulate constant attention to various mini-homelands – 'news from home'. Far from condemning what some disparagingly call 'regional mentality' ['*ulus mentalitet*'], I see it as encouraging cultural richness and harmless non-chauvinist local patriotism. Another trend, for those who can afford it, is an informal shuttle diplomacy – with many return trips back to the homeland from the capital (compare Beier, 2009). Some of the best known indigenous leaders living in Yakutsk manage to get home at least yearly for the haying season, for life process rituals, and for annual reindeer festivals. Wherever people meet in the city, at weddings, birthdays, curing centers, and universities, diverse indigenous trend-setters, such as toast-masters, curers, entertainers, and teachers, help link people from the same regions so that they can help each other. The sub-text of this is that they are often connecting people from specific indigenous groups. These are important social networking mechanisms for newcomers to cities and towns.

Some indigenous people in Sakha Republic have transcended their disadvantaged 'minority' statuses by finding diverse bases for community solidarity and sanctioned public activity. Post-Soviet politics have been characterized by new levels of self-organization and group consolidation. Since 2003, the Yakutsk base of the Association of Indigenous Small-Numbered Peoples of the North, called 'House of the Peoples of the North' (*Dom Narodov Severa*), has hosted cultural, social and economic development events, including numerous congresses and festivals. The Association has also actively participated in Moscow-based RAIPON projects and congresses, and hosted a significant RAIPON congress, which I attended, in

2007. Synergistic spin-offs have included the creative collective of the TV program *Gevan*, within Sakha TV (led by Natalia D. Smetanina, and Liudmilla A. Alekseeva), and the republic paper *Ilkèn* (edited by Varvara Danilova). Other relevant indigenous organizations include the student youth group 'Arctic', a republic branch of the Reindeer Breeders Association; and the local association 'Natives of Nizhne Kolyma'.

The politics of cross-border communication and solidarity, within Russia and beyond, have broadened indigenous people's contacts and potential for self-realization and activism. Examples include enhanced ties between the Even of Sakha and Magadan; the Chukchi of Sakha and Magadan; Evenki of Sakha and China; and a less predictable Yukaghir friendship with a Forest Finn that has turned into concrete, productive projects through the Snow-change Cooperative. This process becomes a somewhat paradoxical multileveled globalization politics for cultural defense. Indigenous partici-pation in folk festivals in Europe, Canada and the United States boosts morale and promotes cultural dignity. Indigenous peoples' annual meetings at the United Nations, the Arctic Council, and the Northern Forum are usual-ly good examples of crucial and dynamic alliance building and ecological defense. However, for Native leaders, the indigenous people's UN conference in May, 2014 was deftly hijacked by a high-level speech proclaiming all of Russia as a multi-ethnic model, by former president of Russia, Dmitri Medvedev, who headed Russia's delegation. The ominous curtailment trend was continued in Fall, 2014 when Russian authorities tried to stop several indigenous leaders from attending another UN conference.

Networks, outreach and communication at multiple levels can help expose the land expropriation and ecological devastation that have been proceeding in Sakha Republic, as energy companies GAZPROM, ROSENERGO and ROSHYDRO have moved in with megaprojects in the past decade. In Northern Sakha Republic, Even and Yukaghir were concerned in 2012 that their nearest airport, in Tiksi, the Northern Sea Route port town with defense industry infrastructure, had temporarily closed to the public without local consultation. In relatively southern parts of the republic, indigenous activists, attempting to make the best of conditions that are increasingly adverse for reindeer breeding, have lobbied for local Evenki to have training and quotas for work placements on megaprojects, and to have economic stimulus agree-ments for their recent service and tourism businesses (compare Murashko, 2013: 167–8).

The most notorious example of a megaproject influencing indigenous communities is the oil pipeline that then Prime Minister Vladimir Putin in 2009 ordered to be diverted from the Lake Baikal area, after public protests. Re-routed into mountainous terrain and then along the Lena River, in order to eventually supply energy to China, it has proved to be extraordinarily dangerous, with at least three spills into the Lena River publicly acknow-ledged, caused by technology that has incompletely tunneled the line. Multi-ethnic ecology activist groups have sponsored public information and protests, and have gotten in trouble with their 'Save the Lena' campaign. A republic advisor to the Sakha president privately acknowledged in 2013 that some serious pipeline spills had harmed local communities. He linked this to careless migrant workers new to the republic, saying: 'there's a gap in qualification of cadres. The republic is trying to educate our local people in technical skills so that they can take jobs, for example in the energy industry.... These locals are people who might be able to defend ecology better. There needs to be a sense of a stake in the region'.[14]

An activist told me in 2012, 'GAZPROM is buying up all the land that Even and Evenki reindeer breeders use, that they need'. This fits with information I have been given for the past 5 years. 'With renewed plans to auction off our lands to the highest bidders, we are once again in danger of the collectives being left with nothing', bitterly complained Afanasy Koriakin in 2010 in Yakutsk. Afanasy, an Evenki elder, had been head of the *ulus* of Zhigansk, Sakha Republic, before moving to the capital, Yakutsk. He was doing everything he could from his prestigious, retired urbanized position in the city to help his fellow Evenki back home. His lessons were significant. First, Evenki loyalties are continually defined by the connections of urban kin back to their 'small homelands' elsewhere in the republic. Second, for Evenki the main problem continues to be land and how to manage it. Evenki framing of their 'identity' is constantly defined and intertwined with their concerns about possible loss of their 'homelands'. Third, ethnic tensions are implicit, with potential to be activated or calmed, depending on interethnic contexts. Any 'highest bidders' in the latest round of land grabs are likely to be Russian businessmen 'outsiders' or perhaps non-local 'Yakut', rather than Evenki.

The business plan Afanasy Koriakin referred to was massive, involving 10 large reindeer herds, a legal designation as a 'territory of traditional land-use', and a bank loan coordinated in the village of Menkerz, with urban Evenki management. Republic officials, including former Sakha president M.E. Nikolaev, thwarted their land plan, calling it 'illegal', and even 'secessionist'.[15] Assumptions that Natives cannot be good businessmen are belied by creative activists such as Afanasy Koriakin. Indeed, some argue that cognitive skills of reindeer breeders, adapting to situational uncertainty, are congruent with those of businessmen.[16]

A relatively more positive example of recent Evenki business success has been an Evenki community collective given a license to participate in a gold mining conglomerate in the Niuringri region, beginning in 2014. Sixty per cent of the start-up capital comes from a republic fund to enhance Evenki well-being in compensation for losing lands to the planned Kankun hydro-electric dam, and forty per cent comes from an existing gold company inexplicably called 'Amber' (*Yantar*), based in the Evenki Iengra district [*nasleg*]. The new director is Nikolai Aribalov.[17]

Many indigenous leaders are attuned to the ecological hazards of too much development, including the Evenki activists Andrei Issakov of

Yakutsk, who has chaired the youth wing of RAIPON; and Anatoly Chomchoev, a former general in the Soviet army, with insider experience as head of the Yakutsk Energo company. Interested in solar energy, he is one of the Siberians whose opposition helped postpone and possibly halt the horribly misnamed Evenki Hydro-Electric Power station that would have flooded large parts of Evenki territory within Krasnoyarsk region on the Yenisei River. Such mega-projects have caused the Yukagir leader Viacheslav Shadrin to intensify his ecological and climate change warnings. As he explained in an interview after Lena River flooding, 'Nature is returning to people their bad actions'.[18]

A gender aspect is relevant to any discussion of Native leadership. Evenki leaders are often women, including former parliament deputy Avgusta Marfusalova and young activists of the Evenki Association of Sakha Republic (Yakutia) Ezhana Vasilieva and Aitalina Alekseeva. As Gail Fondahl (1998) and others have pointed out, a by-product of Soviet education was that indigenous women tended to go further in school than men, and thus they became more ready mediators and interlocutors with Russians and Sakha.[19]

In sum, these and other Native leaders consider their top priorities to be land, ecology sensitivity, political status, and the need to stabilize or reverse Sakhaization and Russification trends. They are working through dispersed local 'collectives', town and city homeland community organizations, and cultural associations at all levels. Against considerable odds, they have had occasional victories, such as eventual recognition of the Zhigansk Evenki National *ulus*, the Olenek National district, and the Iengra Evenki National *nasleg*. These victories are especially notable because they counter a Russian Federation trend to 'consolidate' small nationality-based regions. But territorial recognition in itself does not indicate full measures of self-rule and self-confidence.

Uliana Vinkurova, former Sakha parliamentarian, sociologist, originally from Northern Sakha Republic (Sredne-Kolyma) has gloomily accessed Sakha Republic's indigenous peoples' morale, given recent political and economic pressures: 'The issue is not just bureaucratic struggles [over land and rights], but that social trauma has gone deep, that there has been a destruction of the will to live'. After mentioning several suicides, she added:

> There is a sense of hopelessness, that one cannot do anything to put right one's fate. That everywhere those who live with nature are being hemmed in, herded into smaller territories. We must change this atmosphere, turn around the despair. There seems to be a threshold, whereby quantity [of suicides] has become quality: they can't take it anymore. As the new generation is coming along, some are dying and some are rebelling. It has been 5 years since our Sakha Republic Declaration of Native Peoples – people had high hopes. We are trying to balance the competing claims.[20]

'Balance' means protection without paternalism, the ability to provide for indigenous nomadic families' basic resource needs, and the right of young people to move back and forth between rural and urban environments without feeling they have been driven off their lands.

Conclusions: how many times do people have to cry 'crisis' before they are heard?

Native urban leaders with international experience have repeatedly emphasized to me that effective leadership is key in the chances for indigenous communities to recover from Soviet and post-Soviet pressures, and to guide collaborative participation in development. Enabling conditions for Native communities and individuals to flourish with flexibility, in rural, urban, and everything in between venues, are also crucial (Simpson and Smith, 2014: 11–12). Leadership cannot exist in a vacuum, without resonance, especially when people are being forced off their lands, losing access to affordable transport, and fearing ecological destruction.

As Native spokesman Dmitri Berezhkov analyzed in 2012 after RAIPON was suspended: 'Indigenous peoples... are involuntary contenders and unwanted competitors in the vast expanses of the Arctic'.[21] Rodion Sulanzandiga, when asked in 2012 whether Sakha Republic could be a model, explained:

> There are relative degrees of attention to indigenous rights and ecological problems. The main places that have some track record of attention to indigenous concerns are Yamal-Nenets [region], Khanty-Mansi [region], and yes, Sakha Republic. These are all places with some wealth to share. Other areas are much more depressed – such as the reindeer breeding Todja community in Tuva.

In other words, occasionally the 'trickle down' of natural resources wealth can be harnessed to help Native cultural, social, and ecological projects. This is far from any full-fledged territorially based 'sovereignty'.

A major indicator of rare indigenous political success inside Russia is Native parliaments, or quotas inside existing regional parliaments. Valentina Sovkina, the dynamic and articulate head of the Saami parliament, based in Murmansk, affirmed in 2011: 'places that have allowed a Native parliament best enable indigenous voices to be heard, and development to be somewhat cooperative'.[22] But this means only the Saami, Khanty and Mansi are models, and the small, token Khanty-Mansi National Assembly, based in Khanty-Mansiisk, has been threatened with a downgrade to committee status within the regional parliament. In Sakha Republic, efforts to enable a stable quota for indigenous representatives in the republic parliament have thus far failed, despite the valiant efforts of Evenki leader Andrei Krivoshapkin. Sakha (Yakut), the dominant indigenous people for whom the republic is named, continue to be privileged.

In conditions of changing relationships to the land, relative degrees of 'indigeneity' should be acknowledged, as well as multiple identities, situational identities and fluctuating ability to defend one's people.[23] Indigeneity, as a specific variation of ethnicity, is fluid and relational, yet also grounded in homeland roots (compare Barth, 1969; Anderson, 1991; Appadurai, 1996). Leaders who stray too far from their homelands become less effective and unpopular, although some may reclaim the capital cities of their republics as home turf. It matters greatly whether you have titular republic boundaries to defend and to imagine your community within, such as Altai, Buriatia, Sakha, Tuva, and Khakassia, or *okrug* level boundaries, such as the Khanty-Mansi and Yamal-Nenets regions. Those with poorly defined land-based status, as pertains to the majority of Siberian peoples, for example the Aleut, Chukchi, Chuvants, Dolgan, Enets, Evenki, Eveny, Itelmen, Kamchadal, Ket, Koriak, Negidal, Nganasan, Nanai, Nivkh, Orok, Sel'kup, Shor, Soiot, Taz, Telengit, Teleut, Tofa, Todja, Udege, Ulcha, and Yukagir, are in far weaker positions.[24]

Russia's multiethnic history as well as comparative ethnic studies, suggest that officially acknowledged homelands and state definitions may influence, shape or validate identity. In theory, negotiated rather than repressed political awareness could lay the groundwork for a functioning multi-leveled federalism based on eclectic forms of indigeneity, greater degrees of sovereignty, and various ethnonationalisms, including pragmatic Russian patriotism that is not chauvinist and transcends (neo) colonialism.

Potential 'indigenous cosmopolitan' models outside of Russia include the Inuit of Canada, where the territory of Nunavut (meaning 'Our Land') has a flourishing capital, Iqaluit (formerly Frobisher Bay), a founding Native lawyer who became its first democratically elected premier, and an effective Native legislative assembly. Farther south, the Inuit community in Ottawa has been struggling with urban life, with some, albeit more limited, success:

> As transnational spaces evolve and communities are constructed in urban centers, new forms of Inuitness emerge. These are not disconnected from Inuit cultural and linguistic practices, and political claims to Arctic sovereignty. Indeed the Inuit ethnoscape is changing and Inuit are an important part of this transformation.[25]

To enable new forms of indigeneity and empowerment, a dynamic civil society is crucial. In Russia, for those groups with minimal official territorial support, the importance of umbrella groups like RAIPON is structurally magnified. Indeed the recent threat to RAIPON's existence drew frequently in-fighting indigenous activists closer to solidarity with each other. They are threatened particularly when they have advocated against specific excesses of the state-connected, non-transparent energy companies GAZPROM, ROSENERGO, and ROSHYDRO. RAIPON's NGO status has been in effect converted into a beholden GONGO (governmentally organized non-governmental organization). Russia's 2011 NGO law that stipulates registration of NGOs as foreign agents when they receive money from abroad is also alarmingly relevant, because RAIPON has received money from a 'Scandinavia Fund'.

Serious structural threats to Russia's civil society include the lack of fair elections of regional leaders after they were abolished in 2004, reinstated under President Medvedev with filters, and recently again constrained. Abolishing of lower level territories by merging them into 'mega-region amalgamations' also has been detrimental to Native empowerment. Since 2005, Komi-Permiak, Koriak, Ust-Orda, and Aga territorial mergers have been polarizing and radicalizing many affected Komi, Koriak, and Buriat, according to my non-Russian interlocutors.

Another set of civil-society-related ramifications derives from President Putin's 2012 announcement that regional leaders are responsible for keeping interethnic relations 'tolerant' in their republics, regions and districts. Ironically, this has exposed interethnic tensions in some places. In the Sakha Republic it may have more productively resulted in greater official attention to publicly exposed problems of 'small-numbered indigenous people'. For example, eight Evenki communities received compensations for lands taken by the Kankun hydroelectric dam, in a controversial 2013 decision that is supposed to extend for the next twenty years. A positive cultural development is a new Sakha republic program establishing a 'small-numbered indigenous people's theatre', with an urban base and local outreach, approved in 2013. Hopefully, these are not simply programs that 'look good on paper'.

Competing sources of authority have been particularly difficult for loosely organized indigenous groups. Despite some enabling conditions for activism and healthy debate, increasingly more people are being put into 'opposition' and 'dissident' categories, to use a (neo) Soviet word. This is not how most indigenous leaders define themselves. Certainly long established groups like RAIPON or the human rights advocacy groups Memorial, or Helsinki Watch do not see themselves as 'traitors' or 'separatists'. But government authorities are applying a strategic chill on various emblematic, targeted actors – and the indigenous peoples of the 'North, Siberia and the Far East' as represented by RAIPON are examples in a line of others under threat.

A Native leader and ecology activist who frequently travels throughout the Sakha Republic has been advocating that indigenous people with grievances, whether group or individual, must stop taking every obstacle they encounter as an insult directed personally at them, but rather refuse to receive words or deeds from 'ethnic others' as insults. This may be a noble and self-empowering idea whose time is overdue. However, a broader perspective analyzing potential social change in Russia must acknowledge that one of the hallmarks of civil society is how well its indigenous peoples are able to express and act upon their grievances. Primary among these are increasing tensions over territorial rights, and the correlated decline in Native power at all levels to negotiate situational and fair balances among ecological preservation, access to long-established subsistence and sacred heritage sites, and shares in development profits and processes.

References

Anderson, Benedict (1991). *Imagined Communities: Reflections on the Origin and Spread of Nationalism*. London: Verso.

Appadurai, Arjun (1996). 'Sovereignty Without Territoriality: Notes for a Post-national Geography'. P. Yaeger (ed.) *The Geography of Identity*. Ann Arbor, MI: The University of Michigan Press, 40–58.

Axelsson, Per, Sköld, Peter (eds) (2011). *Indigenous Peoples and Demography: The complex relation between identity and statistics*. New York: Berghahn.

Balzer, Marjorie Mandelstam (1999). *The Tenacity of Ethnicity: A Siberian Saga in Global Perspective*. Princeton, NJ: Princeton University Press.

Balzer, Marjorie Mandelstam (2006). 'The Tension between Might and Rights: Siberians and Energy Developers in Post-Socialist Binds'. *Europe-Asia Studies* 58(4): 567–588.

Barth, Fredrik (ed.) (1969). *Ethnic Groups and Boundaries*. Boston, MA: Little, Brown.

Beier, J. Marshall (ed.) (2009). *Indigenous Diplomacies*. New York: Palgrave Macmillan.

de la Cadena, Marisol (2010). 'Indigenous Cosmopolitics in the Andes: Conceptual Reflections beyond "Politics"'. *Cultural Anthropology* 25(2): 334–370.

de la Cadena, Marisol, Starn, Orin (eds) (2007). *Indigenous Experience Today*. Oxford: Berg.

Commaroff, John, Camaroff, Jean (2009). *Ethnicity Inc.* Chicago, IL: University of Chicago.

Dean, Bartholomew, Levi, Jerome (eds) (2003). *At the Risk of Being Heard: Identity, Indigenous Rights, and Postcolonial States*. Ann Arbor, MI: University of Michigan.

Donahoe, Brian, Habeck, Joachim Otto, Halemba, Agniszka, Sántha, Ivan (2008). 'Size and Place in the Construction of Indigeneity in the Russian Federation'. *Current Anthropology* 49(6): 993–1020.

Fondahl, Gail (1998). *Gaining ground?: Evenkis, land and reform in southeastern Siberia*. Boston, MA: Allyn and Bacon.

Fondahl, Gail (2003). 'Through the Years: Land Rights among the Evenkis of Southeastern Siberia'. *Cultural Survival Quarterly*. Spring 27 (1): 28–31.

Fondahl, Gail, Sirina, Anna (2003). 'Working Borders and Shifting Identities in the Russian Far North'. *Geoforum* 34: 541–556.

Forte, Maximilian C. (ed.) (2010). *Indigenous Cosmopolitans: Transnational and Transcultural Indigeneity in the Twenty-first Century*. New York: Peter Lang.

Funk, Dmitri A. (2012). 'Sokhranenie i razvitie iazykov korennykh malochislennykh narodov Severa Rossiiskoi Federatsii'. Novikova, Natalia I, Funk, Dmitri A. (ed.) *Sever i Severiane: Sovremennoe polozhenie Korennykh malochislennykh Narodov Severa, Sibiri I Dal'nego Vostoka*. Moscow: RAN, Institut Etnologii i Antropologii, 51–61.

Kharyuchi, Sergei N. (2013). 'Doklad Presidenta Assotsiatsii korennykh malochis-lennykh narodov Severa, Sibiri, i Dal'nego Vostoka'. *VII S'ezd korennykh malochislennykh narodov Severa, Sibiri, i Dal'nego Vostoka*. Salekhard: Severnoe Izd.

Klokov, Konstantin B. (2012). 'Sovremmenoe polozhenie olenevodov i olenevodstva v Rossiia'. Novikova, Natalia I, Funk, Dmitri A. (ed.) *Sever i Severiane: Sovremennoe polozhenie Korennykh malochislennykh Narodov Severa, Sibiri i Dal'nego Vostoka*. Moscow: RAN, 38–50.

Krivoshapkin, Andrei V. (2013). 'Praktika zakonodatel'nogo obespecheniia organizatsii I deatel'nosti obshin korennykh malochislennykh narodov Severa i ikh traditsionnoi khoziastvennoi deatel'nosti v Respubliki Sakha (Yakutia)'. Shtyrov, Viacheslav A. *et al.* (ed.) *Sovremennoe sostoianie I puty razvitiia korennykh malochislennykh narodov Severa, Sibiri i dal'nego vostoka Rossiiskoi Federatsii*. Moscow: Sovet Federatsii, 249–256.

Kumpula, Timo, Forbes, Bruce C., Stammler, Florian, Meschtyb, Nina (2013). 'Dynamics of a Coupled System: Multi Resolution Remote Sensing in Assessing Social Ecological Responses during 25 Years of Gas Field Development in Arctic Russia'. *Arctic Urban Sustainability*, 5/30-31/2013, conference, George Washington University, www.gwu.edu/~ieresgwu/programs/conference.cfm (accessed 26 June 2915).

Laruelle, Marlene (2014). *Russia's Arctic Strategies and the Future of the Far North*. M. E. Sharpe.

Mamontova, Nadezhda A. (2014). 'What Language do Real Evenki Speak?'. *Anthropology and Archeology of Eurasia* 52(4): 37–75.

Mestikova, Akulina E. (2010). *Sotsial'nyie Osnovaniia Realizatsii Iazykovykh Prav Korennykh Malochislennykhikh Narodov Severa v Sisteme Obrazovaniia*. Ulan-Ude: *Aftoreferat* Vostochno-Sibirskogo Gos. Tekhnologicheskogo U.

Murashko, Olga A. (2013). 'Uchet kul'turnykh, ekologicheskikh i sotsial'nykh posledstvii promyshlennogo razvitiia v mestakh traditsionnoi khoziastvennoi deatel'nosti korennykh malochislennykh narodov Severa'. Shtyrov, V.A. *et al.* (ed.) *Sovremennoe sostoianie I puty razvitiia korennykh malochislennykh narodov Severa, Sibiri i dal'nego vostoka Rossiiskoi Federatsii*. Moscow: Sovet Federatsii, 158–168.

Neizen, Ronald (2003). *The Origin of Indigenism: Human Rights and the Politics of Identity*. Berkeley, CA: University of California Press.

Novikova, Natalia I. (2014). *Hunters and Oil Workers: Studies in Legal Anthropology*. Moscow: Nauka.

Novikova, Natalia I., Funk, Dmitri A. (ed.) (2012). *Sever i Severiane: Sovremennoe polozhenie Korennykh malochislennykh Narodov Severa, Sibiri i Dal'nego Vostoka*. Moscow: RAN, Institut Etnologii i Antropologii.

Pivneva, Elena A. (2012). 'Khanty-Mansiiskii Avtonomnyi okrug – Yugra'. Novikova, Natalia I, Funk, Dmitri A. (ed.) *Sever i Severiane: Sovremennoe polozhenie Korennykh malochislennykh Narodov Severa, Sibiri i Dal'nego Vostoka*. Moscow: RAN, Institut Etnologii i Antropologii, 84–99.

Romanova, Ekaterina N., Alekseeva, Evdokiia K., Ignat'eva, Wanda B. (2012). 'Respubliki Sakha'. Novikova, Natalia I, Funk, Dmitri A. (ed.) *Sever i Severiane: Sovremennoe polozhenie Korennykh malochislennykh Narodov Severa, Sibiri I Dal'nego Vostoka*. Moscow: RAN, Institut Etnologii i Antropologii, 100–120.

Shoumatoff, Alex (2008). 'Oil Rush'. *Vanity Fair*, 239.

Shtyrov, Viacheslav A. *et al.* (ed.) (2013). *Sovremennoe sostoianie I puty razvitiia korennykh malochislennykh narodov Severa, Sibiri i dal'nego vostoka Rossiiskoi Federatsii*. Moscow: Sovet Federatsii.

Simpson, A. and Smith, A. (eds) (2014). *Theorizing Native Studies.* Durham, London: Duke University Press.

Sirina, A.A. (2008–9). 'People Who Feel the Land: The Ecological Ethic of the Evenki and Eveny'. *Anthropology & Archeology of Eurasia* 47(3): 9–37.

Slezkine, Yuri (1994). *Arctic Mirrors: Russia and the Small Peoples of the North.* Ithaca, NY: Cornell University Press.

Starn, Orin (2011). 'Here Come the Anthros (Again): The Strange Marriage of Anthropology and Native America'. *Cultural Anthropology* 26(2): 179–204.

Todyshev, M.A. (2013). 'O Problemakh dokumental'nogo podtverzhdeniia prinadlezhnosti grazhdan k korennym malochislennym narodam'. Shtyrov, V.A. *et al.* (ed.) *Sovremennoe sostoianie I puty razvitiia korennykh malochislennykh narodov Severa, Sibiri i dal'nego vostoka Rossiiskoi Federatsii.* Moscow: Sovet Federatsii, 87–102.

Tomiak, Julie Ann and Patrick, Donna (2010) 'Transnational Migration and Indigeneity in Canada: A Case Study of Urban Inuit'. *Indigenous Cosmopolitans* Forte, M.C. (ed.) New York: Peter Lang, 127–144.

Ulturgasheva, Olga (2012) *Narrating the Future in Siberia: Childhood, Adolescence and Autobiography among the Eveny.* New York: Berghahn.

Vinokurova, Uliana A. (2011) *Tsirkumpolarnaia tsivilizatsiia.* Yakutsk: Min. Kul'tury.

Wessendorf, Kathrin; Olga Murashko, (eds) (2005). *An Indigenous Parliament? Realities and Perspectives in Russia and the Circumpolar North.* Copenhagen: Eks-Skolens Trykkeri for IWGIA and RAIPON.

Yakel', Julia Ya. (2012). 'Obshchaia khrakteristika deistvuiushchego zakonodatel'stva. Problemy praktiki primeneniia'. Novikova, Natalia I, Funk, Dmitri A. (ed.) *Sever i Severiane: Sovremennoe polozhenie Korennykh malochislennykh Narodov Severa, Sibiri I Dal'nego Vostoka.* Moscow: RAN, Institut Etnologii i Antropologii, 8–21.

Notes

1 This high estimate comes from the July, 2011 report of Elena A. Pivneva at the IX Congress of Ethnographers and Anthropologists of Russia in Petrozavodsk, Karelia. See also Novikova and Funk (2012); Novikova (2014); and Pivneva (2012: 84–99).

2 See also Todyshev (2013); Donahoe *et al.* (2008); and Vinokurova (2011). Sakha sociologist Uliana Vinokurova defines 'minorities' as those peoples who are relatively politically defenseless (email 5/16/11). Russian documents asserting indigenous rights can belie their own propaganda, for example one submitted to the Council of Europe in 2010 affirmed the 'preservation of ethnic identity of the peoples of the Russian Federation' on page 12 while reporting the abolition of national district names on page 200. 'Third Report submitted by the Russian Federation pursuant to Article 25, para. 1 of the Framework Convention of National Minorities' to the Council of Europe, 9/4/2010 www.coe.int/t/dghl/monitoring/minorities/3_fcnmdocs/PDF_3rd_SR_RussianFed_en.pdf (accessed 1/14/2011).

3 They are the Yeltsin administration's 1999 'On guarantees of the rights of indigenous small-numbered peoples of the Federation of Rossiia' (82); the 2000 'On basic principles of organization of communities of the indigenous small-numbered peoples of the North, Siberia and the Far East' (104); and the 2001 law 'On territories of traditional land-use of the small-numbered peoples of the

North, Siberia and the Far East of the Federation of Rossiia' (49). For analysis, see especially Yakel' (2012).

4   On diverse language programs, compare Mestnikova (2010); Ulturgasheva (2012); Funk (2012); Mamontova (2014).

5   This disturbing 2012 description was confirmed with additional interlocutors in 2015. The sources are reliable but prefer anonymity in view of threats.

6   See for example www.raipon.info/en/component/content/article/8-news/83-evenki-intend-get-to-the-strasbourg-court.html (accessed 1/26/2013).

7   For context, see her excellent review of laws relevant to indigenous peoples' cases, Yakel' (2012: 8–21).

8   This data comes from 2010–2014 interviews with indigenous leaders at the Moscow and local levels, but is too sensitive to name the interlocutors. For a more positive assessment, see material from the ongoing international project of Kumpula *et al.* (2013), at the Arctic Centre of the University of Lapland, Rovaniemi, Finland. See also www.gwu.edu/~ieresgwu/programs/conference.cfm (accessed 5/16/2013); and http://vnao.ru/news/chto-budem-delat-kogda-neft-zakonchitsya (accessed 3/29/2013).

9   Olga Murashko presented the results of this survey in July, 2011 at the IX Congress of Ethnographers and Anthropologists of Russia in Petrozavodsk, Karelia. See also her data-filled journal *Mir Korennykh Narodov: Zhivaia Arktika*; Novikova (2014); and Novikova and Funk (2012: 22–37).

10   Nine attendees were interviewed on the Congress, of various ethnic and educational backgrounds. While this sample was not comprehensive, it included a range of opinions. See also the second edition of the Congress proceedings, Shtyrov *et al.* (2013).

11   See their site: http://assembly.ykt.ru/obshiny/associaciya-korennyx-malochis lennyx-narodov-severa-yakutii/.

12   See http://sakha.gov.ru/depnarod (accessed 5/16/2013). Department premises share space with the Association of Indigenous Peoples of Sakha, as well as a club house. The building complex was lobbied for by Even linguist Vasily Robbek and Andrei Krivoshapkin with President V. Shtyrov. For Sakha Republic Scheme 2020 plans that include indigenous peoples' development, see www.sakha.gov.ru/sites/default/files/story/files/2010_10/114/shema2020 (accessed 5/16/2013).

13   I am grateful to Andrei Krivoshapkin for many interviews, including one in his Il Tumen office July 21, 2010. See also Krivoshapkin (2013: 249–256); Romanova *et al.* (2012: 100–120); and Klokov (2012: 48–49). However, laws alone are not enough, and recent Federal laws on fishing and hunting have also been used to restrict indigenous rights, rendering previous 'l'goty' into rental arrangements. President Shtyrov, whose record on indigenous protection was mixed, conceded in a TV interview (8/14/09) that 'every new law seems to make the situation of our indigenous small numbered peoples worse'. The 2013 law on nature preserves is a relevant example.

14   Interview with Sakha sociologist Anatoly D. Bravin, director of the govern-mental 'respublikanskoe-informatsionno-konsaltingovoe agentsva' (RIKA), 6/28/13.

15   Afanasy was one of the leaders calling for the *nasleg* to be called 'Evenkiia'. He explained: 'If the authorities would only let us handle our own economy, our own 'business plan' for a successful reindeer breeding base at the level of a *nasleg*, we could begin selling reindeer products on a larger scale, and living better. We were blocked ... when about 73 per cent of us were Evenki in our own *nasleg*'.

16 Adam Mickiewicz University (Poznan) scholar Ivan Peshkov, studying growing Evenki nationalism and cross-border contacts with China optimistically concludes: 'The northern Evenki play a special role in the cultural-integration process, since they have preserved their traditional culture, they inhabit exceptionally vast territories and they participated in socialist modernization selectively'. http://asiandynamics.ku.dk/pdf/Indig_abstracts (accessed 14 January 2013). Compare Fondahl and Sirina (2003); and Sirina (2008–9).

17 See Vitaly Alekseev 2013 'Evenki zaimutsia zolotodobychei' www.gazetay akutia.ru/component/k2/item/3712 (accessed 3/21/2013). See also ROS HYDRO's report on Kankun: www.yakutia.rushydro.ru/file/main/yakutia/ company/investprojects/17376.html/Kniga_2.pdf; and Vera Solovyeva's U.N. report: http://unsr.jamesanaya.info/study-extractives/index.php/en/cases (both accessed 5/16/2013).

18 Alex Shoumatoff (2008:239). I have periodically met with the impressive Viacheslav Shadrin, who worries that his message of 'never take more than you need' has been ignored by Natives and non-Natives alike.

19 See Gail Fondahl (2003): www.culturalsurvival.org/publications/cultural_sur vival_quarterly/russia/_evenkis_land_and_reform_southeastern_Siberia.

20 Uliana Vinokurova email 1/ 23/2013, my translation.

21 Dmitri Berezhkov 'Why the Russian Government shut down indigenous organization RAIPON' December 4, 2012: www.huntingtonnews.net/50853 (accessed 12/15/2012).

22 This is from V. Sovkina's presentation in July, 2011 at the IX Congress of Ethnographers and Anthropologists of Russia in Petrozavodsk, Karelia, and from a follow-up conversation. See also Wessendorf and Murashko (2005).

23 Many anthropologists, grappling with diverse understandings of 'indigeneity', understand it as contextual and a matter of degree. See especially the scholarship of Orin Starn (2011: 179-204) and Marisol de la Cadena (2007; 2010: 334–370). See also Axelsson and Sköld(2011); Balzer (2006; 2010); Comaroff and Comaroff (2009); Beier (2009); Dean and Levi (2003); Forte (2010); and Neizen (2003).

24 These are all Siberian peoples, by Western geopolitical definitions, some living in Russia's Far East. An excellent analysis of the complex correlations of demography, politics, and land status in Russia is Donahoe *et al.* (2008). Less comprehensive, but with a list of 2010 census statistics for Siberian Natives in English is Laruelle (2014: 33–43).

25 Tomiak and Patrick (2010: 140). 'Ethnoscape' is a term of Arjun Appadurai (1996).

2 From counter-mapping to co-management

The Inuit, the state and the quest for collaborative arctic sovereignty

Barry Scott Zellen

Introduction

Over the last half century, a tremendous wave of structural innovation has transformed the political economy of Arctic North America, stretching all the way from the Bering Sea to Baffin Bay, with the completion of a multi-generational process of negotiating comprehensive Aboriginal land claims treaties to clarify issues of land ownership and to foster an enduring partnership between the region's indigenous peoples and the modern state.[1] This transformation has introduced a variety of new institutions of co-management and self-governance, and the formation of a new economy populated by Aboriginal regional and community corporations, investment corporations, land administration agencies, a variety co-management boards, and a complex patchwork of local, regional and territorial governments created to give a voice to indigenous interests. Once land claims were settled, the next step in the process of Arctic development has been the pursuit of new systems of Aboriginal self-governance, taking various forms and employing various structures over time, with greater powers becoming available as time went by, and earlier policies of assimilation being replaced by more contemporary policies promoting cultural and political renewal.

These new systems of governance ranged from the establishment of municipal or borough governments under existing constitutional law as we saw in Alaska in the 1970s; to the creation newly empowered tribal councils governed by federal Indian law in Alaska and the NWT in the 1980s and 90s; to the negotiation of entirely new systems of governance – with the most ambitious being Nunavut, with their comprehensive land claim settlement in 1993 linked to the subsequent formation of a new territorial government in 1999, creating a complex and potentially powerful system of self-governance applying a public model to a predominantly indigenous region for *de facto* indigenous self-governance. After Nunavut, the evolution toward more distinctly indigenous self-governing structures has continued, as reflected in the Labrador Inuit Land Claim of 2005 with the very first truly Inuit self-governing structure, whose governing principles were articulated in detail in the 2002 Labrador Inuit Constitution. Regardless of the jurisdiction, whether in Alaska or Arctic Canada, or beyond the shores of North America, indigenous peoples have shown tremendous ingenuity in their effort to build new systems for self-governance since the land claims movement took root in the 1960s, creatively adapting existing institutions or creating new ones when possible, lobbying for and negotiating to further advance their powers.

From land title to political power: the path to Inuit re-empowerment

When the Alaska Native Claims Settlement Act of 1971 (ANCSA) was enacted, it aimed to quickly bring Alaska Natives into the modern economy, and at the same time to clarify the extent of Aboriginal title, making it possible to fully develop the state's natural resources and in particular to build the trans-Alaska pipeline. Because its objectives were largely economic, its corporate model became its defining and most transformative characteristic – not without controversy, since the corporate model was viewed with some skepticism by indigenous leaders as a tool of assimilation, and there remains a continuing debate over the appropriateness of the corporate model to the indigenous north. ANCSA formally extinguished Aboriginal rights, title, and claims to traditional lands in the state, while formally transferring fee-simple title to 44 million acres – or some twelve percent of the state's land base – to Alaska Natives, with $962.5 million in compensation for the lands ceded to the state, $500 million of which was to be derived from future oil royalties (as a result of which over half the 'compensation' was to be derived from resources extracted from the Inupiat homeland – an irony not missed by Alaska Natives.) ANCSA also created 12 regional Native corporations, and later a 13th for non-resident Alaska Natives, and over 200 village corporations to manage these lands and financial resources. These new corporate structures introduced a brand new language and culture, as well as a new system of managing lands and resources that seemed at variance with the traditional cultures of the region and their traditional subsistence economy. The early years of ANCSA were famously described by justice Thomas Berger as dragging Alaska Natives 'kicking and screaming'[2] into the twentieth century, and many Native corporations approached the brink of bankruptcy, forced to monetize their net operating losses in a last desperate bid to stay in business. A new cottage industry of northern investment, legal, and policy advisors emerged – sometimes to the benefit of their clients, but often not. In addition to the *corporatization* of village Alaska, ANCSA's original design also had some structural flaws that also nearly proved fatal to the land claims experience, including a 20-year moratorium in transferring shares in Native corporations to non-Natives, which many feared would inevitably result in the dilution of Native ownership, known as the '1991 Time Bomb'. While critics of the land claims process are correct to point out these original structural flaws and the assimilating pressures introduced by new corporate structures, the land claims model has nonetheless proved resilient and adaptive, as Native corporations matured and their boards, managers and shareholders found ways to better balance traditional and modern values, learning from their crash course in capitalism as they went – so today the Native corporations represent a huge economic force in the state of Alaska.

Across the border, the Inuvialuit of the Western Canadian Arctic had a front-row seat to ANCSA, and were impressed by all the money that was flowing north, as well as the new corporate structures created, and the sizeable land quantum formally transferred to Alaska Natives. But they also noted the continuing threat to indigenous culture, and the lack of adequate protections of subsistence rights, traditional culture, and environmental protection, and were determined to do better. They also noted the structural complexity of Alaska's multi-ethnic Native land claim, which settled the claims of all Alaska Natives, and the continuing challenge of balancing the interests of so many diverse Native groups under the framework of a single land claims accord; they sought, instead, a solution that would serve Inuvialuit interests first and foremost. So when the Inuvialuit negotiated the 1984 Inuvialuit Final Agreement (IFA) during the late 1970s, the land claims model evolved significantly – in addition to creating new Native corporations at the village and regional level of the sort created by ANCSA, and accepting the extinguishment of Aboriginal title in exchange for fee-simple title to a substantial quantum of lands, the IFA also made an equal institutional commitment to the preservation of Native culture and traditions, to preserve the land and the wildlife, and to empower not just new corporate interests but also traditional cultural interests as well by creating new institutions of co-management and more powerful hunters and trappers committees. They also ensured that all Inuvialuit became shareholders, and that non-Inuvialuit never would – learning from the Alaskan experience. The Inuvialuit thus successfully modified the land claims concept, so that its structures included a natural institutional balancing – not unlike the U.S. government's under-lying balance of powers concept – that has enabled a greater commitment to cultural and environmental protections. Their land claim entitled the 3,000 Inuvialuit living in six communities to 35,000 square miles of land; co-management of land and water use, wildlife, and environmental assessment; wildlife harvesting rights; financial compensation of $45 million in 1978 dollars, inflation-adjusted to $162 million, for lands ceded to Canada; a share of government royalties for oil, gas, and mineral development on federal land; the formation of new national parks in their settlement area that further protect their land base from development, while allowing subsistence activities unhindered; and a commitment to meaningful economic partici-pation in any development in their settlement area. This model has remained largely intact in subsequent Inuit land claims, showing a continuing endurance as a model for Arctic development.

But one issue that was not yet on the table when the Inuvialuit chose to pursue their own regional land claim – and thereby gain some control over the intense oil boom in their homeland – was the establishment of new institutions of Aboriginal self-governance, something that the Inuit of the central and eastern Arctic – the future Nunavut territory – decided to wait for. The Inuvialuit felt they did not have the luxury of time given the frenetic pace of oil and gas exploration in their lands. But the territories of what became Nunavut remained more isolated, providing additional time to re-think, and re-design, the land claims model. In the years separating the signing of the Inuvialuit land claim in 1984, and the signing of the Nunavut land claim in 1993, much progress was made on the political question, and an increasing respect for Aboriginal rights in Ottawa enabled the establish-ment of a new concept: reshaping political boundaries to correspond to a land-claims settlement area, and establishing a new government to administer this region, augmenting the land claims with real political power. In 1993, with their signing of their historic accord, the Inuit of Nunavut were awarded $1.1 billion and title to 135,000 square miles of land, including 13,600 with subsurface rights, on top of various co-management boards, clearly defined rights protecting subsistence, and royalty sharing from resource development activities. Nunavut has a population of around 30,000 in 28 communities spread out across over 770,000 square miles, or one fifth of Canada's land mass, including the High Arctic islands and the central-arctic coastal main-land. While its population is tiny, its jurisdiction is vast and its resource base extensive, and the sea lanes that cross through its territory, including the famed Northwest Passage, are of emergent strategic economic and military value.

Perhaps the most striking innovation of the Nunavut claim, and the one which generated headlines around the world, was the way the land claim settlement was formally linked to the subsequent division of the Northwest Territories, and the formation of a brand new territory resulting in the 1999 birth of Nunavut. Nunavut has now been up and running for over 15 years, gaining valuable experience in self-governance – but also showing many strains as it struggles to confront some daunting social and economic chall-enges in one of the most challenging geophysical environments imaginable. There have been intergovernmental frictions with Ottawa over implemen-tation, and a growing perception of a crisis in Canada's youngest territory. But there is still much reason for hope for the future; while the roots of the challenges facing Nunavut go deep and are not likely to be quickly overcome, the solutions developed are new, northern solutions, custom-tailored to the Arctic region. Since its population is predominantly Inuit, Nunavut's public government can, at least for now, govern in an indigenous style – as the principles of the Nunavut land claim and the governing power of the new territorial government mutually reinforce one another. For now, at least, with its Inuit demographic predominance, a public model in an indigenous context is a creative way to create indigenous self-government by other means.

Half a decade after Nunavut made headlines around the world, the final Inuit land claim along the North American Arctic and Subarctic coast – the

Labrador Inuit (Nunatsiavut) Land Claims Agreement – was settled. It was ratified in December 2004 and came into effect a year later, presenting a new stage in the evolution of Inuit governance, making the two-step process more of a one-step process, further redefining the limits of self-government within a land settlement area – transcending the public model applied by the Inuit of Nunavut and the Inupiat of the North Slope. The agreement created the 28,000 square-mile Labrador Inuit Settlement Area with an adjoining 18,800 square mile ocean zone extending as far as Canada's territorial waters. The settlement area includes 6,100 square miles of Labrador Inuit Lands, five predominantly Inuit communities, and 3,700 square miles set aside for the Torngat Mountains National Park Reserve (following a tradition established by prior Inuit land claims to create vast national parks in which subsistence was protected) – with the Inuit retaining special rights in each of these areas. The Government of Canada will pay the Labrador Inuit $140 million in 1997 dollars in compensation for lands ceded to the Crown. Just as the formation of the Nunavut territory was the salient innovation of the Nunavut land claim, the emergence of truly Inuit self-government is the hallmark of the Labrador claim. As described in section 17.2 of the claim, it 'exhaustively sets out the law-making authorities and self-government rights of Inuit', with the newly created Nunatsiavut Government to be governed by the 'fundamental law of Inuit' as enunciated by the 159-page 2002 Labrador Inuit Constitution. The constitution, among its many components, included an Inuit charter of human rights, recognized Inuit customary law and its application to 'any matter within the jurisdiction and authority of the Nunatsiavut Government', and embraced laws to protect Inuit culture, language, and traditional knowledge.[3] The Labrador Inuit Constitution created a blueprint of Inuit values and a pathway to the rapid formation of a truly Inuit system of government in a region that's adjacent to coastal waters of emergent strategic significance, with active commercial and subsistence fisheries, major strategic mineral deposits such as the Voisey's Bay project, and the prospect of much future economic potential. It also showed a new path toward Aboriginal self-government, one that did not require the formal secession of Inuit communities like we saw in Nunavut, but instead forged a regional sub-government within an existing province, one with unique governing principles.

The Arctic land claims model, with its subsequent modifications, has become an inspiration to many from the Arctic to the tropics, proof-positive of what can be gained through a determined effort to rebalance and modernize the relationship between the indigenous people of the North and the modern state through negotiated settlements, sometimes taking decades to come to fruition. As with any land reform effort, changes in land tenure can have a profound impact on the domestic balance of power, shifting not just title to land, but the wealth created from that land, resulting in concentrations of economic power in the hands of a small indigenous population numbering in the thousands or tens of thousands, and creating new tensions between different Native groups. In Alaska and the Canadian Arctic, the Inuit have become owners of vast tracts of land, making them a landed elite with control over numerous economic, and increasingly, political levers. While not formally sovereign, they are poised to become increasingly influential stakeholders, partners in the consolidation of state sovereignty, and in the economic development of the northern frontier. A comparable situation exists in the post-Ottoman Middle East, with extended tribal families and clans sitting at a powerful and lucrative nexus of land owner-ship, natural resource wealth, and political power. While the indigenous peoples of Arctic North America are not in command of the ultimate levers of sovereign state power, such as military forces, diplomatic embassies, or national treasuries, they do have in their possession – or within reach – many tools of regional power, making them dominant regional elites in today's Arctic.

Sovereignty by other means: counter-mapping and the foundation for Inuit land claims

Despite their notable gains in land, wealth, and power, the Inuit have experienced a continuing exclusion by the Arctic rim states from several policy areas that national governments believe remain the prerogative of the sovereign. On April 28, 2009, the Inuit Circumpolar Council released the Circumpolar Inuit Declaration on Arctic Sovereignty which responded to this continuing exclusion – particularly from the making of Arctic defense, security and diplomatic policies, as had been experienced at Ilulissat the year before and continues today with the exclusion of defense and security affairs from the mandate of the Arctic Council. The Inuit nonetheless aspire to shape policies in the Arctic on military, security, and diplomatic issues, and during the Cold War endeavored to denuclearize the Arctic basin and to help unify east and west through northern displays of collaboration and cooperation – years before Soviet Premier Mikhail Gorbachev adopted such an approach as state policy in his ultimately unsuccessful bid to end the cold war on terms favorable to Soviet power. The 2009 declaration emerged from the first Inuit Leaders' Summit, held on November 6–7, 2008 in Kuujjuaq, Nunavik, where they 'gathered to address Arctic sovereignty' and 'expressed unity in our concerns over Arctic sovereignty deliberations, examined the options for addressing these concerns, and strongly committed to developing a formal declaration on Arctic sovereignty'.[4] In Kuujjuaq, the Inuit leader-ship had noted with disappointment that the '2008 Ilulissat declaration on Arctic sovereignty by ministers representing the five coastal Arctic states did not go far enough in affirming the rights Inuit have gained through interna-tional law, land claims and self-government processes'.[5] In many ways, their declaration was a direct response to the foreign ministers of the Arctic rim states for the exclusion of the Inuit at Ilulissat, and it counters this exclusion with a strong argument for a central Inuit role in determining the fate of the

Arctic. As the ICC observed at this start of its effort in November 2008:

> Sovereignty is a complex issue. It has a variety of overlapping elements, anchored in international law. But fundamentally it begins with the history and reality of Inuit use and occupation of Arctic lands and waters; that use and occupation is at the heart of any informed discussion of sovereignty in the Arctic. Arctic nation states must respect the rights and roles of Inuit in all international discussions and commitments dealing with the Arctic.[6]

While the institutional map within the Arctic has grown into a complex mosaic of joint- and self-governing structures, empowering and enriching the Inuit, the gap between the dominant narrative on extensive Inuit indigeneity and the historical reality of their cross-border and internal migrations in both the early- and the mid-twentieth century – in particular from Alaska to the Western Arctic in the early twentieth century, and from Northern Quebec to the High Arctic at mid-century – should not be overlooked as they so often are, in part because the state has allied itself with the Inuit in a joint effort to mutually recognize each other's claims, and in so doing, to mutually strengthen both Canada's sovereign claims to the Arctic and the conditions of the Inuit within the Arctic. Ottawa has thereby gained much credibility in world politics with regard to its assertion of sovereignty over its northern territorial frontiers – which remain lightly settled and in some places, entirely unsettled – into contemporary times, while the Inuit have received the many benefits described above. The land swap that has defined a half century of Arctic history has been mutually beneficial to both the state and the Inuit.

Some forty years ago, a team of pioneering anthropologists helped to lay a new foundation for Inuit land claims across Arctic Canada through the Inuit Land Use and Occupancy Project, mapping modern Inuit land use and helping to demarcate the boundaries that would solidify into the Inuit and Inuvialuit land settlements in the 1980s and 1990s, and which would inspire a revolution in indigenous mapping that has come to be known as 'counter-mapping' by which indigenous peoples have turned the map, long a tool of the state to assert sovereignty over new lands and peoples, back upon the state as a tool of empowerment and reclamation of indigenous land rights. Like our generation's human-terrain mapping teams operating in remote conflict zones, this small group of dedicated field anthropologists, with a deep love for the North and a sincere appreciation of Inuit culture, made history by fundamentally transforming the way Ottawa perceived its own Arctic territories – from largely uninhabited frontier lands to productive lands under extensive Inuit land use and occupation. Their work has proved of unequivocally high value to the Inuit who hired them in pursuit of their historic land claims settlement, fostering what became an unquestioned consensus between the Inuit and the state on the narrative of Inuit use and occupation of Arctic lands as presented by the Inuit and illustrated by the distinctly individualistic 'map biographies' sketched by Inuit hunters and trapper for these anthropological fieldworkers across the Arctic.

In his 2010 book, *Rethinking the Power of Maps* – a follow-up to his seminal 1992 *The Power of Maps* – Denis Wood examines the phenomenal rise of counter-mapping amongst indigenous peoples worldwide, crediting the Inuit Land Use and Occupancy Project and its three-volume report issued in 1976 as a powerful historical catalyst of increasing use of indigenous mapping as a tool to persuade states to recognize indigenous land rights. Wood writes that it's 'counter-mapping that shows us where mapping is headed' and 'it's the new attitudes, visions, and radical philosophies of the counter-mappers that are really taking maps and mapmaking in a whole new direction, a direction with the potential to free maps at last from the tyranny of the state'.[7] He describes how 'counter-mapping practices played an essential role in the creation of the Territory of Nunavut where the Inuit became the first Indigenous peoples in the Americas to achieve self-government in recent times'.[8] After the Canadian Supreme Court found in 1973 that 'there was an aboriginal title, and one that dated to a Royal Procla-mation of 1763', Ottawa 'adopted a policy of trying to extinguish such titles by negotiating treaties with the peoples who had never signed them; and beginning in 1974 it offered financial support for work that could lead toward such negotiations. The Inuit Tapirisat of Canada accepted funding to study Inuit land occupancy in the Arctic as a first step. This study resulted in the landmark publication in 1976 of the three-volume Inuit Land Use and Occupancy Project that pioneered the use of individual map biographies' in which 'hunters, trappers, fishermen, and berry pickers mapped out all the land they had ever used in their lifetimes, encircling hunting areas species by species, marking gathering locations and camping sites – everything their life on the land had entailed that could be marked on a map'.[9] These '"map biographies" were unlike anything that had existed before, and they inaug-urated a new trajectory in the history of mapmaking', and 'the Inuit maps went on to play a key role in the negotiations that enabled the Inuit to assert an aboriginal title to the 2 million km² of Canada today known as Nunavut'.[10] Wood observes with the stunning achievements of the Inuit and their mapmakers, the 'role of Indigenous mapping in this process was lost on no one',[11] and 'similar mapping projects were initiated among the Inuit, Settlers, and Naskapi-Montagnais of Labrador, the Beaver and Cree along the Peace River in northeastern British Columbia, the Dene of the Mackenzie River Basin, the Indians of the Yukon, and the Inuit and Cree of northern Quebec, among others'.[12] By 1992, further indigenous mapping projects 'were under way in Asia, Africa, and Latin America',[13] as a 'worldwide wave of Indigenous mapping' arose, 'substantially driven by the interests of granting agencies and philanthropic foundations'.[14]

The Inuit Land Use and Occupancy Project categorized land use in a curiously contemporary manner, not tracing Aboriginal land use deeply back in historical or prehistorical time, but looking at more recent Inuit land use over the course of just a few generations. As described in a section of the introduction to the third volume of the report on the 'Empirical and Inductive Nature of the maps', the maps 'represent a distillation of an immense quantity of highly detailed and precisely mapped information about the use of the Arctic land within each Inuit respondent's own adult lifetime. The information that has gone into these maps ... is the compilation of thousands of real and personal land uses, the partnerships of individual Inuit people with the land's resources', based on some 1,600 individual 'map biographies' chronicling Inuit hunting and trapping on a species-by-species basis.[15] The maps present the 'land use in the lifetime of respondents' that 'occurred during recognizable blocks of social time' as 'categorized' into three periods. Period I covers the 'years prior to the local arrival of traders'.[16] Period II includes the 'years of the fur trade, which occurred when a local or near local fur trade post was established, until fur trapping ceased to be a major economic activity for most people' – generally when 'government-sponsored construction programs provided wage employment opportunities', such as when the DEW Line was constructed. Period III includes the 'years marked by growth of permanent settlements in the north, during which time many Inuit chose to reside for most of the year at enlarged trading centers that provide new education, health care, administrative and housing programs'.[17] The authors of the report point out that '[u]ntil recently, the people who hunted the areas shown ... were not resident' in settlements, which mark the 'central point' on the land use maps, but instead 'were migratory, moving between the seasons and the years throughout a wide-spread area', and that 'settlement living is a relatively recent innovation' which 'for the majority of Inuit, in fact, defines the beginning of Period III in this report'.[18] The Inuit land use maps are categorized by whether they depict Phase I, II, and III, as well as by hunting and trapping; from these data are aggregated 'Regional Summary Maps' showing the 'Extent of Inuit Land Use' for each of the regions including the Western Arctic, West-Central Arctic, East-Central Arctic, Keewatin District, Eastern High Arctic, Baffin Island, Hudson/Ungava Bays, and for the whole of the Northwest Territories, where the full extent of Inuit land use aligns with great fidelity to the future boundaries of the Nunavut Territory.[19] In addition to the pioneering use of 'map biographies' and the contemporary context for the mapping of Inuit land use and thereby avoiding historical ambiguities and the many uncertainties shrouded by the mists of time, the seminal three-volume *Inuit Land Use and Occupancy Project Report* presents a number of additional methodological curiosities which, in the aggregate, suggest that the foundation to much of the Inuit land claim may be built upon subjective assumptions supported by hearsay evidence provided by partisan participants in what is at heart a highly politicized and inherently political process. Nonetheless, it remains noteworthy for its ambition, its effort to empower the Inuit and to redress perceived past injustices and insensitivities by governmental authorities, and its introduction of a powerful new mapping paradigm that essentially re-appropriated mapping as a tool of state, placing it firmly into the hands of indigenous peoples who literally re-charted their destiny.

Old claims, new lands: mapping and the migration paradox

A problematic legacy of the Inuit Land Use and Occupancy Project for the Western Arctic region is that other indigenous peoples (and not just the Inuit) traditionally used some of these very same lands, but these other Natives were not the ones paying their salaries – and as a result were largely marginalized from the report's re-framed narrative on Arctic land use and occupancy. The report's title says it all; it was the *Inuit Land Use and Occupancy Project*, and while other indigenous peoples live in the Arctic, the report was not designed to emphasize their claims, but rather the claims of the Inuit. A few of the report's contributors – most notably Peter J. Usher, who authored the portion of the report on the Western Arctic, and Robert McGhee, who contributed a chapter excerpted from his 1974 book, *Beluga Hunters: An Archaeological Reconstruction of the History and Culture of the Mackenzie Delta Kittegaryumiut* – do mention the important place of the Dene peoples of the Western Arctic in their discussions. But the report would nonetheless become a foundational document substantiating the claims of the Inuit to Arctic lands. So while the dual-use by the Gwich'in of the Western Arctic was mentioned briefly in the report's pages, the tension between the historical record of dual-use and the aspiration of the Inuit for an ethnically-homogeneous settlement area, was never fully reconciled. These anthropologist-certified boundaries, based on largely self-reported map-biographies, would ultimately become constitutionally entrenched in law, bringing tremendous political and economic gain to the Inuit organization that hired them, and to the individual Inuit land claim activists who became political and economic leaders in the post-settlement era.

For many of the Inuvialuit, these claimed lands were lands they had only settled in the early 20th century, migrating to Arctic Canada from their home communities in Alaska where they found rich hunting and trapping lands traditionally used and occupied by the Kittigazuit Eskimos before epidemics nearly wiped them out early in the century.[20] McGhee describes the decline of the Mackenzie Eskimo population and the arrival of Alaskan Inupiat in these abandoned hunting and trapping lands at the start of the 20th century.[21] He cites Vilhjamur Stefannson's 1919 observations of this influx of Alaskan Inuit into the Mackenzie Delta region: 'A large number of the Nunatama have come either overland by themselves or eastward from Point Barrow or Kotzebue Sound as passengers on whaling ships, while those from Bering Strait have ordinarily come as whalers or servants on board. The net result is that the Mackenzie Population is becoming mixed in blood, is already deeply influenced in its culture, and has taken up many strange words into the spoken language'.[22] McGhee concludes that 'Aboriginal Mackenzie

Eskimo culture could probably be considered to have become extinct between 1900 and 1910'.[23]

It is no secret that many Inuvialuit are of relatively recent Alaskan Inuit descent; many became members of the 13th Alaska Native Corporation for non-resident Alaska Natives. Some even enrolled as beneficiaries of the Dene/Metis Land Claim prior to the rapid acceleration of the Inuvialuit land claims process in the 1970s, when they changed affiliation and re-framed their identity as Inuvialuit, or 'the *real* people'. Over the years, many an Ottawa-based politician felt obligated to visit the Western Arctic for a photo-op, including the efforts of Keith Spicer, whose 1990 Citizen's Forum on National Unity sought to alleviate tensions between Native and non-Native after the violent clash at Oka, Quebec, and at the same time to defuse the festering dispute between English and French Canada. Spicer told residents of the Western Arctic region that he felt compelled to come first to speak with Canada's very first citizens – not knowing that he was talking to some of Canada's newest immigrants who had called Alaska home only a few decades earlier. Just four days after being appointed chairman of the Citizen's Forum on Canada's Future, Spicer headed to Inuvik and Tuktoyaktuk to launch his effort to reconcile Canada's fractious populace; his visit was meant to be 'an attitude-changing gesture ... I want people in the South to think of Aboriginal people first because they were first'.[24] Little did he know that many, indeed most, of the Inuvialuit in attendance that day were relative newcomers to Canada. Most Inuvialuit were not among the first peoples to inhabit the Canadian Arctic, but rather the last – part of a relatively recent migration to newly vacant trapping lands. 'Inuvialuit' is not a traditional Inuit descriptor for the newly-arrived Uummarmiut (the 'people of the green trees') who had long resided near the treeline in proximity to the neighboring Gwich'in, or for the indigenous Siglit peoples of whom only a small number survived the epidemics that had decimated their hitherto robust population. The Gwich'in inhabited the same region as the Inuit of the trees, sharing the very same lands and resources, but who would witness the resource-rich coastal lands that they long shared with the Inuit becoming Inuit-owned and -controlled lands, and thus denied to them.

As Usher has observed, 'There is considerable overlap between lands used by the Inuit and lands used by the Indians in the Delta region, especially in the area between Aklavik and Inuvik in the Delta itself, in the marten trapping area east of Inuvik, and in the caribou hunting range in the Richardson Mountains between Aklavik and Fort McPherson. Some Indians also go to Whitefish Station to hunt white whales in July. Both Aklavik and Inuvik have Indian populations nearly as large as Inuit populations. There is a tendency among both groups to see their lands as Native lands collectively, on a community basis, and not to divide them up into 'Inuit lands' and 'Indian lands' which would in any case be impossible'.[25] In his discussion of muskrat trapping in the Mackenzie Delta, Usher writes that the 'fur economy of the Delta has always been centered primarily on the muskrat. North of a line roughly from Aklavik to Inuvik, there is probably not a single lake or creek that has not been exploited by the Inuit muskrat trappers. (South of that line, the Delta is used mainly by Indians)'.[26]

The neatness of such a north/south split along an artificial 'line' that would become the land claim settlement area boundary seems to contradict Usher's above-cited remarks – especially given Usher's later comment on historic dual-use by both Inuit and Dene, and their mutual perception of these lands as being commonly 'Native', and not differentiated according to specific Native ancestry, which is not only logical, but consistent with Usher's observations regarding caribou hunting: 'There has been a noticeable shift in caribou hunting range over time from the mountains down to the coast',[27] a shift that is consistent with Dene cultural memory of seasonal use of the Arctic coast by Gwich'in hunters, in addition to Usher's own observation of Dene whaling along the Arctic coast as well, a logical eventuality considering the plentiful nature of the Beluga whale resource, and the proximity of its habitat to traditional Dene hunting lands. Thus this shift in the caribou range that Usher uses to validate Inuit claims to the coast could substantiate as well the claim by Gwich'in to these same lands. Usher explains the shift is 'largely because in the early 1900's, before the widespread ownership of whale boats and schooners, many people, especially those of Alaskan origin, spent most of the summer on the high ground inland, where travel by foot and pack dog was easier, caribou more plentiful, and mosquitoes fewer. They moved with the caribou and had no permanent summer camps'[28] – a hunting pattern that could describe the Gwich'in caribou hunters as well.

The traditional Mackenzie Inuit population nearly died out from exposure to western diseases, and was described by McGhee as becoming culturally extinct early in this century. He lists the original Mackenzie Eskimo sub-groups, which included the Kigirktarugmiut, Kupugmiut, Kittegaryumiut, Nuvorugmiut, and Avvagmiut, and notes there was both a trading relationship with the neighboring Dene peoples as well as a history of conflict between them – and that the Gwich'in at the time of European contact 'were in frequent but wary contact with the Eskimos of the East Channel area' and that a 'good deal of trade took place between these groups before 1852 when the Eskimos began to visit Peel's River Post, but that several instances of fighting in connection with this trade have been noted'.[29] He cites the 1853 observations of Hooper who 'states that the Mackenzie River Eskimos ... traded with the 'Mackenzie River Loucheux' (probably the poorly known Nakotcho Kutchin) but were probably at 'war to the knife' with the Peel River Loucheux (the Vunta Kutchin or Rat Indians who had trade relations with the Kigirktarugmiut at Barter Island.) After the Eskimos began to trade at Peel River's Post, there was some intermarriage with Indians, and at least one Vunta Kutchin lived at Kittigaruit during the late 19th century'.[30] Thus the cultural history of the Mackenzie Delta region is quite diverse, and its lands were dually used by both the Inuit and Gwich'in. This dual-use would appear to suggest the Gwich'in have as strong an historical claim to the lands and resources of the region, particularly since the Gwich'in have demon-strated uninterrupted continuous historical use and occupancy of these lands while most of the Inuit of the Mackenzie Delta region are by comparison relative newcomers to the region. While Usher does acknowledge Gwich'in use of these lands, the emphasis of the *Inuit Land Use and Occupancy Project Report* would come to disproportionately favor the Inuit. This seem-ing tilt in favor of Inuit traditional use at the expense of another indigenous people from the same region is reinforced by the economic relationship between the report's sponsor, the Inuit Tapirisat of Canada, a national political body representing the political interests of the Inuit; and the federal government, which partnered with the Inuit in this process of documenting Inuit land use and advanced the funds for the project, even though the choice of anthropological fieldworkers was determined by the Inuit, who were in the process of negotiating their land claim with the federal government – and in the end, Ottawa accepted their findings at face value.

As described in the report's preface: 'In February 1973 Inuit Tapirisat of Canada proposed to the Minister of Indian and Northern Affairs that research be undertaken to produce a comprehensive and verifiable record of Inuit land use and occupancy in the Northwest Territories of Canada', and the 'record so obtained would delimit the present and past use and occu-pation of the land and marine environment and would categorize the uses which any particular area served. In view of the continuing role which land plays in defining the cultural and ecologic circumstances of Inuit society, the research was also to provide an explicit statement – *by the Inuit* – of their perception of the man-land relationship'.[31] The perceptual nature of these observations is acknowledged, but through the subsequent processes of land claims negotiation, formalization, and implementation, perception would eventually become legal fact. The preface to the report acknowledges that 'with the exception of the short settlement histories presented for each contemporary community, virtually all textual material was derived from fieldworkers' discussions with Inuit informants. By thus restricting the material presented to that derived directly from recent fieldwork, we have attempted to meet our objective of setting down the Inuit view relating to land use and occupation'.[32] The report's findings would gain tremendous political, indeed historic, momentum, contributing to the formalization of these perceptions into law, and while this would be of great benefit to the Inuit, it would harm the Dene peoples who had long shared these same lands. The report's authors note in the end of their preface that the 'main deter-minant of the final form of this report' has 'necessarily been consideration of balance in trying to describe accurately the voluminous documentation now available describing the different Inuit groups occupying and using the approximately 1.5 million square miles of northern Canada that constitute their domain'.[33]

As described in the foreword of the *Inuit Land Use and Occupancy Project Report*: 'The Inuit Land Use and Occupancy Project was initiated at the request of the Inuit Tapirisat of Canada. Following preliminary discussions in 1972 and 1973, Milton Freeman Research Limited was incorporated on 18 June 1973, in order to undertake research into Inuit use and occupancy of the land, with funds advanced by the Department of Indian and Northern Affairs. After the research had begun a Steering Committee regularly met to oversee the interests of the federal government and Inuit Tapirisat of Canada in the Project'.[34] This committee is described on the next page: 'The contract between Her Majesty and Milton Freeman Research Limited to carry out the Inuit Land Use and Occupancy Project called for the establishment of a Steering Committee to advise the Minister on the overall progress of the Project. The Steering Committee, consisting of two members appointed by the Minister and two by the Inuit Tapirisat of Canada, met five times, reviewed the progress reports and financial statements of the Project, and found them satisfactory'.[35] The Inuit representatives were Connie Hunt and Tagak Curley and the government representatives were A. Stevenson and Dr. M.J. Ruel.[36] Among those 'fieldworkers, interpreters, and interviewers' individually thanked in the acknowledgements on page nine from the western Arctic portion of the project are: Victor Allen, Nellie Cournoyea, Bertram Pokiak, Sam Raddi, and Peter Thrasher, several of whom would become important land claims activists, as well as important political and economic leaders – with Nellie Cournoyea rising to become the Premier of the North-west Territories and later the Chair of the Inuvialuit Regional Corporation, and Sam Raddi, who served as COPE President and is widely viewed as a founding father of the Inuvialuit land claim.[37]

That so many of the field researchers and interviewers who played the role of gatekeeper of the information provided by the Inuvialuit hunters and trappers on their traditional land use were so closely affiliated with the land claims process and personally gained political and economic power from the very land claims process their research helped to substantiate, reveals the inherently political nature of the land claims process and the potential to politicize results of research undertaken in pursuit of such a political process. Reminiscent of Carl von Clausewitz, the famed nineteenth century Prussian theorist of war who coined the famous aphorism, 'war is the continuation of politics (*politik*) by other means', one could conclude that Aboriginal land claims are also a continuation of politics by other means – and reflect the bilateral effort a peacemaking to reconcile a fundamental land dispute between indigenous peoples and the modern states that assert sovereignty over indigenous lands. For the Inuit, land claims have become an important mechanism for conflict resolution that endeavors to reconcile the interests of the Inuit and the state, and to create lasting institutions for economic modernization and development, land and resource management, and increasingly self-governance – and to ensure that peace and stability are maintained across the vast northern territories that 'constitute their domain'.

The third volume of the *Inuit Land Use and Occupancy Project Report*, as noted above, presents numerous land use and occupancy maps derived from the project's 1,600 map-biographies, and similarly shares with the preceding two volumes methodological issues, including a reliance upon claims made and biographical maps sketched by Inuit hunters and trapper without cross-checking their claims against those of other users of those lands. If you add to this the political role of the fieldworkers, translators and interviewers, and the fact that the report was commissioned by a political organization with funds advanced by the national government, and implemented by a research consultancy that was not a public institution with a broad communal responsibility to all stakeholders in society, then these maps can be understood to be subjective aspirations and not necessarily reflections of objective reality, as wishful thinking rather than established ground truth. And yet these maps, as discussed above and widely noted by indigenous peoples worldwide, played an important role in determining Inuit land claim boundaries. Summing up the extent of Inuit land use on page 153 and 154 of the report's third volume is a map describing the 'Full Extent of Inuit Land Use', and it comes as no surprise that the extent of land use depicted is so very full – covering what would become the Inuvialuit Settlement Area in the west and the Nunavut Settlement Area in the north and east, a vast expanse of land covering nearly one-third of Canada.[38] The map presenting the 'Full Extent of Inuit Land Use' thus conveyed extensive, contiguous territorial possession across the heart of Arctic North America, a domain so vast that to many, it looks like the map of a sovereign state.

The maps presented in the third volume of the *Inuit Land Use and Occupancy Project Report* are extensive, but their time frames are curiously contemporary and a far-reaching historical analysis largely absent. Thus the extent of Inuit land use portrayed is not necessarily a zone of *traditional* indigenous land use, as the vast majority of its constituent maps illustrate recent patterns of land use – but the end result has been to incorporate these lands into the final agreements for the Inuit of both the Western and Eastern Arctic, agreements based upon *Aboriginal* use and occupation of these lands. The persuasive power of these maps cannot be overstated, and it has never really been questioned by anyone except for the Dene peoples whose claims to territories in both the Inuvialuit and the Nunavut settlement areas overlap with those of the Inuit. Both the Inuit and the state gained much by accepting the compelling logic of these maps, and not to look very far beneath the surface or back in time. There was no room for third-party interests here, and a mantra of the post-settlement era has been that there are in fact almost no third-party claims in the settlement areas, something the Dene peoples of the Arctic dispute.

Indeed, the land use maps prepared for volume three of the *Inuit Land Use and Occupancy Project Report* for the Inuvialuit of Aklavik convey a sense of Inuit exclusivity to lands that are known to have been used by both Gwich'in as well as Inuit, and so noted by Usher in his report. But in the end it was the compelling logic of these maps that would influence the land settlement boundaries, and thus determine ownership of lands that had been jointly used and which may well have been as if not more legitimately claimed by the Gwich'in, owing to the historical continuity of their usage and the relative newness of many Inuit residents of the Mackenzie Delta region. As a consequence, the Gwich'in Settlement Region includes lands found only to the south of those claimed by the Inuvialuit – even though lands north of that boundary line were historically used by the Gwich'in, and the migration route of the Porcupine Caribou herd, a principal food source for the Gwich'in that was jointly hunted by both the Gwich'in and Inuit, crosses from one side of that boundary line to the other – helping to substantiate the claim by Gwich'in to be traditional users of these lands. Such a legacy of traditional land use can be further substantiated by the rich heritage of traditional Gwich'in placenames throughout the region, a heritage that stands in marked contrast to the Inuvialuit, who could not persuasively demonstrate such in their land claims effort, hence their reliance on the anthropologist-sanctioned *Inuit Land Use and Occupancy Project Report*. Consider the observations of University of Alberta geography professor William C. Wonders, who author- ed the 1987 article, 'Native Claims and Place Names in Canada's Western Arctic', in *The Canadian Journal of Native Studies*: 'The Western Arctic/ Lower Mackenzie sector was and is the area of most extensive overlap in the Northwest Territories. The Dene and Metis regarded it as of top priority even to the point of trying to have the investigation restrict itself to this area, a request rejected as it was contrary to the agreed-upon terms of reference. The much greater economic development in the Mackenzie Delta and the oil and gas activity in the Beaufort Sea make this area particularly important. It also is the most complex ethnically, with large numbers of all major groups intermingled and increasingly intermarrying'.[39]

As Wonders recalled, 'In 1978 the Federal Government and the Inuvialuit (C.O.P.E.) had signed an Agreement In Principle towards a comprehensive land claims settlement and the boundaries thus delineated greatly alarmed the Dene/Metis. They believed that their traditional rights were threatened within parts of the area involved, despite reassurances by the Inuvialuit. By 1983 there still had been no agreement reached ... in the matter of overlapping areas of land use and occupancy', and yet 'such agreement was a pre-requisite of the Government of Canada for settlement of any comprehensive Native land claims'.[40] While the Native associations 'had held discussions on an on again/off again basis for some years but without reaching agreement', Wonders noted that 'finally in September 1983, with consent of all parties', he was 'appointed 'fact finder' to the Minister of Indian Affairs and Northern Development, to research and determine Native land use and occupancy in overlap areas in the Northwest Territories as part of a process to resolve the overlap problem. Major emphasis was to be placed upon existing docu- mentary evidence supplemented by first hand local input where desirable, though the five-month time frame permitted was disconcertingly short. The report was forwarded to the Minister on January 20, 1984',[41] prior to the enactment of the Inuvialuit Final Agreement in June of that year.

While there was comparatively much traditional place-name information from the Dene peoples of the region, there was a noted shortage of information on the Inuvialuit place-names; as Wonders explains, a 'major gap existed in the indigenous place names of this particular area. Except for limited treatment by Petitot, Inuvialuit toponomy had been almost entirely neglected by researchers. The interpretive results accordingly are really an indication of the extent of Dene/Metis presence in the overlap area but without comparable toponymic information for the Inuvialuit (though other sources of information on the latter people's presence is available). As noted previously however, the former group felt the urgent need to demonstrate its presence within part of the designated 'Traditional Inuvialuit Lands' according to the Agreement in Principle'.[42] The irony is that the Dene peoples of the region were better able to establish their traditional use of these very same lands; hence their consternation with the delineation of Inuvialuit and Dene lands along a seemingly arbitrary north-south boundary line.[43] Wonders observed that 'joint Inuvialuit-Dene place names are noted for the Richardson Mountains west of the Delta and for the Peel River above Fort McPherson. Eastwards, joint Inuvialuit-Dene names are recorded for the lower Anderson River and Horton River. The concentration of exclusively Dene place names west of the Horton River stops short of the Arctic coast but extends west as far as the Mackenzie Delta beyond Sitidgi and Campbell Lakes. One isolated Dene place name occurs north of Parsons Lake and south of the site of the Inuvialuit village of Kittigazuit, at the base of the Tuktoyaktuk Peninsula'.[44] He further noted, 'It is clear that Dene place names do occur extensively within the areas designated as 'traditional Inuvialuit lands' in parts of the mainland in the Western Arctic and lower Mackenzie Valley area, thereby substantiating the Dene's claim to a traditional presence within parts of those areas. The Mackenzie Delta initially seems to have been used seasonally at least by Inuvialuit, who focussed primarily on the coast. Not until the present century did both Inuvialuit and Dene move into the Delta on a permanent basis'.[45] And yet in the end it was the Inuvialuit who eventually gained title to the resource-rich coastal lands, and as a consequence, the post-settlement era, with its new property boundaries separating Inuvialuit lands from those of the more southerly Gwich'in lands, has continued to experience land disputes between the two peoples.[46] With the Inuvialuit land claim firmly settled, new boundaries were drawn corresponding to the maps depicted in the *Inuit Land Use and Occupancy Project Report*, and these became entrenched in law – despite the long historical record of dual-use by both Gwich'in, thus depriving many Gwich'in full access to, use of, and economic benefits derived from their own traditional lands along the Western Arctic coast.

With their new wealth and status as major land owners and power brokers across the North American Arctic, it is hard to view the Inuit of today as victims any more. And yet, Inuit leaders continue to position their people as victims of past historical injustices in their quest for compensation from the

Government of Canada, as evident in the case of the High Arctic exiles who were relocated to the High Arctic communities of Grise Fiord and Resolute in the 1950s. There has been much controversy over the plight of the exiles, with numerous accounts written describing their poor treatment and near-abandonment by Canadian authorities during the early years of their relocation, such as Wil Haygood's August 1992 feature in the *Boston Globe*, 'The Lie at the Top of the World', and several books including Alan Rudolph Marcus' 1995 *Relocating Eden: The Image and Politics of Inuit Exile in the Canadian Arctic*, and Melanie McGrath's 2008 *The Long Exile: A Tale of Inuit Betrayal and Survival in the High Arctic*. Thomas Berger correctly pointed out that the 1950s relocation of the Inuit to the High Arctic was driven largely by Ottawa's desire to establish a permanent population, and thus bolster its otherwise tenuous sovereign claims to the region.

Because of the painful history of their relocation, and the chronicled neglect and mistreatment by government officials, Ottawa agreed to a $10 million financial settlement with the survivors of the relocation and their descendants in 1996, known as the High Arctic Relocatees Trust or HART fund. But because Ottawa argued that its intention was to alleviate the threat of famine near Port Harrison, it did not proffer an apology at the time, waiting instead another 14 years before capitulating and formally presenting an apology. University of British Columbia international law professor Michael Byers passionately argued the case for a formal apology to the exiles, and in a 2008 op-ed in *The Globe and Mail* made his case: 'Mr. Harper, apologize to the 'High Arctic Exiles': Not only is this the right thing to do, but it would help cement Canada's northern claims'.[47] Byers saw a link between the apology issue and Canada's recent efforts to strengthen its sovereignty in the Arctic, and believed Ottawa's decision in the 1950s to move the exiles to the Elizabeth Islands 'was motivated by concerns about possible Danish or American claims', and that 'the Inuit, identified by government officials by numbers rather than their names, were essentially treated as flagpoles'.[48] As he described, 'for the Inuit, it was like landing on the moon'.[49] Byers suggested that 'for a Prime Minister who cares about sovereignty, apologizing to the High Arctic Exiles would be an excellent next step'.[50] But while an apology would be dramatic, and when it finally came was exuberantly cheered by Inuit, the situation of the exiles was complicated by the fact that their presence in the High Arctic has resulted in substantial benefits to the Inuit, and that their presence dates back only to the 1950s – a point successfully argued by the exiles themselves in their quest for historical justice.

Among the benefits received by the Inuit were large tracts of High Arctic lands selected for the Nunavut land claim, which contribute substantially not only to the land- and resource-wealth of the Inuit, but also to the territorial breadth of the Nunavut territory. By many measures – including the size of the new territory, the amount of land now owned outright by the Inuit (lands not utilized by the Inuit in modern times, and thus integrated into the modern Canadian state well before modern Inuit land use in the High Arctic islands even began), the extent of their subsurface rights as well, and the inclusion of the High Arctic communities of Grise Fiord and Resolute and their continuing flow of operational funding and infrastructure investment as part of Nunavut – the relocation of the exile families to the High Arctic has proven, on the whole, to be a long-term gain for the Inuit overall. Further, as Byers himself has noted, Inuit leaders like John Amagoalik – considered by many to be the 'Father of Nunavut' – emerged from the crucible of the relocation experience; so as difficult as the experience was for the families involved, it made the Inuit stronger and not weaker for their suffering, contributing to the emergence of a strong and dedicated leadership that ultimately triumphed by negotiating the very creation of Nunavut.[51] They now run municipal governments and a variety of new Inuit corporations, and own tens of thousands of square miles of land outright, with vast surface and substantial subsurface rights, influence over the development of those lands through co-management boards, and millions of dollars in compensation for ceding the remaining lands to the Crown. By virtue of their relocation to the High Arctic, the Inuit have become the dominant landowners of a largely Inuit territory that covers one-third of Canada's land mass. If they are truly exiles to these lands, with historical roots to lands far away – 1,933 kilometers to the south – one could reasonably conclude that they could not rightfully claim *Aboriginal* titled to these new lands, nor to any of the compensation Ottawa has provided in turn for surrendering Aboriginal title to them.

Indeed, a historical case for an Inuit claim to the High Arctic lands to which they were relocated in the 1950s is further undermined by recent research that questions any ancestral link to the original inhabitants of the High Arctic – the Dorset or paleo-Eskimo peoples who settled the Arctic in a single migratory wave hundreds of years before today's Inuit arrived. *Tech Times* reporter Jim Algar reported in September 2014 that DNA studies show the first migration into Arctic North America 'left no genetic traces in modern Inuit', and that as a consequence, the Inuit 'were not the first humans to inhabit the Arctic'.[52] According to the new research, 'DNA from ancient remains showed the Saqqaq and Dorset peoples, considered a single genetic line dubbed Paleo-Eskimos, originated in a single migration from Siberia across the Bering Strait into North America that started around 6,000 years ago', who then 'spread from Alaska to as far as Greenland, but died out about 700 years ago'.[53] Further, the study shows 'DNA from those ancient people and modern day Inuit show no match'.[54]

The foundation of the successfully negotiated claim by Inuit to lands they never historically used or occupied is fascinating; but as a consequence one could argue that Canada's own sovereign claim to these lands is weakened, having been justified in large part by the consent of these self-professed original peoples who turn out to be relative newcomers to these lands – lands that they persuasively argued that they only came to settle under the duress and deceit of the very same Government of Canada that now asserts a sovereign claim to these lands, a tautology too circular to remain credible upon close scrutiny. It is from this very same government that the Inuit negotiated their comprehensive land settlement, while at the same time demanding compensation and an apology for having been exiled to these distant lands, winning vast land holdings, lucrative cash compensation for ceded lands, and continuous implementation funds that flow to their new communities of Grise Fiord and Resolute, plus an additional $10 million that Ottawa paid in 1996 as further compensation for their suffering prior to issuing a full apology 14 years later. That apology did not come until 2010, when the Minister of Indian and Northern Affairs at the time, John Duncan, announced after years of controversy that: 'On behalf of the Government of Canada and all Canadians, we would like to offer a full and sincere apology to Inuit for the relocation of families from Inukjuak and Pond Inlet to Grise Fiord and Resolute Bay during the 1950s. We would like to express our deepest sorrow for the extreme hardship and suffering caused by the relocation. The families were separated from their home communities and extended families by more than a thousand kilometers. They were not provided with adequate shelter and supplies. They were not properly informed of how far away and how different from Inukjuak their new homes would be, and they were not aware that they would be separated into two communities once they arrived in the High Arctic. Moreover, the government failed to act on its promise to return anyone that did not wish to stay in the High Arctic to their old homes'.[55] As recognized by both the state and by the Inuit, Inuit use and occupancy of these new High Arctic lands only began in the 1950s. Without a history of traditional use or occupation, the Inuit of Nunavut would thus appear to have no bona fide Aboriginal claim to any land in the Elizabeth Islands.

Reporting on the October 16–18, 2014 Arctic Circle conference in Reykjavik, Iceland, prolific blogger and insightful Arctic scholar Mia Bennett has discussed the complexity inherent in defining indigeneity in the modern Arctic, writing 'who is indigenous and who is not – is actually quite complex'.[56] She pointed out that 'Norse settlers, for instance, sailed from Iceland and Norway to southwest Greenland at the end of the 10th century, likely arriving there before the Thule Inuit moved down from present-day northern Greenland and Canada', and though the Norse colonies eventually died out, 'one has to wonder, if they survived, would Norse Greenlanders be considered indigenous?'[57] Bennett further noted that a 'map of indigenous peoples in the Arctic shown during a presentation at Arctic Circle did not include Icelanders as indigenous people, even though the island was settled at the end of the 9th century – before the Thule Inuit made it to southern Greenland. By contrast, the Yakuts living in the Republic of Sakha are considered an indigenous people, even though they migrated from the steppes of Central Asia in the 13th century, centuries after the Settlement in Iceland. How long does a group of people need to reside in one place before they are considered indigenous?'[58]

It is universally accepted that the Inuit are indigenous to the Arctic, but can one group of Inuit originally from Northern Quebec rightly claim Aboriginal title to lands over nineteen hundred kilometers to the north, on a High Arctic island they had never used or occupied before their arrival in the middle of the twentieth century? And can another group of recently migrated Inupiat, whose home communities are in Alaska, across an international boundary, rightly claim Aboriginal title to lands in Canada's Western Arctic, lands utilized by the Gwich'in for centuries, and the traditional homeland of another, linguistically distinct Inuit community whose population had tragically collapsed after epidemics swept through their community earlier in the century? For the Inuvialuit and the Arctic exiles, the answer was a clear yes: they could, and they did. We thus find ourselves at a fascinating moment in the history of Inuit empowerment – where an indigenous people with historical roots outside their land claims settlement area has now twice persuaded the state to accept an Aboriginal claim to their newly inhabited lands – first, when a group comprised primarily of recent Inupiat migrants from Alaska rechristened themselves the Inuvialuit of the Western Canadian Arctic within a generation of their arrival; and again, when a group of more recent Inuit migrants from Northern Quebec asserted an Aboriginal claim to lands in the High Arctic that they had settled only a generation earlier – receiving, through their successful negotiations, fee-simple title to extensive lands, bountiful financial compensation, and multiple levers of political power in exchange for ceding Aboriginal rights to lands never before part of their traditional homeland, which in the case of the Inuvialuit was located across an international border in the United States, and in the case of the High Arctic exiles was located almost two thousand kilometers to the south in the Province of Quebec.

These impressive – indeed unprecedented – gains through successful negotiation achieved by these two Inuit groups reflect a great triumph for the Inuit, and are evidence of their remarkable resilience, strategic and tactical ingenuity, and determination – enabling them to reframe and re-map the very narrative of their origins to include new lands located far from their traditional territories, on the other side of national, state, and provincial boundaries, lands they had never before either used or occupied. In so doing, the Inuit have asserted a concept of indigeneity so far-reaching, and on such a truly continental scale, that it resembles something altogether different: modern sovereignty itself.

Notes

1   This historical process has been described in greater detail in the author's *Breaking the Ice: From Land Claims to Tribal Sovereignty in the Arctic* (Lanham, MD: Lexington Books, 2008) and *On Thin Ice: The Inuit, the State and Challenge of Arctic Sovereignty* (Lanham, MD: Lexington Books, 2009).
2   See Thomas R. Berger, *Village Journey: The Report of the Alaska Native Review Commission* (New York: Hill and Wang, 1985).

3   Land Claims Agreement Between the Inuit of Labrador and Her Majesty the Queen in Right of Newfoundland and Labrador and Her Majesty the Queen in Right of Canada, 17.3.4e, 252.

4   Inuit Circumpolar Council, Circumpolar Inuit Declaration on Arctic Sovereignty, April 28, 2009, www.inuitcircumpolar.com/sovereignty-in-the-arctic.html.

5   Inuit Circumpolar Council, Circumpolar Inuit Declaration on Arctic Sovereignty, April 28, 2009, www.inuitcircumpolar.com/sovereignty-in-the-arctic.html.

6   Inuit Circumpolar Council, Circumpolar Inuit Declaration on Arctic Sovereignty, April 28, 2009, www.inuitcircumpolar.com/sovereignty-in-the-arctic.html.

7   Denis Wood, 'Chapter 5: Counter-Mapping and the Death of Cartography', *Rethinking the Power of Maps* (New York: Guilford Press, 2010), 111.

8   Wood, *Rethinking the Power of Maps*, 111-12. While Wood focuses on Nunavut, which literally remapped Canada through the 1999 formation of this new, predominantly Inuit territory, the Inuit Land Use and Occupancy Project also laid the foundation for the groundbreaking Inuvialuit land claim that was signed in 1984.

9   Wood, *Rethinking the Power of Maps*, 130.

10   Ibid.: 130.

11   Ibid.: 131.

12   Ibid.: 131–32.

13   Ibid.: 132.

14   Ibid.: 135.

15   Milton M.R. Freeman, *Inuit Land Use and Occupancy Project Report, Volume III: Land Use Atlas* (Ottawa, ON: Supply and Services Canada, 1976), xv.

16   Freeman, *Inuit Land Use and Occupancy Project Report, Volume III*, xxiii.

17   Freeman, *Inuit Land Use and Occupancy Project Report, Volume III*, xxiii. In addition, the report notes, in 'some cases Period IV was also recognized as residents acknowledged the occurrence of a significant new event during Period III'. The authors of the report found '[v]ery few Period I land use maps were obtained, due to the scarcity of surviving individuals active that many years into the past' and so for 'many localities Periods I and II land use maps were combined and represented in the atlas as a single map'. They add that 'as land use does not change sharply as one time period grades into the next, this decision has not resulted in any significant misrepresentation of historical fact'. In contrast, in 'certain other recently established communities' including the High Arctic community of Grise Fiord, 'social time cannot be subdivided at all, and is represented as continuous Period III occupation'.

18   Freeman, *Inuit Land Use and Occupancy Project Report, Volume III*, xxiii.

19   Freeman, *Inuit Land Use and Occupancy Project Report, Volume III*, xv–xvi. Sample map biographies are presented on xvii, and a figure presenting a map-index for all the maps is presented on xviii–xix. On xx is a list of all wildlife categorized along with the cartographic symbol developed to portray each species, including seal, fish, whale, walrus, polar bear, wildfowl, caribou, moose, muskox, grizzly bear, wolf, wolverine, red fox, lynx, marten, beaver, muskrat, Arctic hare, ground squirrel, and sheep, as well as symbols for traplines (almost exclusively for fox), and fox trapping areas. For the Western Arctic region, the maps are organized as follows: Map 1 Aklavik: Trapping Periods I and II (pre-1955); Map 2 Aklavik: Hunting Periods I and II (pre-1955); Map 3 Aklavik: Trapping Periods III (1955–1974); Map 4 Aklavik: Hunting Periods III

(1955–1974); Map 5 Inuvik: Trapping Periods I and II (pre-1955); Map 6 Inuvik: Hunting Periods I and II (pre-1955); Map 7 Inuvik: Trapping Periods III (1955–1974); Map 8 Inuvik: Hunting Periods III (1955–1974); Map 9 Tuktoyaktuk: Trapping Periods I and II (pre-1955); Map 10 Tuktoyaktuk: Hunting Periods I and II (pre-1955); Map 11 Tuktoyaktuk: Trapping Periods III (1955–1974); Map 12 Tuktoyaktuk: Hunting Periods III (1955–1974); Map 13 Paulatuk: Trapping Periods I and II (pre-1959); Map 14 Paulatuk: Hunting Periods I and II (pre-1959); Map 15 Paulatuk: Trapping Periods III (1955–1974); Map 16 Paulatuk: Hunting Periods III (1955–1974); Map 17 Sachs Harbour: Trapping Periods I and II (1928–1961); Map 18 Sachs Harbour: Hunting Periods I and II (1928-1961); Map 19 Sachs Harbour: Trapping Periods III (1962-1974); Map 20 Sachs Harbour: Hunting Periods III (1962–1974). Additional, part of the West-Central Arctic region that joined the Inuvialuit Settlement Area, is the settlement of Holman: Map 40 Holman Island Hunting Period II (1923–1939); Map 41 Holman Island Trapping Period III (1939-1965); Map 42 Holman Island Hunting Period III (1939–1965); Map 43 Holman Island Trapping Period IV (1965–1974); Map 44 Holman Island Hunting (1965–1974). For the High Arctic, the maps are organized as follows: Map 140 Resolute Bay: Trapping Period II (pre-1960); Map 141 Resolute Bay: Hunting Period II (Pre-1960); Map 142 Resolute Bay: Trapping Period III (1960-1974); Map 143 Resolute Bay: Hunting Period III (1960–1974); Map 144 Grise Fiord: Hunting Period III (1963–1974); and Map 155 Grise Fiord: Trapping Period III (1963–1974).

20 Milton M.R. Freeman, (ed.)., *Inuit Land Use and Occupancy Project Report, Volume 2: Supporting Studies* (Ottawa, ON: Supply and Services Canada, 1976), 141. 'As recounted by Robert McGhee in his chapter in volume 2 of the Inuit Land Use and Occupancy Project Report: Before the arrival of Europeans in the 19th century, the people who are now called Mackenzie Eskimos inhabited the Western Canadian Arctic coast between Barter Island and Cape Bathurst. They were numerous people with a population variously estimated at between 2,000 and 4,000, a figure larger than the total remainder of the Eskimo population inhabiting the Arctic regions between Mackenzie River and Hudson Bay. Despite the large size of this group, very little is known of the history and Aboriginal culture of the Mackenzie Eskimos. This is primarily a result of the early extinction of local Aboriginal culture due to a series of epidemic diseases which swept through the population during the late 19th and early 20th centuries. By 1910, the Mackenzie Eskimos were reduced to a few score survivors scattered among the more numerous Alaskan Eskimo immigrants who flooded into the Delta in the company of European whalers and traders'.

21 Freeman, (ed.)., *Inuit Land Use and Occupancy Project Report, Volume II*, 144. 'After the appearance of the American whaling fleet along the Mackenzie Delta coast in 1889, and with the increasing association between the indigenous population and the whalers wintering at Herschel Island and elsewhere, the effects of disease and the disruption of Aboriginal social patterns accelerated rapidly. The population was subjected to two devastating measles epidemics in 1900 and 1902. By this time, according to police reports, the Mackenzie Eskimo population had declined rapidly from an estimated 2,500 people in 1850 to about 250 in 1905 and under 150 in 1910. At the same time as Eskimos were being decimated by disease, local Aboriginal culture was being submerged beneath a wave of American and Alaskan Eskimo introductions. Shocked by the materially

rewarding involvement with the American whaling ships, Mackenzie Eskimo culture was susceptible to wholesale adoption of the cultural traits of American-oriented Alaskan Eskimos. The latter were either brought to the area as caribou hunters by the whaling ships, or had moved in on their own in search of new hunting grounds after the North Alaskan caribou herds had been killed off to supply the excess demands of the whaling fleet'.

22 Freeman, (ed.)., *Inuit Land Use and Occupancy Project Report, Volume II*, 144. McGhee is citing Vilhjalmur Stefansson, *The Stefánsson-Anderson Arctic Expedition of the American Museum: Preliminary Ethnological Report*, Volume 14, Issues 1–2, New York: American Museum of Natural History, 1914, 195.
23 Freeman, (ed.)., *Inuit Land Use and Occupancy Project Report, Volume II*, 144.
24 Barry S. Zellen, 'Keith Spicer Visits The Western Arctic', *The Sourdough*, November 28, 1990.
25 Milton M.R. Freeman, (ed.)., *Inuit Land Use and Occupancy Project Report, Volume I: Land Use and Occupancy* (Ottawa, ON: Supply and Services Canada, 1976), 24.
26 Freeman, (ed.)., *Inuit Land Use and Occupancy Project Report, Volume I*, 22.
27 Ibid.: *Volume I*, 22.
28 Ibid.: *Volume I*, 22.
29 Ibid.: *Volume II*, 148.
30 Ibid.: *Volume II*, 148.
31 Ibid.: *Volume I*, 19.
32 Ibid.: *Volume I*, 19.
33 Ibid.: *Volume I*, 19.
34 Ibid.: *Volume I*, 6.
35 Ibid.: *Volume I*, 6.
36 Ibid.: *Volume I*, 7.
37 Ibid.: *Volume I*, 9.
38 Ibid.: *Volume III*, 153.
39 William Wonders, 'Native Claims and Place Names in Canada's Western Arctic' *The Canadian Journal of Native Studies* VII, 1 (1987): 113.
40 Wonders, 'Native Claims and Place Names in Canada's Western Arctic', 113.
41 Ibid.: 113.
42 Ibid.: 114.
43 Wonders, 'Native Claims and Place Names in Canada's Western Arctic', 114. As Wonders recalls: 'At the time that the investigation was undertaken there were four major sources of indigenous toponomy available for the area involved. These were the journals and the analyses of the journals of Father Emile Petitot, the 19th century missionary; the work of anthropologist Cornelius Osgood; the work of linguist John T. Ritter; and current research into Dene place names based at Fort Good Hope, Colville Lake, and Fort Franklin, N.W.T. The presence of the Dene Mapping Project headed up by my anthropology colleague Michael Asch on the University of Alberta campus greatly facilitated access to the latter material. The informative special 'Arctic Archaeology' issue of *The Musk-Ox* with Hanks and Winter's 'Dene Names' article (1983) for example, had not yet been distributed'.
44 Wonders, 'Native Claims and Place Names in Canada's Western Arctic', 118. Wonders observed that 'Arctic Red River place names occur through the eastern part of the Mackenzie Delta about as far north as Inuvik, thence eastwards

around Campbell and Sitidgi Lakes, along the Miner and Kugaluk Rivers with some evidence even along the lower Smoke River. They extend eastwards to merge with the Fort Good Hope/Colville Lake names along the Wolverine River and around the Crossley Lakes. Fort McPherson place names are particularly numerous along the Peel River and its western tributaries, Rat River and Stony Creek, leading through the Richardson Mountains. Kutchin place names occur through the western channels of the Mackenzie Delta. Local informants also reported some in the western Delta to an area northwest of Aklavik, with a wider dispersal over the higher land immediately to the west, and extending into the northern Yukon'. He further noted that 'Dene toponyms for 'Arctic Ocean' are documented from both Fort Franklin and Fort Good Hope. Osgood's map of Bearlake Indian place names (1975) based on his 1928 research in the area for the National Museum of Canada, shows a general encirclement of the lake and close similarity with the pattern of Dene place names collected recently by the Fort Franklin people. The presence of Dene names in the northeast area of Great Bear Lake is particularly significant in terms of Inuit overlap from the Arctic coast. Osgood notes Dene toponyms for the Coppermine River, for the Arctic Ocean, and for Dismal Lakes where 'in this area the Indians occasionally came into contact with Eskimo' (Osgood, 1975:532), and he comments that Stick Island in Dease River was used by both Indian and Eskimo hunting parties. Ritter's work with the Kutchin people of the Dene (n.d.) provided 680 indigenous place names within the N.W.T. and maps supplied by the Dene Mapping Project fixed their location'. Wonders, 'Native Claims and Place Names in Canada's Western Arctic', 115–116.

45   Wonders, 'Native Claims and Place Names in Canada's Western Arctic', 118.
46   A similar process was used to lay claim to the High Arctic lands that are now an important part of both the Nunavut land settlement and the Nunavut territory, delineating its northern territorial boundaries and representing a significant portion of the Inuit land quantum and cash compensation transferred upon settlement of their land claim. While the Inuit claims to the High Arctic did not displace a neighboring Aboriginal people as took place in the Delta, it did empower the Inuit on a historically dubious claim of traditional land use in a region that was historically unoccupied and which the Inuit themselves claim they were forcibly and deceptively relocated to in the mid-twentieth century – thus entitling them to not only the land and cash compensation of the land claims process, but also further compensation for the suffering they endured during their exile to these very lands that now form such an important source of their new wealth and power. On top of this the Inuit demanded an apology from the Ottawa, and further implementation funds from the Canadian treasury to top-off their already unprecedented financial gains – even though they had previously gladly accepted the substantial land and cash transfers that accompanied their successful land negotiations and the formation of the Nunavut Territory more than a decade ago.
47   Michael Byers, 'Mr. Harper, Apologize to the 'High Arctic Exiles': Not Only Is This the Right Thing to Do, but It Would Help Cement Canada's Northern Claims', *The Globe and Mail*, June 12, 2008.
48   Byers, 'Mr. Harper, Apologize to the "High Arctic Exiles"', June 12, 2008.
49   Ibid.
50   Ibid.

51 Interestingly, at any time since commercial aviation reached into Canadian archi-
pelago in recent decades, any resident of Grise Fiord or Resolute could board a
plane and fly south, something many routinely do for medical services, higher
education, and family vacations. There is no restriction on travel and at any point
during the last two generations, the entire population of these villages could have
moved back to Northern Quebec. But they did not want to: the Inuit of these
communities don't want to go home because they *are* home. This very much
challenges the brilliantly constructed and compelling narrative that these land-
rich, largely self-governing, and increasingly autonomous communities are in fact
exile communities at all.

52 Jim Algar, 'Paleo-Eskimos, and not Inuit, were the first settlers in Arctic, DNA
study reveals', *Tech Times*, September 1, 2014, www.techtimes.com/articles/
14516/20140901/paleo-eskimos-and-not-inuit-were-the-first-settlers-in-arctic-
dna-study-reveals.htm.

53 Algar, 'Paleo-Eskimos, and not Inuit, were the first settlers in Arctic, DNA study
reveals'.

54 Algar, 'Paleo-Eskimos, and not Inuit, were the first settlers in Arctic, DNA study
reveals'.

55 Aboriginal Affairs and Northern Development Canada, 'Apology for the Inuit
High Arctic Relocation: Speaking Notes for The Honourable John Duncan, PC,
MP, Minister of Indian Affairs and Northern Development and Federal
Interlocutor for Métis and Non-Status Indians at the Apology for the Inuit High
Arctic Relocation', August 18, 2010, Inukjuak, Nunavik, www.aadnc-aandc.
gc.ca/eng/1100100016115/1100100016116.

56 Mia Bennett, 'Arctic Circle 2014: Welcome to the New Global Arctic', *Cryo-
politics*, November 3, 2014, http://cryopolitics.com/2014/11/03/arctic-circle-
2014-welcome-to-the-new-global-arctic/.

57 Bennett, 'Arctic Circle 2014: Welcome to the New Global Arctic'.

58 Ibid.

3 Re-imagining indigenous space

The law, constitution and the evolution of Aboriginal property and resource rights in Canada

Ken Coates and Greg Poelzer

Of growing international importance are the constitutional provisions and legal processes that indigenous peoples often view as 'the last cannon shot' in their defense of resource rights and interests. This 'shot' represents the efforts of indigenous populations to use constitutional protection and recourse to the courts to carve out indigenous space within nation-states, thus ensuring themselves the land, resources, and political power necessary to survive in a globalized, multi-cultural world. Where colonial domination once suppressed indigenous rights, courts and legislative actions are now gradually restoring them. These efforts have a long and complex history.

Indigenous peoples in Canada have endeavored to define their rights within the constitutional and legal frameworks of their nation-states. Over the past three decades, these efforts have produced many important legislative acts, court judgments, and land claim settlements that have expanded the scope and degree of indigenous rights. How effective has this strategy been in serving indigenous peoples and, in particular, their quest to secure property and resource rights? Is the legal recognition and constitutional protection of indigenous rights an end in itself or a means to something else? Canada provides a good case for exploring the constitutional and legal protections in place for indigenous or Aboriginal peoples' property and resource rights. In Canada indigenous peoples are formally recognized as the Aboriginal peoples of Canada – First Nations, Inuit, and Métis – and thus the rest of this chapter follows Canadian legal nomenclature.

The Canadian case reveals several important developments. First, over the past thirty years Aboriginal peoples in Canada have made significant advances in defining and shaping constitutional recognition of their rights in the written constitution itself, through court decisions, and by negotiated land claims agreements. In the process, these advances have challenged the state to rethink its relationship with Aboriginal Canadians and to reexamine the manner in which it accommodates Aboriginal interests.

The unfolding of Indigenous rights has been time consuming, expensive for Aboriginal communities far from linear in its progress and rarely characterized by implementation and acceptance by non-Indigenous Canadians. Indeed, advances in Aboriginal rights appear to produce a routinely backlash amongst non-Indigenous peoples. Put simply, constitutional provisions have not guaranteed rights themselves; rather, the trust building and the creation of new and enduring political relationships that followed have the potential to provide the foundation for full recognition of constitutional rights.

Governments in Canada, including provincial and territorial governments that control natural resources, moved slowly to respond to the growing legal authority of Indigenous peoples. First Nations, in particular, resented the slow legislative and administrative progress on the recognition of land and resource rights and pressed the governments to speed up the process. Ironically, corporations shifted their strategies more quickly, working on impact and benefit agreements that recognized Indigenous rights over traditional territories. A Supreme Court decision in 2014, relating to the Tshilqot'in case from central British Columbia, altered the national debate dramatically, creating considerable uncertainty around Aboriginal land and resource rights and foreshadowing a reconsideration of Indigenous influence over their traditional territories.

The written constitution

For indigenous leaders, securing constitutional protection of Aboriginal land and resource rights is fundamental to the long-term protection of both their legal authority and their cultures. For this reason Aboriginal politicians and lawyers have single-mindedly pursued constitutional recognition. The 'constitution' of Canada is not simply a single document but instead comprises many parts: the Constitution Act (1982), the Canadian Charter of Rights and Freedoms, the Constitution Act (1867), and the Canada Act (1982).[1] The constitution also includes certain acts passed by Canadian and British parliaments; court decisions from Canada and Britain; and important customs, traditions, and conventions.[2]

The British Parliament passed Canada's original constitution, the British North America (BNA) Act, in 1867. It included modest recognition of lands reserved for Aboriginal peoples who were considered the fiduciary responsibility of the federal state. It also provided a platform for defining Aboriginal control over portions of their traditional territories and for providing them with the continued ability to use resources for traditional – and occasionally commercial – purposes. However, the decision of Prime Minister Pierre Trudeau's government to patriate the Canadian constitution from the United Kingdom in the early 1980s altered the national role of Aboriginal rights. First Nations protested their initial exclusion from constitutional processes and lobbied hard, and successful for the recognition of Aboriginal rights.

It is important to appreciate that, prior to 1982, Aboriginal Canadians enjoyed little political or legal recognition of their land and resource rights. That most Aboriginal people lived in remote regions, far from non-Aboriginal settlements and with little competition for harvestable resources provided greater protection of Indigenous hunting, fishing and gathering than did protection under the law. Through to the 1970s, the Department of Indian Affairs held sway in Indigenous communities, controlling land and assets and working more on assimilation or integration than the protection of traditional lifeways and Aboriginal access to land and resources. In a series of cases, including White and Bob[3] (1965) and Sparrow (1990), First Nations secured limited recognition of harvesting rights.[4] A major turning point came in the middle of these cases when, in 1973, the Nisga'a unsuccessful petitioned the Supreme Court of Canada for recognition of their rights to their traditional lands. The Government of Canada was rattled by the legal near-miss (the Supreme Court voted 3-3-1, with one justice ruling against the Nisga'a on a procedural technicality) and reversed its opposition to Aboriginal claims negotiation covering non-treaty lands, which at that juncture represented over half of Canada's land mass.[5]

The strengthening of formal recognition of Aboriginal rights in the 1982 written constitution was a result of evolving circumstance rather than the prime minister's original design. Aboriginal leaders who demanded inclusion in the patriation process – only to be rebuffed by federal and provincial politicians – carried their protests to the United Kingdom, soliciting the support of British parliamentarians. The effort encountered considerable opposition from provincial premiers but the willingness of the federal government to accept the Aboriginal requests and public affirmations, in Canada and the United Kingdom, or Aboriginal determination carried the day politically. Intense negotiations led to critical changes in federal and provincial government plans, culminating in formal recognition of greater Aboriginal rights by Canada's new constitution. The language of Section 35, which addresses Aboriginal rights in the 1982 Constitution Act, is limited in scope and definition but carries considerable legal authority.[6]

The section recognizes and affirms 'existing Aboriginal and treaty rights', emphasizes that new claims and other agreements are tantamount to legal treaties, and assures equality between male and female Aboriginal peoples.[7] The treaty rights element of the section is clear; specific provisions in existing and future treaties with Aboriginal peoples have constitutional protection. The Aboriginal rights element, however, is much less clear, for it essentially means that any right defined as an 'Aboriginal right' – either by the Supreme Court of Canada or by the Parliament of Canada – would gain constitutional protection. These rights cannot be easily changed or eliminated through legislation or regulation, nor are they defensible through other legal considerations. In other words, the constitutional guarantee of Aboriginal rights is neither an immutable nor a vulnerable concept; rather, it is an assurance that all Aboriginal rights recognized by the courts or parliament would enjoy a long-term legal foundation. The constitution thus allowed government and indigenous leaders to extend constitutional protection to hitherto contested rights, such as self-governance arrangements.

However, the inclusion of Aboriginal rights in the Constitution Act (1982) did not soon resolve the status of Aboriginal land and resource rights. It took several decades for administrative and political practice to fall in line with constitutional provisions, and thirty years later much remained unresolved. In most of Canada, these rights are defined in pre-1921 treaties or post-1980 treaties, particularly with respect to land. While all of these codified rights enjoy constitutional recognition under Section 35, ongoing efforts to define harvesting and resource rights are proving more contentious. These rights, such as hunting and fishing for subsistence purposes, are separate from negotiated agreements. The gradual extension of resource rights to treaty members, non-treaty and off-reserve Aboriginal peoples, beneficiaries of modern treaties, and people of Métis ancestry also broadened the controversy surrounding such rights. Repeated recourse to the courts has provided a series of victories as well as a handful of setbacks for Aboriginal groups.[8] Thus, using the law to define and clarify constitutional provisions has proven to a complex and difficult process and one that continues to the present.

Courts and the inclusion of property in the constitution

Even before the 1982 Constitution Act affirmed and entrenched Aboriginal and treaty rights, Canadian Aboriginal peoples used the courts to secure greater constitutional recognition of their land and resource rights, but the victories came dearly and only incrementally. Across the country Aboriginal peoples had two main concerns: the ability to use land and resources in a similar manner as their ancestors, and the capacity to control resource development on traditional territories. It required years of litigation before they realized these aspirations and received recognition of their legal authority over their lands.

Early in the twenty-first century, the legal contests shifted to concerns about indigenous influence over general resource use. Several court challenges, particularly those of *Haida Nation v Ministry of Forests* (2004), *Taku River Tlingit First Nation v British Columbia* (2004), and *Mikisew Cree First Nation v Canada* (2005), produced a set of court rulings decreeing that the state had a duty to consult with, and accommodate, Aboriginal peoples before development proceeded on Aboriginal lands.[9] Put simply, Aboriginal communities and organizations insisted on being part of the planning and decision-making process.[10] They also expected a significant return – in cash, jobs and business opportunities – from the resource developments. Governments had, under Supreme Court direction, an obligation to deal with Aboriginal communities, determine their interest in the territories in question and provide appropriate compensation for any disruptions. These latter cases are already having a dramatic impact in Canada and, over the next decade, may prove to be among the most powerful property and resource rights enjoyed by the country's Aboriginal peoples.

The issues associated with the duty to consult are central to the protection and assertion of Aboriginal rights. Initially, observers assumed that the duty to consult constrained third-party interests – mining companies, land developers, pipeline operators, and the like – rather than the governments that authorized the use of Aboriginal lands. Canadian courts, however, made it clear that the duty applied first to the Crown and not these other agents. The success of First Nations in the Haida, Taku River, and Mikisew Cree cases necessitated the development of appropriate guidelines. The cases also expanded the duty to consult, putting it ahead of other remedies – statutory and regulatory arrangements, land claims agreements and treaties, contractual arrangements, and common law requirements – that remained in force.

The new court-imposed obligations on the Crown include the recognition that the honor of the Crown is at stake in these discussions and that consultation is an integral part of reconciliation between indigenous groups and other Canadians. The government must act in a reasonable and responsive way through sincere, meaningful consultations throughout the process. Furthermore, courts have mandated that the discussions show mutual respect, accessibility, inclusiveness, and transparency, and that they move forward in a timely and efficient manner. These are strong and compelling requirements, designed to ensure that the government show respect for indigenous cultures, needs, and interests. At the same time, these requirements pose a formidable barrier for development interests on lands connected to indigenous groups.[11] For example, the mutual respect mandate requires that debates concerning land and resource rights reach mutually beneficial arrangements. As an indicator of the requirement's importance, the Perrins Report on the future of uranium mining in Saskatchewan made explicit mention of the duty to consult.[12] Additionally, First Nations in northern Alberta used their newfound empowerment to block further oil sands development, which included a compensation agreement worth $1 billion. For their part, governments in British Columbia, Alberta, Saskatchewan, and the Yukon are quickly coming to terms with the new legal environment that mandates close attention to Aboriginal rights. Specifically, the duty to consult enables clear legal repercussions for governments that permit development without first securing Aboriginal support and approval.[13]

The duty to consult and accommodate requirements do not provide Aboriginal people with a veto over proposed resource development. The legal test is not Indigenous support for the project. Rather, the requirement is that governments and companies give affected communities the right to explain the potential implications of a resource development and that the accommodation offered, by way of cash or other benefits, be commensurate with the impact of the project. Some Aboriginal communities asserted that their approval was needed before a resource initiative could proceed, often citing the United Nations Declaration on the Rights of Indigenous Peoples, specifically the 'free, prior and informed consent' clause, in defense of this position.[14]

Land claims and indigenous constitutionalism

One of the most important aspects of indigenous affairs in Canada has been the emergence of indigenous constitution-making as a consequence of land claims settlements and constitutional changes. Indigenous peoples and organizations have wrestled with the appropriateness of using and modifying Western and European systems for defining governance and rights regimes within their communities. For example, the Mohawk in south-central Canada have resisted these pressures by relying heavily on traditional governance models (including blood quantum requirements for membership), although considerable internal dissension over the management of local affairs still exists.[15] Modern land claims settlements describe the scope and nature of indigenous governance as well as outline the extensive provisions defining governance included in these settlements. Using the 1982 Constitution Act as a new starting point, a series of modern treaties – most covering large tracks of land in northern Canada – have included substantial provisions covering land, land use, planning, conservation, harvesting, and development. [16]

The agreements between the Government of Canada, and the Inuvialuit, Nisga'a and the Council for Yukon First Nations (CYFN) exemplify the complexity of Aboriginal constitution-making in the modern era. In the case of the Inuvialuit – one of the first to settle a comprehensive, modern treaty – the 1984 accord covered a homogenous group in the Western Arctic and provided very precise definitions of land, resource, and financial authority. The 1993 CYFN Agreement – an umbrella accord that spelled out general arrangements among the fourteen First Nations – focused on territory-wide provisions for governance and the general allocation of settlement resources among its parties.[17] A series of comparable agreements with each of the First Nations describes these specific arrangements. The Inuit of the Eastern and Central Arctic subsequently signed a settlement with the Canadian government that, in 1999, created the new territory of Nunavut. With over 80 percent of the population in Nunavut, the Inuit secured effective control of public governance in the region, managing their affairs with substantial authority over the use of land and resources. The Nisga'a, who live inland from the British Columbia coast along the Nass River, started negotiations with the Canadian government in the late 1800s and saw their final agreement come into effect in 2000.[18] This complex agreement outlines the operations of the Nisga'a Lisims government, which embeds the people's cultural system within regional governance arrangements. The codification of the Lisims system – and the resulting regulation of fisheries, hunting, and land use according to Nisga'a customs and decision-making structures – represents a sophisticated and largely successful attempt to capture the concepts, structure, and purpose of Western-style constitutions, using them to exercise extensive property and resource rights.[19]

As these cases illustrate, modern treaty and legal processes have convinced Aboriginal peoples of the legal and political value of the Canadian constitutional model.[20] Through land claims processes, Aboriginal Canadians have steadily defined and described their aspirations and expectations in legal and constitutional terms. Land claims, more so than other legal avenues, represent the degree to which Aboriginal peoples in Canada have capitalized on constitutional protections as a means for regulating and guaranteeing their rights now – and in the future.

But there are significant limits to the effectiveness of land claims processes as a means of reconciling Indigenous land and resource rights. In British Columbia, home to over one third of the Aboriginal people in Canada, land claims negotiated moved slowly and expensively after the settlement of the Nisga'a negotiations. The British Columbia treaty process, which a significant number of First Nations boycotted, ran up over $1 billion in negotiation costs but led to few agreements and has not provided a viable solution. The vast majority of the province remains outside the Canadian treaty process. This did not, however, stop resource development. First Nations, using their rights under duty to consult and accommodation, negotiated with companies and governments. The fact that the British Columbia government accepted resource revenue sharing on a project-by-project basis – reversing long-standing opposition to such measures – eased the process considerably.[21]

The Tshilqot'in decision and the recasting of indigenous rights in Canada

The Canadian legal landscape took an unexpected shift in June 2014, when the Supreme Court of Canada released its decision on the William (Tshilqot'in). The Tshilqot'in First Nation live in an isolated valley in west-central British Columbia. Over the years, they resisted numerous efforts by outsiders to move into their territories. A dispute over forestry plans in the area convinced the Tshilqot'in to take the Government of British Columbia to court, asserting their right over traditional lands and resources. The legal process took many years and cost the First Nation – and the two levels of government – millions of dollars in legal and court fees. The land in question had never been covered by a treaty; the Tshilqot'in asked the court to recognize their Aboriginal title to their traditional lands and to thereby ensure their control over subsequent resource developments.

The Supreme Court offered a decisive ruling in the favour of the Tshilqot'in. In a surprise unanimous decision, they accepted the First Nation's argument that they had not lost control of their traditional lands. The court expanded on its earlier duty to consult and accommodate rulings and established a significantly higher bar regarding Aboriginal approval on resource projects. The justices stopped short, but only barely, of providing the Tshilqot'in with a veto over future resource development activity. The provincial governments – whose continuing right to establish resource policy was re-affirmed in a subsequent court decision on the Grassy Meadows case – were required to provide a clear statement about the principles they would use in over-ruling Aboriginal decisions. In addition, the judgment indicated that, in using traditional territories and resources, First Nations had to attend to the needs and expectations of subsequent generations, a requirement that places as yet unknown constraints on Indigenous use of their lands.

In the first instance, the Supreme Court decision applied only to non-treaty areas. This, however, included substantial sections of the country, including almost all of resource-rich British Columbia, significant sections of the Yukon and Northwest Territories, and much of the Atlantic provinces. (The latter case is interesting in that the Mikmaq and Maliseet signed 'peace and friendship' treaties in the 18th century, agreements that did not include land surrenders. There are, therefore, no land-based treaties in the region. The First Nations wish to update and modernize the existing accords; the Government of Canada, in contrast, prefers to negotiate a fully modern accord to replace the more vague and unclear centuries-old accords.) As part of a larger body of law on the maintenance of Indigenous rights over traditional lands and resources, however, the Tshilqot'in judgment continues a process of expanding and strengthening Aboriginal land and resource rights.

The Tshilqot'in decision re-enforced the Aboriginal position that, under British and Canadian law, they retained substantial territorial and resource rights. Alone, it was a striking and important re-affirmation of the contemporary authority of Indigenous peoples. As part of a long string, stretching back over fifty years, the Tshilqot'in case made it clear that, in the eyes of the Supreme Court of Canada, if not yet all the governments in Canada, the Aboriginal rights remained less than fully defined. In reaching its decision, the Supreme Court once again reiterated its wish that First Nations and governments would resolve their differences through negotiations rather than legal battles, a possibility that remains unrealized.[22]

Future prospects and next steps

High-level constitutional provisions require legal definition, and the resulting contestations can take years, if not decades, of extremely expensive court procedures. Unfortunately, numerous national governments, including Canada's, have found administrative, political, budgetary, and legal ways of delaying the implementation of constitutional provisions and court decisions that ratify Aboriginal rights. This is because constitutional provisions, beyond attending to mere Aboriginal demands and rights, rely on political leverage as well. Consequently, governments are often reluctant to test the legal waters, fearful that an unexpected court decision could extend constitutional rights in practical but potentially disruptive ways. As a result even vague provisions in a national constitution can exert influence effectively equal to or greater than detailed provisions.

The empowerment of Aboriginal peoples in Canada has proceeded quickly, codified in the constitution and given meaningful authority through land claims, duty to consult requirements, and informal political arrangements. However, much remains unfinished. In particular, a series of options available to the federal, provincial, territorial, and Aboriginal governments of Canada might well pave the way for more meaningful and effective recognition of Aboriginal land and resource rights. The effort must focus on ensuring indigenous input on resource and environmental matters and recognizing the state's responsibilities to indigenous peoples.

First, governments should facilitate greater indigenous participation within existing land and resource management regimes. Routine engagement of Aboriginal peoples and organizations in management systems is a clear and meaningful way of ensuring ongoing indigenous consultation on resource development plans. Provincial and regional governments should provide for Aboriginal peoples' memberships on boards concerning planning, wildlife management, water control, and other relevant topics, doing so in a manner consistent with the arrangements of the comprehensive treaties. They could also construct mechanisms to include Aboriginal traditional knowledge within environmental management systems, although this might prove controversial in some areas. At present, Aboriginal engagement in resource management is inconsistent and often not assured. The inclusion of Aboriginal peoples in the decision making and appeal processes would ensure that indigenous voices are heard and would provide Aboriginal peoples – and the courts – with evidence of extensive consultation and engagement in the resource-use process. In effect, this would commit governments to a series of strategic assessments and studies that would incorporate indigenous perspectives and accommodate Aboriginal interests and rights at the earliest possible stages of the development review process.

Second, the government should also develop guidelines with and for the private sector so that there is a more uniform understanding of which legal steps satisfy the duty to consult. At present, there is a great deal of uncertainty about the meaning, authority, and processes associated with this standard. Contrary to some beliefs, the duty does not confer a veto to indigenous organizations, nor does it allow governments or corporations to operate sham consultations. The requirements calling for sincerity, efficiency, and mutually beneficial solutions apply to all participants in the development process, including indigenous peoples and governments. By developing a set of guidelines and ensuring that the duty to consult has been exercised properly, governments, indigenous groups, and private sector developers can proceed with the level of certainty and shared understanding necessary for more constructive relations. In the absence of such guidelines, land and resource use processes will unfold on an ad hoc basis, remaining a source of contention and frustration for all concerned. Currently, few participants understand the legal, political, and financial parameters involved in discussions, meaning that most negotiations start from foundational elements and move slowly toward a resolution.

Finally, the incorporation of off-reserve and urban aboriginals in decision-making processes presents a serious challenge. Off-reserve and urban Aboriginal peoples have cultural, financial, and personal relationships with traditional territories and seek assurance that mechanisms for consultation and management accommodate their interests. Most political structures, however, are reserve-focused, effectively disenfranchising off-reserve members. This in turn leaves consultations and decisions subject to criticism and legal challenge. Consulting with and incorporating off-reserve peoples will head off potentially serious, long-term struggles; mechanisms can include recognizing urban members through separate band structures, providing voting and political privileges on the reserve, and instating comprehensive outreach programs to ensure adequate engagement.

There are of course other steps local and regional governments in Canada can take. They can move quickly to conclude remaining land claims negotiations and to fully implement the agreements that have already been reached. They can change their current approach to negotiations with indigenous groups, which seeks to establish the minimum amount that they are legally required to provide to Aboriginal groups. Both governments and indigenous partners can publicize successful arrangements, publicly acknowledge the growing role of indigenous organizations in resource management, and improve resource management arrangements inside treaties and settlement agreements. In general, Canadians should recognize the fundamental importance that most Aboriginal groups attach to the long-term stewardship of resources, and should maximize the financial return they provide to local communities. Since development on aboriginal lands is crucial to the financial stability of many parts of the country, indigenous partnerships throughout Canada are important to secure long-term benefits from resource development for all Canadians.

As Canadian history demonstrates, constitutional arrangements and Supreme Court decisions shift the foundations of law and politics. Even if constitutional and legal rights do not immediately improve and protect Aboriginal land and resource rights, they do alert governments, private firms, and the public at large to new legal realities. Slowly, if not dramatically, constitutional arrangements can reinforce Aboriginal control, expand their sense of what is possible, and convince society to rethink the place of Aboriginal peoples within the nation-state. In the end success will depend on trust building and the creation of new and enduring political relationships crucial to full recognition of constitutional rights. Canada has already taken several key strides toward appropriate, sustainable, and well-understood arrangements for protecting indigenous land and resource rights. Further efforts are necessary to ensure that these promising initial stages become the foundation for true and sustainable reconciliation between the state and its Aboriginal peoples.

Canada has, as of 2014, a potent illustration of the risks associated with leaving the question of Aboriginal resource and land rights to the courts. The Tshilqot'in decision, in recognizing the unresolved land and resource rights of First Nations on non-treaty land, shifted the national discussion considerably. Indigenous peoples in non-treaty areas feel re-empowered, even if it is not entirely clear precisely where and when the Supreme Court decision applies. Some Indigenous leaders from non-treaty areas assert that the Tshilqot'in decision relates to their territories as well. While the apocalyptic forecasts of a serious downturn in the British Columbia resource economy are likely exaggerated – many First Nations desire the jobs, business opportunities and other benefits associated with resource development – the reality is that the basic rules have changed. Indigenous peoples in Canada do not have comprehensive control over land and resources that they desire and that they believe are theirs by right of law, treaty and constitution, but they have made significant progress in the past few decades in making the transition from outsiders in the development process to key decision-makers and beneficiaries from the use of their traditional lands.

Notes

1   Constitution Act, 1982 (U.K.) 1982; Constitution Act, 1867 (U.K.), 30 & 31 Victoria.
2   Patrick Monahan, *Constitutional Law* (Toronto: Irwin Law, 2006), 4–6.
3   *Regina v White and Bob*, 52 D.L.R. (2d) 481, 1965 SCC (1965).
4   *R. v Sparrow*, 1 S.C.R. 1075, 1990 SCC (1990); Thomas Isaac, 'An Analysis of the Aboriginal Government'. Thomas Isaac, *Aboriginal Law: Commentary and Analysis* (Saksatoon: Purich Press, 2012).
5   For the details on the treaty, as presented by the Nisga'a, see 'Understanding the Treaty' (www.nisgaanation.ca/understanding-treaty). Tom Milloy, *The World is Our Witness: The Historic Journey of the Nisga'a Into Canada* (Calgary: Fifth House, 200).
6   Gordon Christie, 'Aboriginal Citizenship: Sections 25, 25 and 15 of Canada's *Constitution Act*, 1982', *Citizenship Studies* 7 (2003): 481–495: James (Sa'Ke'j) Youngblood Henderson, *Treaty Rights in the Constitution of Canada* (Toronto: Thomson Carswell, 2007).
7   Constitution Act, 1982, S.35(1) & (4).
8   Bill Gallagher, *Resource Rulers: Fortune and Folly on Canada's Road to Resources*. Bill Gallagher, 2012 surveys the evolution of the law on this matter.
9   *Haida Nation v British Columbia* (Minister of Forests), 3 S.C.R. 511, 2004 SCC 73 (2004); *Taku River Tlingit First Nation v British Columbia* (Project Assessment Director), 3 S.C.R. 550, 2004 SCC 74 (2004); *Mikisew Cree First Nation v Canada* (Minister of Canadian Heritage), 3 S.C.R. 388, 2005, SCC 69 (2005).
10 Sonia Lawrence and Patrick Macklem, 'From Consultation to Reconciliation: Aboriginal Rights and the Crown's Duty to Consult', *The Canadian Bar Review* 79 (2000): 252-79; Patricia Ochman, 'Recent Developments in Canadian Aboriginal Law: Overview of Case Law and of Certain Principles of Aboriginal Law', *International Community Law Review* 10 (2008): 319–350.
11 Government of Canada, 'Aboriginal Consultation and Accommodation: Interim Guidelines for Federal Officials to Fulfill the Legal Duty to Consult', www.ainc-inac.gc.ca/ai/mr/is/acp/intgui-eng.pdf (date accessed: February 2008).
12 Dan Perrins, 'Future of Uranium Public Consultation Process [Perrins Report]', prepared on behalf of the Uranium Development Partnership (Regina: Government of Saskatchewan, 2009).

13 For an overview of these developments, see Ken Coates, and Brian Lee Crowley. *New Beginnings: How Canada's Natural Resource Wealth Could Re-shape Relations with Aboriginal People*. Macdonald-Laurier Institute for Public Policy, 2013.

14 Terry Mitchell, (ed.)., *The Internationalization of Indigenous Rights: UNDRIP in the Canadian Context* (Waterloo: CIGI, 2014).

15 Gerald Alfred, *Heeding the voices of our ancestors: Kahnawake Mohawk politics and the rise of native nationalism.* (Donmills: Oxford University Press Canada, 1995).

16 For an overview, see Michael Asch, *On Being Here to Stay: Treaties and Aboriginal Rights in Canada* (Toronto: University of Toronto Press, 2014). See also Greg Poelzer and Ken Coates, *Treaty Peoples to Treaty Nation* (Vancouver: UBC Press, 2014).

17 Indian and Northern Affairs Canada, 'Umbrella Final Agreement Between The Government of Canada, The Council For Yukon Indians and The Government of The Yukon', 1993, www.ainc-inac.gc.ca/al/ldc/ccl/fagr/ykn/umb/umb-eng.asp (date accessed: 18 October 2009).

18 Nisga'a Final Agreement Act [SBC 1999] (Victoria: Queen's Printer, 2000); Richard Krehbiel, 'Common Visions: Influences of the Nisga'a Final Agreement on Lheidli T'enneh Negotiations in the BC Treaty Process', *International Journal on Minority and Group Rights* 11 (2004): 279–88; Paul Rynard, 'The Nisga'a Treaty: Are We On the Right Track?' *International Journal on Minority and Group Rights* 11 (2004): 289–98.

19 Edward Allen, 'Our Treaty, Our Inherent Right to Self-Government: An Overview of the Nisga'a Final Agreement', *International Journal on Minority and Group Rights* 11 (2004): 233–49.

20 Christopher Alcantara, 'Explaining Aboriginal Treaty Negotiation Outcomes in Canada: The Cases of the Inuit and the Innu in Labrador', *Canadian Journal of Political Science* 40 (2007): 185–207. See his broader study, *Negotiating the Deal: Comprehensive Land Claims Agreements in Canada* (Toronto: University of Toronto Press, 2013).

21 Resource revenue sharing reviewed in Ken Coates, *Sharing the Wealth* (Ottawa: Macdonald-Laurier Institute, 2015).

22 The Tshilqot'in decision is examined in Ken Coates and Dwight Newman, *The End is Not Nigh: Reason over alarmism in analyzing the Tsilhqot'in decision* (Ottawa: Macdonald-Laurier Institute, 2014).

4 President Lugo and the indigenous communities of Paraguay

Cheryl Duckworth

Introduction

When Padre Lugo's election was confirmed, and the *Partido Colorado* candidate conceded (which was no foregone conclusion), the indigenous communities dedicated sacred dances to him to celebrate a victory they clearly felt they shared (Estigarribia, 2008). Indeed, they along with student groups, socialist groups, *campesinos* and other similar groups were central to Lugo's victory, won by a coalition called the Patriotic Alliance for Change (PAC). Candidate Lugo spoke frequently on the stump about justice for the indigenous and other landless communities; at one point, while campaigning, he said that, 'Since 1992, the 500th Anniversary of the arrival of the Europeans, there has been a discovery of indigenous dignity. And it's got a long way to go yet' (O'Shaughnessy, 2008). Having worked for around two decades as a priest and then a bishop with Paraguay's poorest, Lugo spoke with what most felt was a great deal of moral authority and credibility. His election was a seismic event in Paraguay's history after generations of military dictatorship and colonial occupation. When he took office, hopes for Paraguay's future had never before been so high. Many considered his election the true beginning of Paraguay's democracy, owing to the defeat of the Colorado Party, which had ruled Paraguay through military dictatorship both before and during General Stroessner's regime, and which has been synonymous with corruption even after his fall in a 1989 military coup. With roughly a year passed since his ouster in 2013, this chapter will revisit the context of his election, his campaign platform and promises regarding Paraguay's indigenous peoples, his policies and any progress (or regress) made.

I noted in my previous book, *Land and Dignity in Paraguay,* that while clearly the election of Lugo was a seismic shift for the political landscape in Paraguay, a number of economic and political structural factors remained in place that Lugo would find extraordinarily difficult to change (Duckworth, 2011; Brun, 2007). Lugo and his supporters were in the end unable to find ways to negotiate, maneuver or mobilize to provide him with the political support needed for lasting change, and the results were marginal and transient. With the Colorado Party representing ranchers and land owners now back in power, the small gains he was able to implement are likely in my view to be reversed. The difficulties have been clear. In my view, the genuine and hefty base he consolidated throughout his campaigning was his greatest strength and this seems the greatest resource for indigenous and other activists moving forward after his ouster. Lugo seemed clearly far more skilled at connecting with people and mobilizing them than at political maneuvering, which was always going to be a difficult feat given the wealthy and powerful interests represented in the Colorado Party which opposed him.

What Lugo inherited: political obstacles

Lugo, it hardly need be said, inherited an extraordinarily difficult context in which to lead genuine transformation towards greater justice and equality. Students of Paraguay are familiar with the authoritarian political culture that dominated Paraguay throughout the 20th century, and in particular with the corruption and brutality of the military regime led by the late Gen. Stroessner ('el Stronoto'). Following Stroessner's ouster in something of a 'palace coup' by Stroessner's one-time ally, Gen. Rodriguez, Rodriguez instituted some genuine democratic reforms. Specifically, the 1992 Constitution was a stunning victory, at least on paper, for the indigenous communities in that it specifically recognized them as citizens of Paraguay whose political, social and cultural rights it explicitly protected. Perhaps most significantly, it protected communal land ownership, which remains central to indigenous cosmology and way of life (see Renshaw, 2002, for example). Despite these advances, the ruling *Partido Colorado* remained (and some would argue, remains) deeply corrupt. For example, human rights abuses, especially those targeting indigenous and *campesino* activists, were a concern throughout Paraguay's period of democratic consolidation after Stroessner (Duckworth, 2011; Horst, 2007).

Stroessner built an incredibly durable political machine in *Partido Colorado*, and it retains its strength in Congress. Indeed, Lugo at one point had to make a deal with the Colorado Party to fill Senate seats (La Nación, 2009). This reportedly cost him a major coalition ally, the Authentic Radical Liberal Party (PLRA). Second to *Partido Colorado*, the PLRA holds the most seats in Congress (Nickson, 2008a). This made passing and then implementing genuine land reform even more difficult than it has been. In addition, Lugo's coalition won him the presidency, but not a majority in Parliament. As Nickson writes, 'Despite their strong support for the Lugo campaign, Congressional representation by left-wing parties remains the same – three senators and two deputies – as in 2003-8. A major reason was the failure of 10 different left-wing parties in the APC, including Lugo's own *Movimiento Popular Tekojoja* (MPT), to agree on fielding a single list of candidates' (Nickson, 2008b).

Something of a paradox restricted Lugo during his time in office. Part of Stroessner's legacy is a deep fear of an executive with the ability to consolidate too much power. Hence Lugo inherited firm limits on presidential power. This made it very difficult for him to ensure the passage of legislation which would deliver on key priorities. Land reform, in particular, strikes at the heart of deeply entrenched privilege of the wealthy landowners which dates back to Stroessner (and before). Many of these ranchers are themselves in Congress or have ties to Representatives, another legacy of *el Stronoto* (Duckworth, 2011; Kidd, 1995, 71). In addition, Lugo won the Executive, but again has never had a true majority in Congress. With these two structural factors against him, enacting his agenda was difficult in the extreme. As a result, there were only isolated and small victories Lugo can point to.

Lugo's time in office was insufficient to have righted generations of land theft and oppression of Paraguay's indigenous communities. Nor is it enough time to have changed a political culture with entrenched elements that remain brutal and corrupt. This being the case, my question here remains not whether Paraguay's most pressing problems have been solved, but whether progress has been made and whether it looks likely to be made in the future. Prior to Stroessner's fall and throughout the years in between Stroessner and Lugo, demonstrations and protests were regular features of Paraguay's sociopolitical landscape. Under Stroessner, of course, one risked disappearance, torture or death if one participated in such a protest; this reality improved some but not sufficiently in the following administrations. Focused as before on land reform, health and education, indigenous *manifestaciónes* continue today. Far from having been problematic for Lugo, I would argue that such activism during his term was essential to successfully challenge the wealthy land-owners who continue to thwart the land reform which is a necessity, for socio-political stability in Paraguay. The gains he could achieve were limited, but pressure from activists and civil society played a role in making them possible.

Despite Lugo's emphasis on good governance and human rights, Amnesty International, the U.N. and Paraguayan civil society continues to express concern about beatings and harassment of indigenous and other democracy leaders. Indeed, even under Lugo's watch, several demonstrations were brutally put down, according to media coverage (Rodriguez, 2008). According to journalist Lorena Rodriguez, Lugo was not in the country during one set of such demonstrations by the FSP (the Social and Popular Front, a coalition of campesinos, indigenous, students and so on created after Lugo's inauguration) and arrived back in the country without commenting. I view such situations as a missed opportunity causing his base to be disillusioned when he needed them most. However, Lugo did reportedly meet with the FSP to discuss their agenda, which includes the return of land illegally sold, access to credit and the distribution of seeds (Rodriguez, 2008). Reports of police brutality emerged from these demonstrations, to include beatings and tear gas. The FSP called for the resignation of the Attorney General (Rodriguez, 2008). By speaking out and acting consistently on just such abuses as he did on the campaign trail, in my opinion, Lugo could have accomplished two valuable objectives simultaneously. One, he might have signaled to his opponents that he was not about to surrender the principals of human rights and the rule of law behind his agenda. Two, he might have built on his greatest strength as a politician, which at least as demonstrated by his campaign, was his charisma and ability to mobilize popular support. Unfortunately he was never able to advance land reform or human rights and this cost him support throughout his tenure. Technically in fact it was violence surrounding a rural land occupation, which left seventeen Paraguayans dead according to media coverage at the time (The Economist, 2012), which Lugo's political enemies cited as the reason for his impeachment. I emphasize the opportunities Lugo missed here because the other systemic obstacles he faced, which include economic factors and the structural factors in Paraguayan politics such as lacking a Parliamentary majority, were far less under Lugo's control.

Additionally Lugo was struggling with political scandal related to a number of paternity suits dating back to his time as a bishop; I have nothing to say about this fallout beyond noting that it weakens him politically, and serves as a distraction from an already difficult agenda. As his defeated opponent, Blanca Ovelar, put it when her *Partido Colorado* was accused of conspiring against Lugo: 'President Lugo conspired against himself' (Barrionuevo, 2009). This, rather tragically, had implications for the impoverished communities of Paraguay, both indigenous and non-indigenous alike, who rallied around him, hoping that he would finally deliver what previous Colorado Party presidents had not. The tragedy, of course, was the ammunition the scandal could help but provide to his opponents in *Partido Colorado*.

The crucial issue for Paraguay's impoverished, both indigenous and nonindigenous *campesinos* alike, remains land reform. The Agricultural Minister which Lugo originally appointed, Cándido Vera Bejarano, opposed returning land illegally seized during (and after) *el Stronato* by *Partido Colorado*. He also opposed the occupations which have been a mainstay of protest by landless citizens. His replacement, former Senator Enzo Cardozo, had promised to study some of the issues which indigenous communities and environmental activists have been mobilizing around, such as pesticides, but did not deliver the end to pesticides that some protestors demand (ABC Color, 2009b). Cardozo began expanding Paraguay's agricultural ties, for example with Iran, a move that did not suggest to me the prioritization of indigenous demands for land reform (Iran Daily, n.d.) Yet despite this centrism, Lugo's decades of work with the indigenous communities as a priest and then bishop seemed to lend credibility to his intentions to deliver on his election promises. Certainly, Paraguay's indigenous leaders thought so. Justice and equity for indigenous peoples were a principle part of his campaign rhetoric, and since Stroessner's fall, Paraguayans have demonstrated the willingness to protest and rally when they deemed it necessary to demand reform. Optimistically, this in itself bodes well for Paraguay's continued democratic development, even if Lugo ultimately was not able to deliver the economic growth, land reform, transparency and integrity he campaigned on. A vibrant civil society always strengthens good governance.

The centrality of land reform to Paraguay's indigenous communities made the turmoil at INDI (the National Indigenous Institute) under Lugo's administration of grave concern. One devastating setback for President Lugo's agenda for Paraguay's indigenous communities was the forced resignation of Margarita Mbywangui; she made history by becoming the first indigenous person to head INDI. Established rather paradoxically by the dictator Stroessner, INDI's charge is to purchase and title land for indigenous communities in compliance with Law 904 (1981), which made illegal the private sale of land belonging to indigenous communities. An interim Director, Hugo Medina, was appointed after her. Significantly, Mbywangui was forced to resign by the repeated protests of indigenous communities, who expressed the fear that she would favor her own Aché tribe over other indigenous tribes (Torres, 2009). For some time after Mbywangui's resignation, a lack of clarity existed as to who would replace her. Indigenous leader Alberto Perez reported, after his meeting with the President, that the appointment of his choice (Cardozo and Cañete, 2009) was a certainty, but Penayo Rueben, Lugo's Head of Communications, denied this (Ultima Hora, 2009b). Indigenous communities occupied *Plaza Uruguaya*, in the central of the capital city of Asuncion, demanding the official appointment of Cardozo (ABC Color, 2009c). The matter was unresolved for a time and hence the institution which is arguably the most important for ultimately resolving the deadly conflict over Paraguay's land remained without leadership. More recently, the current head of INDI as of 2013, Jorge Servin, announced that his predecessor had embezzled $700,000 and remains at large (Associated Press, 2013). It is difficult to imagine how progress can be made in such a mercurial environment; effective and legitimate leadership for INDI is essential. Such corruption can only add to the tumultuous journey INDI has had since its inception in 1981, further hindering an institution that has already struggled with perceived illegitimacy, chronic underfunding, and a terrible amount of difficulty in establishing the census and land titling data needed to carry out its mandate (Renshaw, 2002, 125; Duckworth, 2011, Horst, 2007). This latter challenge has hindered INDI's efforts for years now. Due to the extreme sociopolitical, economic and geographic isolation of many indigenous communities, establishing birth and death certificates, as well as land title, has been all but impossible (INDI Official, Personal Interview, June 28, 2006). In addition, a UNICEF official in Paraguay informed me during my field work there that many indigenous communities are still hesitant, when they can be contacted, to cooperate at all with the collection of census data (UNICEF official, personal interview, June 20, 2006). This points to the immediate and urgent need for conflict resolution dialogues between government officials, development officials, land owners and indigenous leaders.

Institutional capacity with regards to the Institute for Land and Rural Development (INDERT), also impacted the achievement of just and sustainable land reform during Lugo's tenure. Malcolm Childress, who oversees *Banco Mundial*'s land reform projects for Paraguay, reported that *Banco Mundial* Paraguay's land administration program will likely be proceeding with the Department of Agriculture instead of INDERT. Apparently INDERT was perceived at the time as too close to the FSP (Personal Interview, July 7, 2009). This exemplified the continuing conflict over not just the land itself, but over the power to shape land policy and ultimately, the right to have one's own narrative about the conflict recognized and validated. Economic growth and development are often praised, with some reason, as a cure for many social and political ills. So they can be. Those who argue this, however, would do well to remember that markets depend on social trust, as with any other human institution. These difficulties that INDI and INDERT face exemplify the contradiction inherent in simultaneously pursuing fast growth through agri-exports and pursuing the return to indigenous communities of their land. Dialogue involving all of the stakeholders, as well as the reform of inequitable political and economic structures, was urgently necessary during Lugo's term and remains so. Yet dialogue in this context can only be productive if it is a dialogue between equals, which is not yet the case. Hence continuing all efforts to empower indigenous communities must remain a prominent conflict resolution strategy.

In *Land and Dignity in Paraguay*, I wrote extensively of the dynamics shaping the indigenous social movement. Drawing on social movement theory, I argued that indigenous leaders mobilized around the Dignity Frame, as opposed to other possible frames, for several reasons quite specific to Paraguay's context (Duckworth, 2011). These factors included the heinous oppression and exploitation of Paraguay's indigenous communities, the dramatic opening of socio-political space after the fall of Stroessner and the ability this opening provided to partner with NGOs who could provide critical financial, legal and social resources. Few social movements have escaped internal discord and Paraguay's, alas, is no exception. Disagreement existed as to both tactics (how much to engage the government) and goals (is the objective participation in the state? Autonomy from it? Both?). Prior to President Lugo, this manifested itself in opposing indigenous groups divided as to whether or not to fight for the implementation of Law 904, the law which originally established indigenous rights, or with a law that had been proposed under a previous president, Frutos, Law 2822. This law would have established a National Council of Indigenous Peoples within the government of Paraguay – precisely the goal many indigenous leaders sought. Other indigenous groups feared that the Council, located so close to wealth and power in Asunción, would be co-opted or even become another tool of state control. The events surrounding Mbywangui's dismissal from INDI suggest that some divisions do still exist among indigenous leaders, even if there is little division among indigenous leaders regarding their ultimate policy platform of land reform, access to health care and access to education. Hence I believe that one important step for civil society in a post-Lugo Paraguay is fostering as much debate and dialogue between Paraguay's seventeen indigenous communities as possible. Indigenous leaders have already initiated such dialogues (Duckworth, 2011). They united behind him as a candidate, and share a common set of policy goals; they also share, of course, some cultural factors in common, even as each indigenous community is distinct from the others. The more trust and unity they can foster, the more united an ally they can be politically, which will no doubt be necessary with *Partido Colorado* back in power. They have always represented land owners and ranches, but here we must remember that some elements of Lugo's own electoral coalition, for example the PLRA, hold private property rights as a central tenant, in direct opposition to the demands for land reform of many indigenous and *campesino* leaders. Lugo's administration at the time argued this was necessary to build a coalition large enough to govern.

Cabinet reshuffling occurred during Lugo's first year outside of INDI, as well, to include the crucial post of Minister of Agriculture. Candido Vera Bejarano was replaced by Enzo Cardozo, as noted just above. Luis Alberto Riart replaced Horario Galeano Perrone at the Ministry of Education and Culture (MEC). Similarly, Francisco Rivas became the new Minister of Industry and Commerce, replacing Martin Heisecke. Given Paraguay's continued struggles with corruption and the rule of law, the Ministry of Justice and Work is another essential post with respect to accomplishing the objectives Lugo campaigned on; Humberto Blasco replaced Blas Llano at this Ministry (China Economic Net, 2009). Such a thorough reset of powerful cabinet positions obviously suggests that Lugo was not pleased with their performance. Alternatively, this 'reshuffle' (as the media termed it) may have been the result of political coalition management, survival or other similar pressure.

Hope is not change: economic obstacles

Could President Lugo have possibly chosen a different global economic environment in which to attempt substantive economic reforms, surely he would have done so. While rising food prices in one sense raise the value of some of Paraguay's exports, especially soy and cattle, they also of course result in higher food prices for Paraguayans. Global economic recession during points of his tenure also made it more difficult to diversify economically as both countries and private consumers spend less, and as development aid budgets shrink. That said, Paraguay's macro-economics were stronger than they had been in the past. ECLAC reported 5 per cent growth for Paraguay and the government reported a 1 per cent surplus (ECLAC Online). Although unemployment rose, from 24 per cent to 25 per cent, the minimum wage also rose 10 per cent in nominal terms. Foreign direct investment (FDI) increased 13.8 per cent. Paraguay's trade deficit also improved somewhat (from 6 per cent to 4.5 per cent). It is difficult to overstate the significance of the continued growth of Paraguay's crop farming, which rose 24 per cent in 2007 alone (ECLAC Online). The question, as ever when considering the contradictions between economic development and human well being, is how much macroeconomic indicators can in fact tell us about, as they refer to it in Bhutan, Gross National Happiness. The very sector fueling the conflict with Paraguay's indigenous communities (as well as indigenous communities throughout Latin America) has exploded, portending continued violence, weak food security, illness and human rights abuses for the indigenous communities of Paraguay. Without a change in the dominance of this sector, in my analysis there will be very little Lugo can ultimately do to achieve a sustainable resolution to this conflict. Yet continued growth of this sector is almost certain with the new administration of Cartes which seems classically neoliberal in economic policy. Elsewhere (Duckworth, 2011), I noted the paradox in which so many developing countries find themselves, a paradox observed by numerous other scholars (see, for example: Gill, 2000 on Bolivia; Yasher, 2005; or Brysk, 2000). The bind is thus: new democracies now find themselves more accountable than ever to their constituents to provide social services such as health care, education and infrastructure. Clearly this requires funding. Yet simultaneously, developing countries throughout the Global South have been pressured by multinational corporations and international financial institutions (IFIs) to pursue development in a manner which has displaced many indigenous and *campesino* communities. The very manner in which Paraguay is currently funding their development, in my analysis, is the source of the conflict; yet growth remains necessary if roads, clinics and schools are to be built and staffed.

One hope which Lugo had expressed to resolve this Catch-22 was been pushing for the renegotiation of the Itaipú treaty with Brazil. This of course has long been a source of tension between Brazil and Paraguay. A regional economic powerhouse who has only grown in strength in the past several years, Brazil dominates MERCOSUR (with Argentina closely behind). Hence some Brazilians (or '*Brazilguayos*' as they are sometimes derisively called) have increasingly been buying land in Paraguay, especially along the Brazil/Paraguay border. Both before and after Lugo's inauguration, this has been the source of violent conflicts as Brazilian land owners in Paraguay defend what they consider to be their property, while indigenous communities and *campesinos* have staged demonstrations and occupations. The conflict escalated to the point which, in October 2008, Brazil even took the step of deploying troops to the Itaipú Dam in a clear demonstration of military and economic power. As Raúl Zibechi reported: 'On Oct. 17th, soldiers were deployed in a massive operation known as Southern Border II, in which they utilized planes, tanks, ships, and live munitions. The press in Asunción reported that the operation included exercises such as occupying the Itaipú Dam while rescuing Brazilian citizens. The Lugo government weighed in and assured that Brazil only wanted to negotiate peace for the soybean farmers for the benefit of Itaipú' (Zibechi, 2009).

In what may emerge as his most significant contribution to Paraguay's economic future, Lugo continued to push publicly for the renegotiation of this treaty such that Brazil would be paying a more fair market price for Paraguay's electricity, and was successful in 2009. Lugo pushed strenuously for this achievement. For example, at a meeting of the Organization of American States, Lugo suggested that the military exercises were intended as a warning from Brazil about Itaipú. He also issued a statement, during a visit to Washington, DC, arguing that, 'No agreement is sustainable when inequality is established nor is it ethical when disparities are generated as a result of a shared effort' (Zibechi, 2009). This issue had, as I say, long been a source of grievance between Paraguay and Brazil. Lula, for his part, had said that this issue was not on the table, though he did suggest that development aid to Paraguay might be possible (Lemus, 2009), highlighting what an achievement it was for Lugo to have ultimately secured some renegotiation. To be clear, Brazil was buying electricity from Paraguay, in accordance with the stipulations of the treaty, at rates significantly below market value. Billy Lemus of Energy Publisher reported that Brazil paid $2.7 per megawatt when market value was closer to $60 per megawatt (Lemus, 2009). In addition, the first Itaipú Treaty dated back to 1973, when both Brazil and Paraguay were under military dictatorships. The lack of legal clarity here perhaps fueled this conflict. The 'Brasilguayos' who purchase the land (at a far better price than they could in Brazil) felt they had purchased it legally; the indigenous communities, for their part, employ an anti-colonial narrative. They rhetorically link their current demands for the return of their stolen land to the exploitation and slavery they experienced under Spanish occupation (Duckworth, 2008; Horst, 2007; Gansen, 2003). Hence their narrative that the land was not anyone else's to sell! Notably the renegotiation, while an important achievement for Lugo, does not directly benefit the indigenous communities in particular, however, unless those funds are used to, for example, settle land theft cases or address food security and health care needs.

Other economic obstacles similarly bedeviled the progress of land reform under the Lugo administration. One such economic obstacle remains the external debt of Paraguay, which the ECLAC reports was 18.7 per cent of GDP in 2008 and currently is 15 per cent according to the World Bank (ECLAC; World Bank). Currently, Paraguay owes external creditors over $5 billion (World Bank). Paraguay also continues to endure a disadvantaged position within MERCOSUR, and the difficulties of two of Paraguay's major trading partners, Argentina and Brazil, given the global recession. (Note Paraguay was suspended from MERCOSUR for a time in response to Lugo's ouster, but has since been reinstated.) The difficulties caused by the global recession, in particular, were singled out by the President of *Banco InterAmericano de Desarrollo (BID)*, Luis Alberto Moreno, during a forum in which BID announced a fund for microfinance support. Of course, there remain concerns that lending will not again begin to flow, with the obvious consequences for development throughout the Global South. President Lugo, who attended this Forum, repeated a theme of his campaign: that the macroeconomic growth Paraguay had been able to achieve had had 'little impact' in addressing inequality ('BID reafirma apoyo', online).

So where to now, then? One significant and noticeable policy shift under Lugo was the non-renewal of Paraguay's agreement with the International Monetary Fund (IMF). This break was made before Lugo was even inaugurated, announced by his Finance Minister, Dionisio Borda (International Financial Institutions in Latin America, 2008). Borda is a respected but hardly left-wing economist; this choice was a clear signal that Lugo did not intend to implement a socialist revolution (followers of Paraguayan politics will likely remember the rampant speculation to this point prior to Lugo's election). Still, such a choice genuinely reflected a desire to restructure Paraguay's economy, a desire Lugo's administration was ultimately unable to implement, especially with regards to economic justice for indigenous communities. In an interview with *The Banker* around the time of his appointment, Borda spoke of the need to diversify Paraguay's economy so that it is less dependent on soy and cattle. He stated, 'At present, the economy is doing very well with two lines we're very strong on, soya and beef. Prices are high and the money's flowing in', he says. 'But it is time for us to take advantage of the other natural assets and add value by processing them' (Pavoni, 2010). Even into 2014, however, agriculture or other industries which require large plantations of land remain vastly dominant (sugar, soybeans, cotton and wood for example).

Access to jobs, health care, education, and the reduction of poverty are all equally important to economic diversification. Perhaps it is also worth stating the obvious point that economies are notoriously difficult to control or even guide, especially when one's country is in the structurally weak position Paraguay has always been in, with respect not just to the global economy, but with respect to the regional economy, and to MERCOSUR specifically. Many economists have also argued, as I do just above, that macroeconomic growth does not automatically result in a reduction of poverty (see for example the work of Paul Krugman, Joseph Stigletz, Ha-Joon Chang, or James Galbraith). Data from the Economic Commission on Latin America and the Caribbean (ECLAC), presented just above, demonstrates this. Recall that Paraguay has been growing, with respect to its GDP, at a quite respectable rate (especially in a time of such a severe global recession) until recently. Yet, as Lugo stated, this has not translated into a reduction in poverty for Paraguay's indigenous or other impoverished citizens; Paraguay continues to endure dramatic (though reportedly falling) inequality in incomes and land ownership (SEDLAC, 2009).

Lugo's term was hardly sufficient time to have made significant progress on, let alone completed, some of the audacious goals he set out. Yet it is inescapable that indigenous communities and *campesinos* continued to occupy national plazas, such as the Plaza Uruguaya and the Plaza Naciónal. Further, Lugo's government was unable to prevent continued human rights abuses. In an anti-government demonstration during his tenure, for example, according to local press coverage, Lugo heard a group of National Peasant Foundation protestors chanting and believed they were chanting for him. Alas, they were protesting and when this became clear, he apparently offered a brief greeting and moved on, saying that his 'government is not insensitive to the demands of the people' ('Lugo fue escarchado' Online). Meanwhile, the Municipality of Asunción had given the protestors several more days (as of Saturday, June 27, 2009) to vacate the *Plaza Uruguaya* or be forcibly evicted (ABC Color, 2009a). *Ultima Hora* reported at the time the eviction – at gunpoint – of fifty indigenous families. This was precisely Lugo's difficulty. He could speak out and even demand accountability, but without a majority in Congress, or a majority of support in local police districts, he was unable to halt these sorts of abuses.

Why did indigenous leaders protest a president for whom they fought? There is clearly some political and movement strategy here; any organizer knows that the proverbial 'squeaky wheel' gets the oil, and indigenous leaders know better than anyone the monied, connected and entrenched interests which fight their efforts to secure the return of their ancestral land. For example, rancher lobby groups, such as *Asociación Rural*, have issued statements that indigenous persons have not ever been exploited or discriminated against in Paraguay and that efforts to return their land are anti-capitalist, and as such, backward and anti-modern (Kidd, 1995, 71–72; Duckworth 2011, 202). This rhetoric is a common response to those seeking economic reform which threatens elite interests, but as Richard Reed (Reed, 1997), for example, has demonstrated, the mobilization around land rights among indigenous communities in Paraguay is not monolithically anti-capitalist (though such elements explicitly exist). Indeed, throughout Paraguay's colonial and military history, some indigenous groups chose willingly to engage in local, private markets. When they were able to do so from the relative security of their ancestral lands, which provided food, water and shelter, indigenous communities profited (quite literally) from such economic relations, Reed argues persuasively. My own field data was quite consistent with his observations (Duckworth, 2011). Hence a more nuanced understanding of indigenous demands would recognize that their central demand is for dignity and the ability to provide for themselves, rather than a wholesale rejection of the existence of free-markets. Underlying this observation is the reality, which I think is not often enough recognized, that capitalism is as much a set of norms and values as it is an economic system.

These stories of protests and plaza occupations are identical to those which emerged from Lugo's predecessors. Lugo never did have a handle on how to hold his extraordinarily ideologically diverse coalition together while maneuvering around the wealth and power trying to prevent him from being able to deliver the genuine land reform which would provide indigenous communities with the ability to sustain themselves in the manner of their choosing. This coalition reportedly included a Vice President who did not necessarily share his agenda; the BBC described this relationship as 'fractious'

(Duffy, 2009) and indeed it was the former Vice President himself who lead the effort to oust Lugo. Lugo's tenuous coalition further included the PLRA, which holds private property as a central tenant. According to *Ultima Hora*, they broke with Lugo's PAC during his Presidency. In response, Lugo stated to the press at the time that they were welcome to 'return to the sidewalk in front' if they wished (Ultima Hora, 2009a). Again, this particular fracture was especially troublesome because, other than *Partido Colorado*, the PLRA had the most seats in Congress.

An example illustrates how important Paraguay's Congress was to implementing, or failing to implement, land reform and critical education and health programs for Paraguay's indigenous communities. One tactic indigenous communities throughout Latin America have used to empower themselves in what are often vastly asymmetrical conflicts is maneuvering around the national state to engage with international bodies such as the United Nations, international human rights organizations or the InterAmerican Court of Human Rights. For example, in 2005, the Yakye Axa community successfully sued the government of Paraguay. The Court ruled that the State had not met their obligations to the community and assessed a fine. President Lugo was reportedly vocal in his support of the national legislation which would comply with the Court's ruling, but Amnesty International reported that 'members of a Congressional Committee in Paraguay have voted against the return of indigenous lands to the Yakye Axa community', which 'undermines a binding decision made by the InterAmerican Court of Human Rights' (Amnesty International, 2009). This speaks to the continued urgency of indigenous concerns being represented in the national Congress as well as the Executive.

The political and economic structural obstacles I have been describing are not at all insurmountable. Indeed, every victory the indigenous communities have won looked impossible beforehand. Law 904, which we recall made it illegal to sell indigenous lands, was enacted under Stroessner. The new 1992 Constitution was a watershed victory, finally recognizing that Paraguay did, in fact, have an indigenous community with social, cultural, economic and political rights. This victory was won (at least on paper) just over two years after Stroessner's fall. With a variety of techniques that include partnering with NGOs, marching, forming regional coalitions, and occupying stolen land or national plazas, indigenous people have ensured the survival of their culture and communities. Yet this should not obscure the cost in human life and suffering required to achieve whatever victories they have managed. Tens of thousands have died of illness, hunger, exposure or due to violence. The mere fact of an opposition candidate's election, especially one who focused so explicitly on poverty and land reform, remains itself a victory of sorts. Yet as I have been describing, the political, social and economic systems currently preventing such reform remain manifest and are arguably strengthened again with the return of *Partido Colorado* to power. The Bishop of the Poor needed his base vocal and united to have the political power necessary to achieve results on the ground in indigenous communities. Ultimately, to be transformative, he may have had to choose between the more moderate, right-wing and left-wing aspects of his coalition. Unable to do so, and facing the 'deep state' of *Partido Colorado,* as well as his own failings as a leader born I suspect of a lack of experience, as this chapter has shown, he was ultimately unable to deliver transformative change for the indigenous peoples of Paraguay.

References

ABC Color, 'Emplazan a Aborígenes a Salir de Plazas Públicas'. *ABC Color*, 27 June 2009a, www.abc.com.py/2009-06-27/articulos/534863/intiman-a-indigenas-a-salir-de-plazas.

ABC Color, 'Enzo Cardozo no se Opone a la Aplicación de Conflictiva Norma'. *ABC Color*, 15 Mayo 2009b, www.abc.com.py/2009-05-15/articulos/521846/enzo-cardozo-no-se-opone-a-la-aplicacion-de-conflictiva-norma.

ABC Color, 'Los Indigenas Insisten Con Cardozo Para INDI'. *ABC Color*, 7 Julio 2009c, www.abc.com.py/2009-07-07/articulos/537667/los-indigenas-insisten-con-cardozo-para-indi.

Amnesty International, 'Paraguayan Congress Risks Lives of 90 Indigenous Families'. Amnesty International, 28 June 2009, www.amnestyusa.org/document.php?id=ENGNAU2009062811157&lang=e# (accessed 26 June 2015).

Associated Press, 'Paraguay: Indian Official Alledgedly Stole $700,00'. All India, NDTV.com, 24 September 2013, www.ndtv.com/article/india/paraguay-indian-official-allegedly-stole-700-000-422810 (accessed 26 June 2015).

Banco Interamericano de Desarrollo (BID), 'BID Reafirma Apoyo a Microfinanzas en América Latina ante Turbulencia Internacional'. *Comunicados de Prensa*, 9 October 2008, www.iadb.org/es/noticias/comunicados-de-prensa/2008-10-09/bid-reafirma-apoyo-a-microfinanzas-en-america-latina-ante-turbulencia-internacional, 4795.html (accessed 26 June 2015).

Barrionuevo, Alexei. 'Paternity Makes Punch Line of Paraguay President'. *New York Times*, 10 May 2009, www.nytimes.com/2009/05/10/world/americas/10paraguay.html?_r=1&scp=6&sq=Paraguay&st=cse (accessed 26 June 2015).

Brun, Diego Abente. 'The Quality of Democracy in Small South American Countries: the case of Paraguay'. Working Paper #343, 2007. https://kellogg.nd.edu/publications/workingpapers/WPS/343.pdf (accessed May 2014).

Brysk, Allison. *From Tribal Village to Global Village: Indian Rights and International Relations in Latin America*. Stanford UP: Stanford, CA, 2000.

Cardozo, Jose and Jorge Cañete. 'Lugo fue escrachado por campesinos en Villarrica'. *ABC Color*, 27 June 2009, www.abc.com.py/edicion-impresa/politica/los-indigenas-insisten-con-cardozo-para-indi-1188924.html.

Childress, Malcolm. World Bank Paraguay Land Administration Specialist. Personal Interview, 8 July 2009.

China Economic Net, 'Paraguayan President Reshuffles Cabinet'. *China Economic Net*, http://en.ce.cn/World/Americas/200904/21/t20090421_18867831.shtml# (accessed 30 June 2009).

Duckworth, Cheryl Lynn. *Land and Dignity in Paraguay*. Continuum: New York, NY, 2011.

Duffy, Gary. 'Paternity Claims Harm Paraguay Leader'. *BBC Online*, 25 April 2009.

Economic Commission on Latin America and the Caribbean. 'Paraguay'. www.eclac.cl/publicaciones/xml/3/33873/Paraguay.pdf (accessed 26 June 2015).

The Economist, 'Lugo out in the Cold: Why did Paraguay's Congress Mount a Constitutional Putsch against the President? And What Happens Now?' *The Economist*, 30 June 2012, www.economist.com/node/21557802 (accessed 26 June 2015).

Estigarribia, J. Eulogio. 'Indi Habilita un Centro Agrícola Para Capacitar a los Indígenas a Cultivar'. *ABC Color*, 26 April 2008, www.abc.com.py/2008-04-26/articulos/409823/indi-habilita-un-centro-agricola-para-capacitar-a-los-indigenas-a-cultivar.

Ganson, Barbara. *The Guarani Under Spanish Rule in the Rio de le Plata*. Stanford University Publications: Stanford, CA, 2003.

Gill, Leslie. *Teetering on the Brim: Global Restructuring, Daily Life and the Armed Retreat of the Bolivian State*. Columbia UP: New York, NY, 2000.

Horst, Rene Harder. *The Stroessner Regime and Indigenous Resistance in Paraguay*. University of Florida Press: Gainesville, FL, 2007.

International Financial Institutions in Latin America, 'Lugo's Paraguay and the IMF'. International Financial Institutions in Latin America Monitor, http://ifis.choike.org/informes/851.html (accessed 26 June 2015).

Iran Daily, 'Agricultural Ties with Paraguay'. *Iran Daily*, n.d., www.iran-daily.com/1388/3410/html/economy.htm.

Kidd, Stephen. 'Land, Politics and Benevolent Shaminism: The Enxet Indians in a Democratic Paraguay'. *Journal of Latin American Studies*, Vol 27, No. 1., February 1995: 43–75.

La Nación, 'Fernando Lugo Pierde al Partido Liberal Como su Principal Aliado'. *La Nación*, 6 Julio 2009, www.lanacion.com.py/noticias_um-255177.htm.

Lemus, Billy. 'Paraguay: Scandal and inertia weigh down Lugo'. Energy Publisher Online, www.energypublisher.com/article.asp?id=19148; no longer active, but reposted on *SperoNews* at: www.speroforum.com/a/19148/Paraguay-Scandal-and-inertia-weigh-down-Lugo#.VIrrgHvp2tw (accessed 26 June 2015).

'Los Indigenas Insisten Con Cardozo Para INDI'. *ABC Color*, 7 Julio 2009, www.ultimahora.com/nativos-anuncian-cambio-director-el-indi-pero-n234991.html (accessed 26 June 2015).

National Indigenous Institute of Paraguay (INDI) Official, Personal Interview Conducted by Cheryl Duckworth, 28 June 2006.

Nickson, Andrew. 'An Opportunity for Paraguay: The Challenges for Fernando Lugo'. *Nueva Sociedad*, Nro. 216, Julio-Augusto 2008a. Online at www.nuso.org/upload/articulos/3529_2.pdf (accessed 26 June 2015).

Nickson, Andrew. 'Paraguay: A Shift to the Left Under Lugo?' *Real Insituto Elcano*, 9 November 2008b. www.realinstitutoelcano.org/wps/portal/rielcano_eng/Content?WCM_GLOBAL_CONTEXT=/Elcano_in/Zonas_in/Latin+America/ARI99-2008 (accessed 26 June 2015).

O'Shaughnessy, Hugh. 'Chavez, Lula and… Lugo'. *The Guardian* Online, www.guardian.co.uk/world/2008/jul/03/religion.catholicism (accessed July, 2008).

Pavoni, Silvia. 'Paraguay Banks on Natural Resources'. *The Banker*, 30 August 2010, www.thebanker.com/Profiles/People/Q-A/Paraguay-banks-on-natural-resources (accessed 26 June 2015).

Reed, Richard. *Forest Dwellers, Forest Protectors: Indigenous Models for International Development*. Allyn and Bacon: Boston, MA, 1997.

Renshaw, John. *Indians of the Paraguayan Chaco: Identity and Economy*. University of Nebraska Press: Lincoln, NE, 2002.

Rodriguez, Lorena. 'Police Repression and Presidential Promises: The Fight for Social Justice in Paraguay'. 12 November 2008, http://upsidedownworld.org/main/content/view/1574/44/ (accessed 3 September 2015).

SEDLAC (2009). Socioeconomic Database for Latin America and the Caribbean, *CEDLAS and the World Bank*, Brief 2, May 2009.

Torres, Gustavo. 'Indigenous Groups Left to Wait'. 1 January 2009, http://lapress.org/articles.asp?art5785 (accessed 26 June 2015).

Ultima Hora, 'Lugo sugiere que si el PLRA déjà la Alianza sera de nuevo oposición'. *Ultima Hora.* 3 Julio 2009, www.ultimahora.com/notas/234988-Lugo-sugiere-que-si-el-PLRA-deja-la-Alianza-ser%C3%A1-de-nuevo-oposici%C3%B3n (accessed 26 June 2015).

Ultima Hora, 'Nativos Anuncian Cambio Pero...'. *Ultima Hora*, 3 Julio 2009, www.ultimahora.com/notas/234991-Nativos-anuncian-cambio-de-director-en-el-INDI,-pero (accessed 26 June 2015).

UNICEF Official, Personal Interview Conducted by Cheryl Duckworth, 20 June 20 2006.

Yashar, Deborah J. *Contesting Citizenship in Latin America: The Rise of Indigenous Movements and the Postliberal Challenge.* Cambridge UP: New York, 2005.

Zibechi, Raúl. 'Is Brazil Creating Its Own Back Yard?' *Americas Policy Report*, 3 February 2009, http://americas.irc-online.org/pdf/reports/0902backyard.pdf.

5 Awkward alliances

Is environmentalism a bonding agent between indigenous and rural settler politics in America and Australia?

Saleem H. Ali and Julia Keenan

Introduction

Assumptions around indigenous proclivities for nature have been rife in popular environmental writings and pronouncements for much of the twentieth century. At the same time, environmentalists and conservation regulators have often marginalized indigenous communities in their quest for rapid protection of lands in what Mark David Spence has referred to as 'dispossessing the wilderness' (Spence, 2000). Modern environmentalism has also been critiqued with similar accusations of marginalizing indigenous rights at the behest of conservation, particularly through well-funded conservation philanthropies. In 2004, anthropologist Mac Chapin wrote an influential article in which he challenged the three largest environmental organizations in the United States (Conservation International, World Wildlife Fund and The Nature Conservancy) to show greater sensitivity towards indigenous perspectives on conservation (Chapin, 2004). Despite some initial defensiveness, there was genuine introspection on the part of the leadership of these organizations. Gestures such as the appointment of indigenous representatives on boards as well as more consultative approaches to protected areas management were instituted to avoid the phenomenon of what Mark Dowie (2011) referred to as 'conservation refugees'.

At the same time, revisionist anthropologists and environmental historians, citing the Pleistocene Overkill, have also questioned the presumption that indigenous peoples have lived in harmony with nature and noted that they too are subject to the same human failings on conservation (Krech, 2000). The debate on whether or not to ascribe any ecological ascendancy to indigenous tradition is often caused by a differential analysis of scale and cultural specificity of particular practices. Historian Calvin Martin's reversal of views about indigenous sensibilities towards the environment is emblematic of this tension. In his first classic work *Keepers of the Game* (Martin, 1982), Martin had noted that given the ferocity of hunting culture within some tribes that 'Even if we absolve him of his ambiguous culpability in certain episodes of despoliation, invoking instead his pristine sentiments towards Nature, the Indian still remains a misfit guru. There can be no salvation in the Indian's traditional conception of Nature for the troubled environmentalist'. However, a decade later when he had a chance to live closer to Native Americans in northern New York State where his wife was serving as a medical doctor, Martin reconsidered his earlier views. His two subsequent books (Martin, 1993 and 2000) were far more sympathetic towards indigenous conservation ethics.

A collectively humanizing discourse on this topic has been offered by Cherokee historian Jace Weaver in the context of Native American environmentalism, and with whom we concur more broadly regarding a self-evaluation of indigenous environmental politics:

> We are not Moses coming down from Sinai with the Ten Commandments of environmental protection. Indians have been stereotyped far too long by the environmental movement as those with the mystical, ancient wisdom that alone can save the planet. Rather we presented and represented the honest and extremely difficult struggles of indigenous peoples to meet ecological challenges confronting them. Though traditional knowledge and ways play an important part in these battles, so do all the tools of technology, modern modes of communication, and the simple investment of time and sweat.
>
> (Weaver, 1996)

Some win-win opportunities for indigenous communities to have an economic development path that is preferred by environmentalists have been identified in the service sector, particularly with eco-tourism developments. The specific features of tourism and other service sector economies that might offer a positive opportunity for indigenous-environmental interface because their growth is predicated on social relationships more so than the sale of a particular commodity (Vivanco, 2007). Thus even though service sector economies consume resources they do not sell a particular material commodity (particularly a nonrenewable one) and hence offer a less pinching area for activity by environmentalists. However, indigenous communities are also conscious of their cooptation by such sectors and becoming 'objectified' as novelties in a sort of naturalized museum. This led to a formal meeting of indigenous communities in 2002 during the United Nations International Year of Ecotourism to counter what was perceived by them as a corporatized agenda for tourism that was neglecting community concerns. In this declaration, however, concerns about cooptation of the indigenous agenda by non-indigenous civil society including environmentalists were also clearly articulated: 'Indigenous Peoples are not objects of tourism development. We are active subjects with the rights and responsibilities to our territories and the processes of tourism planning, implementation, and evaluation that happen in them. This means we are responsible for defending Indigenous lands and communities from development schemes imposed by governments, development agencies, private corporations, NGOs, and specialists' (Oaxaca Declaration, quoted in Zeppel, 2006, appendix).

In contrast with tourism, extractive resource projects pose a far more normative dilemma for environmentalist and indigenous sensibilities. The industrial development of such projects are framed as existential threats to the planet – such as uranium mining and the nuclear industry or more recently fossil fuels and climate change. At the same time, there is also a narrative of negative legacy which past mineral projects have left on indigenous lands and where minimal benefits accrued for the communities. A lack of control on the development trajectory looms large for many indigenous groups. Previous research has indicated that in such contexts the alliances between indigenous communities and environmentalists are robust only if there is a link to sovereign decision-making for the indigenous groups concerned (Ali, 2003). However, within the past five years, there has been a marked increase in the level of global recognition of indigenous interests as well as much greater potential for networked alliances with a broader range of stakeholders. In this chapter our goal is to reconsider the prevalence and efficacy of indigenous-environmental alliances through a comparative case analysis to highlight key evolutionary differences in settler politics in North America and Australia. We have chosen two specific recent cases of extractive development which have seen a parallel level of indigenous and environmental activism.

Indigenous/environmentalist relations in the keystone Xl case

For the North American case, we consider the development of the Keystone XL Pipeline which is a transnational project originating in the oil sands deposits of Alberta and making its way south to the United States with two routings. The project is a particularly useful case to understand indigenous-environmental alliances because it traverses multiple state and federal jurisdictions and covers a broad range of ecological and social landscapes over thousands of miles of infrastructure.

Environmentalist opposition to this project is first and foremost because of a long-standing concern about oil sands exploitation in Alberta and the impact it is having on water and land usage. Climate change activism around fossil fuel developments is also an additional cause for opposition leading with groups such as 350.org (focused on bringing carbon dioxide concentrations to or below 350 ppm in the atmosphere) joining the cause against the project. The lobbying efforts against the project have traversed numerous organizations but it is important to note that environmentalists did not initiate indigenous concerns in this regard. The first unified statement at an organizational level against the Keystone XL project was put forward by the National Congress of American Indians which passed a resolution in September 2011 that stated: 'The United States is urged to reduce its reliance on the world's dirtiest and most environmentally destructive form of oil –

the 'tar sands' – that threatens Indian country in both Canada and the United States and the way of life of thousands of citizens of First Nations in Canada and American Indians in the U.S., and requests the U.S. government to take aggressive measures to work towards sustainable energy solutions that include clean alternative energy and improving energy efficiency...'.[1]

This resolution also reinforced the importance of considering continental North America as a pre-Columbian inhabited entity that defied the current political demarcation between Canada and the United States. The transboundary nature of the pipeline also provided an additional impetus for indigenous activism on this matter as a mark of showcasing a collective indigenous ethos across borders. It is important to note that in the wording of this resolution environmental factors are clearly mentioned as the cause for concern. However, there were several other issues at stake for First Nations in Canada and Native Americans, including cultural heritage protection and ancestral remains being desecrated. On September 19, 2011, a number of leaders from Native American bands in the United States and First Nations bands from Canada were arrested for protesting the Keystone XL outside the White House and thus a direct civic engagement started as well. It is nevertheless worth noting that several Canadian First Nation tribes continue to have interests in oil sands development. In some cases even former leaders who had opposed oil development have gone on to work for the industry despite overall consensus from Canadian organizations such as the Assembly of First Nations critical of oil sands (Prystupa, 2014).

Some of the more vocal activism on the street against the pipeline came from the Indigenous Environmental Network – an organization which has the closest direct alliance with environmental groups and has been galvanized by the charismatic Ojibwe activist Winona LaDuke. She has also founded an organization called 'Honor the Earth' which directly challenges the development paradigm being followed by specific indigenous groups (LaDuke, 1999).

Meanwhile, the project's major owner TransCanada responded to indigenous opposition by focusing on broader research support on indigenous well-being and training of their staff rather than engaging with their specific ecological or social disruption concerns. The company endowed a Trans-Canada Pipelines Chair in Aboriginal Health and Well-being at the University of Toronto. They also started a program of community engagement through applied collaboration in research. According to the company: 'Each community chooses to become involved in its own way. One scenario may see a TransCanada facilitator join Aboriginal community experts and scientists on a biophysical study, during which they'll record concerns. For example, a botanist and an Aboriginal expert in medicinal plants may conduct a survey together'.[2] Such a program undoubtedly has educational value but detracts from the key points of tension that were being articulated by the indigenous communities. There appeared to be a presumption on the part of Trans-Canada that the environmental concerns being voiced by Green groups were somehow divorced from the daily reality of indigenous livelihoods. Indeed, numerous Canadian tribes have supported resource development to the chagrin of some environmental groups. However, what the company did not realize is that where direct benefits are less palpable as compared to potential planetary cost, tribes are exhibiting environmental resistance, and want redress on those measures.

Native concerns about environmental damage are more directly linked to a sense of loss for past lands which had been appropriated for resource development without community consent. Much of the narrative in their dissent harkens back to the struggles about land between encroaching White settlements of yesteryears. The South Dakota Sioux Tribe has collectively called the approval of the Keystone pipeline an 'Act of War' which is quite a far more austere rhetoric than one may hear from environmentalists. Seven tribes of the Lakota Nation, along with tribal members and tribes in Idaho, Oklahoma, Montana, Nebraska and Oregon, have joined forces in opposition.[3] The issue is particularly sensitive because of a history of armed tensions between the U.S. government and the Sioux tribes in this region (Biolsi, 2001). The Osage tribe in Oklahoma has a history of oil extraction but with little to show in terms of development on the reservation, even though at one time the tribe was getting record revenues and was ostensibly one of the wealthiest communities in America. However, through government mismanagement and corruption the oil revenues became a source of discord and decay for the communities (McAuliffe, 1999). Opposition to the Keystone XL pipeline emanated to a large degree from such fears of poor governance of the oil infrastructure which would be beyond the control of the tribes. There have been some insinuations by commentators that indigenous opposition to Keystone XL may have political motivations as well in terms of tribal relationships with the Obama administration (Mufson, 2012). However, the multifaceted nature of the opposition from major Tribal organizations suggests that the opposition is principled and issues-oriented and not predicated on co-optation by environmentalists nor political posturing.

What is also remarkable about the alliance formation in the context of this pipeline development has been the proclivity of Native Americans to form closer relations with conservative ranchers which even environmentalist Bill McKibben (2014) has noted as a 'Cowboys and Indian' alliance. The anatomy of such an alliance defies a history of racism by ranchers against Indians and is predicated on a common primacy to sovereign decision-making at the local level rather than through federal authority. In the words of Paul Seamans, the chair of Dakota Rural Action: 'An alliance might seem unlikely, but it's not really…we have a lot of the same interests. Historically it may have been so, but things are changing. Especially with the advent of social media, which has made it a lot easier to keep in contact. A lot of us have given more consideration to their Native American treaty rights and see things more from their perspective now'.[4]

Thus the Keystone XL resistance case shows that the dynamics of the relationship between indigenous communities and environmentalism have evolved to the point where the following key characteristics were observed:

a   The indigenous resistance to the pipeline emerged independently of environmentalist concerns and was motivated by a concern about the negative legacy of oil extraction and the lack of control tribes felt they had on the trajectory of the project.
b   Environmental concerns were noted by indigenous organizations as a substantive concern in their resolutions against the project but no formal alliance formation occurred between tribal governments with environmentalists except in the case of established Native Green activist groups such as the Indigenous Environmental Network.
c   The transboundary nature of the pipeline project also prompted indigenous communities across the border between Canada and the United States to show collective solidarity. Such a show of unity was aimed at highlighting ecological connectivity but also the importance of transcending post-Columbian border demarcations within the context of indigenous politics.
d   The alliance formation between indigenous communities and ranchers (who might otherwise be at odds with environmentalists as well as indigenous activism) highlighted the importance of sovereign decision-making and local rights discourse within indigenous alliance formation. Transcanada Corporation did not fully engage with this aspect of dissent, focusing instead on technical research on impact mitigation and unrelated cultural training for employees.
e   Climate change concerns about fossil fuels and tar/oil sands deposits themselves were noted as points of concern by indigenous organizations in their opposition to the project. However, there continues to be some willingness to engage with extractive companies more so than the environmentalist's positional stance against tar/oil sands.

Recognizing inherent cultural differences, there is still increasing degree of lesson drawing across indigenous activism worldwide. In the next case analysis we consider how the Australian context may be similar or different from the North American case of activism against extractive industries, and the fossil fuels sector in particular, and whether any comparative lessons can be drawn.

Indigenous/environmentalist relations in the Australian CSG industry

Our Australian case study considers the recent and rapid development of the coal seam gas (CSG, also known as coal bed methane, CBM) export industry in southern Queensland and northern New South Wales, Australia. CSG is extracted from extensive gas fields located near to the Queensland-NSW border, transported over 300kms by pipeline to a regional port facility where it is cooled and pressurised for overseas export as liquid natural gas (LNG). The gas fields region, where the impact is greatest, is home to some of Australia's most highly valued agricultural land and lies above part of the Great Artesian Basin, one of the largest underground water resources in the world.

As with the Keystone XL pipeline, differences in support or opposition to CSG can be observed in the different states' jurisdictions, ecological and social landscapes. Adding to the complexity, the approval and environmental monitoring of petroleum developments is the responsibility of the state government departments while underground aquifers are subject to federal regulatory authority.

While the individual CSG wells have a relatively small footprint (about $20,000m^2$ during drilling and $5,000m^2$ in operation), they are more closely spaced than conventional gas wells. Each well pad is interlinked by access roads and pipelines, producing an almost geometric pattern over thousands of square kilometres of the landscape. The majority of the land gazetted for CSG exploration in Queensland is owned by families or family companies (with a small proportion of national and international corporations) engaged in agricultural production, particularly of food crops, cotton and cattle grazing (Coffey, 2012).

The development of these projects has seen some of the most high profile and widespread protest and activism around resource development in Australia since the proposed establishment of uranium mining in Kakadu National Park. Alliances between Aboriginal and environmental groups has helped to raise the profile of Aboriginal causes, but often clashes over values have set 'green' and 'black' groups at odds (Langton, 2012; Ritter, 2014). Opposition to the development of the CSG industry is evident in a range of stakeholder groups from local communities to Australian society more broadly. Impacted landholders and community activists have aligned with broader environmental and activist movements to bring attention to a broad range of issues. Direct local impacts including loss or contamination of water sources, health impacts, environmental damage and impacts on farmer liveli-hoods and rural lifestyles are prominent in activist discourse, as are broader impacts including climate change, governance and land use transformation (Carey, 2012; De Rijke, 2013a). Impacts on one of Australia's World Heritage sites, the Great Barrier Reef, from shipping and port development are also prominent concerns.

Concerns about impact have been accompanied by concerns about process. Indeed indigenous, activist and landholder groups have all registered concerns about the timeframes, transparency and quality of the approvals process; the capacity of the regulatory agencies; the state of scientific know-ledge, and processes for planning land use change. The speed of the development and inexperience of the proponents (Trigger *et al.*, 2014, 179) and regulators (de Rijke, 2013b, 15) certainly contributed to raising the levels of anxiety and fear among impacted communities and reducing trust in government and industry (Lloyd, Luke and Boyd, 2013, 145).

It has long been acknowledged that environmental groups face a dilemma in determining whether or not to ally with corporations or governments in order to enact change, and that activist groups can be seen on a spectrum from 'activism to engagement' (Beder, 1991). The predominant alliance opposing CSG is the 'Lock the Gate' alliance, which falls firmly on the activist end of the spectrum. The Lock the Gate Alliance declares that it is: 'a national coalition of people from across Australia, including farmers, traditional custodians, conservationists and urban residents, who are uniting to protect our common heritage – our land, water and communities – from unsafe or inappropriate mining for coal seam gas and other fossil fuels'. (Lock the Gate Alliance, n.d.)

In contrast to this high level of oppositional activity, CSG development in Queensland has resulted in unprecedented negotiation of Indigenous Land Use Agreements (ILUAs) with Indigenous peoples. Between 2010 and 2014, 35 ILUAs between CSG companies and Indigenous groups were signed, compared to 16 mining ILUAs in the whole state of Queensland in the same period (Trigger *et al.*, 2014, 178). Under the *Native Title Act 1993* (Cth) (and subsequent amendments), the continuation of a range of Indigenous rights to land can be recognised. Those Indigenous groups with recognised native title rights (or registered claims) to impacted areas have the 'right to negotiate' with proponents about future development on their lands.[5] The 'right to negotiate' does not include the right to veto a development, but does include the ability to negotiate over compensation, cultural heritage and environmental protection, provision of public works and infrastructure, employment, economic opportunities and so on.

While initially resisted by industry, a 'culture of agreement making' with Indigenous peoples is now well established across Australia (Langton and Palmer, 2003; Neate, 2008; National Native Title Tribunal, 1999). A study of agreements in the gas fields region of Queensland noted diverse Indigenous views on CSG development and on the agreements negotiated with CSG companies and the shifting legal and regulatory context: 'The range of concerns, disputes, and unresolved issues illustrated in the legal cases reviewed suggests that development of CSG in eastern Australia is engaging with Aboriginal groups that are internally diverse in terms of articulation of traditional rights in country as well as aspirations for and capacity to manage agreements'. (Trigger *et al.*, 2014, 185)

Key issues to Indigenous groups included: the social wellbeing associated with access to 'country' (i.e., the physical and spiritual property of land and waters); access to economic benefits including employment and contracting opportunities, and dissatisfaction with the agreement process (including pressured timeframes, limited negotiating power, lack of Indigenous organisational capacity and consultation fatigue) (Trigger *et al.*, 2014, 182–3).

There is also a strong congruence between America and Australian with regard to dispossession of the land but the situation was far more acute for Australian Aboriginal people since there were no treaties (no matter how unfairly negotiated) that might provide some moderating influence over the trauma of relocation.

A number of Indigenous people's concerns resonate with the concerns of local non-Indigenous communities and farmers. Indigenous groups were not a dominant voice in anti-CSG activism, although that is not to say that Indigenous voices were absent. In northern New South Wales, where opposition to CSG is notably more widespread and intense than in Queensland, two Aboriginal people described in the media as elders were arrested during a blockade of CSG exploration activities (Feain and Brown, 2013) and local Aboriginal organisations are in conflict over approvals for CSG exploration (Trigger *et al.*, 2014, 18–4). On the other hand, New South Wales Aboriginal Land Council CEO reprimanded the environmentalists for ignoring Aboriginal aspirations for economic development, saying: '[Lock the Gate leader] Hutton was out there saying we should be noble and grow vegetables. Thanks for your advice! It's not noble having people whose sewerage systems don't work; it's not noble having people live on the dole all their life. We want something better and we don't want to rely on government' (MacDonald-Smith, 2013).

The case of CSG development in Queensland gives another example of the dynamics of the relationship between indigenous communities and environmentalism. In this case the following key characteristics were observed:

a   A 'culture of agreement making' and the opportunity for direct negotiation with impacted Indigenous peoples provides an alternative avenue for engagement other than alignment with broad activist movements. Langton notes the similarity in Indigenous and non-indigenous responses to the encroachment of extractive industries: 'With the development of shale gas and fracking projects and their expansion into valuable farming land, farmers, rural and even suburban dwelling Australians have objected stridently, and begun to demand protections much as Aboriginal people did 50 years ago when large scale mining projects impacted on their world' (Langton, 2012).

b   She argues that the 'seat at the table' provided by the 'right to negotiate' has been the 'most important achievement of Aboriginal leaders in law and policy' (Langton, 2013). While farmers and others are still fighting for due consideration via alliances with activists, native title groups are exercising their rights in direct negotiation with project proponents.

c   Where the legal system provides no opportunity to refuse extractive industry development, Aboriginal groups are using their 'right to negotiate' to leverage economic development, local environmental and cultural heritage protection opportunities via agreement making.

Concern for broad environmental issues and climate change were noted among Aboriginal populations, however these issues are beyond the scope of Indigenous Land Use Agreements.

d   There is no consistent 'aboriginal' position on CSG, nor is there an existing institution at the tribal, regional or national level that could present such a position. Aboriginal engagement with environmentalists in the CSG context appears to be motivated by personal or family attitudes towards environment and industry, and related to complex intra and inter-group politics. The native title regime, with its emphasis on recognising the distinct Indigenous social groupings, and the fractured nature of Indigenous social relations in the region, do not encourage unity as a broader Indigenous entity.

Comparative lessons and conclusion

The two case comparisons show that environmental organizations have the potential for providing some measure of knowledge-based connectivity between indigenous and rural-based settler politics in Australia and North America. Environmentalists can thus play the role of an 'epistemic community', to use the nomenclature of Haas (1989), but that role has become less salient as indigenous organizations gain their own scientific knowledge base or are supported by the national government. There continues to be a level of caution exhibited by indigenous communities about the motivation of environmentalists in forming alliances. This has much to do with the history of environmentalist involvement in marginalizing indigenous communities in the name of conservation and the establishment of protected areas as well as their positional stance against hunting and other practices that may be part of indigenous tradition.

In North America, the environmental movement has developed a more organic base within indigenous politics through their own environmental organizations such as The Indigenous Environmental Network. Because of such a base, indigenous organizations may feel more comfortable collaborating with environmentalists for tactical rather than strategic advantage where appropriate. In contrast, indigenous groups have more strategic commonality with ranchers and property rights activists in the current context since their broader strategy for political ascendancy is predicated on exercising such sovereign influence. Thus many indigenous organizations are willing to overlook the history of racism associated with rancher politics in rural America and focus on the current opportunity for strategic cooperation. In Australia, the relationship between ranchers and indigenous groups has not reached that level of maturity since there is less emphasis on 'sovereign' government institutions and more on economic development pathways.

In Australia, there is also a more business-focused model of Aboriginal institutional development through Native corporations (similar to Alaska rather than mainland U.S. and Canada). This has also led to a need for land acquisition on the part of Aboriginal communities that is also facilitated by the federal government via The Indigenous Land Corporation (ILC), which is a statutory authority mandated to 'assist Indigenous people to acquire and manage land to achieve economic, environmental, social and cultural benefits'. This often puts them in direct competition with ranchers and further prevents them for overlooking a negative history of conflict unlike their American counterparts. Environmentalists in Australia have had more common ground with ranchers through the 'Lock the Gate' movement than they have been able to muster with indigenous groups. Indeed, the Green-Rancher alliance makes it more difficult for indigenous groups to feel comfortable in forming environmentalist alliances. Any alliance formation with environmentalists is thus very personality dependent and linked to individual friendships that may have come about extant to the particular anti-CSG campaign.

This chapter has attempted to provide some broad comparative insights regarding the alliance formation between indigenous communities in the Americas and Australia, using two contemporary extractive resource issues with similar level of activism. Further research on the ethnographic aspects of alliance formation or lack thereof could shed light on the strength of any cooperative mechanisms and how sensitive they are to violations of trust. It is important to recognize that human alliance formation is intrinsically dynamic and communities are constantly evaluating their partnerships. For those scholars who are interested in efficient processes for resolving indigenous resource conflicts, an understanding of such alliance dynamics is essential. Through such an understanding indigenous leaders, environmental organizations, corporations and governments can better assess the framing and articulation of issues in the negotiation process.

References

Ali, S.H., 2003. *Mining, the Environment, and Indigenous Development Conflicts.* Tucson, AZ: University of Arizona Press.

Beder, S., 1991. 'Activism versus Negotiation: Strategies for the Environment Movement'. *Social Alternatives,* 10(4), 53-56.

Biolsi, T., 2001. *Deadliest Enemies: Law and the Making of Race Relations on and off Rosebud Reservation,* First Edition. Berkeley, CA: University of California Press.

Carey, M., 2012. 'Coal Seam Gas: Future Bonanza or Toxic Legacy?' *Viewpoint 8,* 26–31.

Coffey Environments Pty Ltd., 2012. *Surat Gas Project – Environmental Impact Statement, Volume 1, Chapter 13: Agriculture.* Prepared for Arrow Energy Pty Ltd. Retrieved 26 March, 2013, from www.arrowenergy.com.au/content/Document/surateis/Volume%201/Chapter%2013%20-%20Agriculture.pdf.

Chapin, M., 2004. 'A Challenge to Conservationists'. *WorldWatch,* November/December.

de Rijke, K., 2013a. 'The Agri-Gas Fields of Australia: Black Soil, Food and Unconventional Gas'. *Culture, Agriculture, Food and Environment,* 35(1), 41–53.

de Rijke, K., 2013b. 'Hydraulically Fractured: Unconventional Gas and Anthropology'. *Anthropology Today*, 29(2), 13–17.

Dowie, M., 2011. *Conservation Refugees: The Hundred-Year Conflict between Global Conservation and Native Peoples*. Cambridge, MA; London, U.K. MIT Press.

Feain, D. and Brown, J., 2013. 'Githabul Elders Arrested at Doubtful Creek CSG Protest'. *Northern Star*. Retrieved from: www.northernstar.com.au/news/web-first-arrest-at-doubtful-creek/1743202/.(accessed 15 November 2014)

Haas, P.M., 1989. 'Do Regimes Matter? Epistemic Communities and Mediterranean Pollution Control'. *International Organization* 43, 377–403.

Krech, S.K., 2000. *The Ecological Indian: Myth and History*. W.W. Norton & Company, New York.

LaDuke, W., 1999. *All Our Relations: Native Struggles for Land and Life*, First Edition. Cambridge, MA: Minneapolis, MN: South End Press.

Langton, M., 2012. *Boyer Lectures 2012: The Quiet Revolution: Indigenous People and the Resources Boom*. ABC Books, Sydney.

Langton, M., 2013. 'Why Aboriginal Issues are no longer Black or White'. *The Age Online*. Retrieved from: www.theage.com.au/comment/why-aboriginal-issues-are-no-longer-black-or-white-20130313-2g0mo.html (accessed 26 June 2015).

Langton, M. and Palmer, L., 2003. 'Modern Agreement Making and Indigenous People in Australia: Issues And Trends'. *Aust. Indigenous Law Rep 8*, 1–31.

Lock the Gate Alliance. n.d. 'About Lock the Gate Alliance'. Retrieved from: www.lockthegate.org.au/about. (accessed 15 November 2014)

Lloyd, D. J., Luke, H. and Boyd, W. E., 2013. 'Community Perspectives of Natural Resource Extraction: Coal-Seam Gas Mining and Social Identity in Eastern Australia'. *Coolabah 10*, 144.

MacDonald-Smith, A., 2013. *Aboriginal Council takes on Greens, Farmers Over Gas*. Australian Financial Review Online. Retrieved from: www.afr.com/p/australia2-0/aboriginal_council_takes_on_greens_OPdixfkeUqHKx0KTnLL14J (accessed 26 June 2015).

Martin, C., 2000. *The Way of the Human Being*. New Haven, CT: Yale University Press.

Martin, C., 1993. *In the Spirit of the Earth: Rethinking History and Time*. Baltimore, MD: Johns Hopkins University Press.

Martin, C., 1982. *Keepers of the Game: Indian-animal Relationships and the Fur Trade*. Berkeley, CA: University of California Press.

McAuliffe, D., 1999. *Bloodland: A Family Story of Oil, Greed and Murder on the Osage Reservation*. Council Oak Books.

McKibben, B., 2014. 'Cowboys and Indians Against Keystone'. *Politico* April 9, 2014. Retrieved from: www.politico.com/magazine/story/2014/04/cowboys-and-indians-against-keystone-105550.html (accessed 26 June 2015).

Mufson, S., 'Keystone XL Pipeline Raises Tribal Concerns'. *Washington Post* September 17, 2012.

National Native Title Tribunal, 1999. *Native Title: A Five Year Retrospective 1994-1998: Report on the Operations of the Native Title Act 1993 and the Effectiveness of the National Native Title Tribunal*. National Native Title Tribunal, Perth, WA.

Neate, G., 2008. *Native title claims: overcoming obstacles to achieve real outcomes*. Paper Presented at the Native Title Development Conference, Brisbane.

Prystupa, M., 2014. 'First Nations chiefs talk tough on oil sands wealth at AFN convention'. *Vancouver Observer*, December 11.

Ritter, D., 2014. 'Black and Green Revisited: Understanding the Relationship Between Indigenous and Environmental Political Formations'. *Land, Rights, Laws: Issues of Native Title,* 6(2), AIATSIS, Canberra.

Spence, M.D., 2000. *Dispossessing the Wilderness: Indian Removal and the Making of the National Parks.* Oxford University Press, Oxford.

Trigger, D., Keenan, J., de Rijke, K. and Rifkin, W., 2014. 'Aboriginal Engagement and Agreement-Making with a Rapidly Developing Resource Industry: Coal Seam Gas Development in Australia'. *The Extractive Industries and Society 1,* 176–188.

Vivanco, L.A., 2007. 'The Prospects and Dilemmas of Indigenous Tourism Standards and Certifications' in R. Black and A. Crabtree (eds), *Quality Assurance and Certification in Ecotourism.* Ecotourism Series No. 5. CAB International, Wallingford, UK/Cambridge, MA: 218–40.

Weaver, J., 1996. *Defending Mother Earth: Native American Perspectives on Environmental Justice.* Maryknoll, N.Y.: Orbis Books.

Zeppel, H., 2006. *Indigenous Ecotourism: Sustainable Development and Management.* CABI Publishing, Wallingford, U.K.

Notes

1   Resolution passed by the National Congress of American Indians MKE 11-030, September, 2011: www.ncai.org/attachments/Resolution_HkgPdeJQmhLst PVJGNoJNsEqcyKxRGcpxBTUlVhIdsinhSAvkgp_MKE-11-030.pdf (accessed 15 December 2014).

2   Transcanada CSR Report 2013: http://csrreport.transcanada.com/Community/ ANAIP/TKP.html. (accessed 15 November 2014)

3   Interview on *National Public Radio,* November 21, 2014: www.npr.org/ 2014/11/21/365761999/native-americans-landowners-protest-keystone-xl-pipeline-in-south-dakota.

4   'Keystone XL pipeline opposition forges 'Cowboys and Indians' alliance', *The Guardian,* www.theguardian.com/environment/2014/nov/17/keystone-xl-pipe line-opposition-cowboys-indians-alliance-oil. (accessed 15 November 2014)

5   For a more comprehensive explanation of CSG, native title and agreement making, see Trigger *et al.,* 2013.

6   Satisfying honour?

The role of the Waitangi Tribunal in addressing land-related treaty grievances in New Zealand

Debra Wilson

Introduction

The recognition of the Treaty of Waitangi as New Zealand's founding document is a relatively recent shift in perspective, only occurring over the last 30 years. Prior to this, from its signing in 1840 until the mid-1980s, the Treaty was considered a 'legal nullity'[1] and the promises made to the indigenous Maori people under its Articles largely ignored. As a result, the Maori people were deprived of the majority of their land (and the rights associated with that land) in a manner that was, in most cases, less than equitable. In 1974 the Treaty of Waitangi Bill established the Waitangi Tribunal, and the process of addressing the increasing conflict between the Maori people and the New Zealand Government began. When the Bill was introduced into Parliament it was explained that it 'is primarily aimed at satisfying honour. It will also give physical and lawful sustenance to the long-held view that the spirit of the Treaty more than warrants our country's continued support'.[2] This chapter will discuss the development of the Waitangi Tribunal in addressing Maori grievances under the Treaty through a consideration of some of its most important inquiries, and consider its role in satisfying the honour of both Treaty partners and fulfilling the promise made in the Treaty, of two peoples working together to create one nation.

New Zealand history and the treaty of Waitangi

The Maori people are the indigenous peoples of New Zealand. Descended from Eastern Polynesians, oral history records their travel to New Zealand some 1000 years before the arrival of European settlers. The word 'Maori' or 'tangata Maori' simply means 'ordinary' or 'ordinary people', a term used to distinguish themselves from the 'Pakeha' or European settlers. Another term commonly used by Maori to describe themselves is 'tangata whenua', or 'the people of the land'. The word 'whenua', meaning 'land', is also the word for 'placenta', and the shared usage of the word clearly emphasizes the importance of land to the Maori people in terms of their identity.

Europeans first became aware of New Zealand in 1642, when it was sighted by Abel Tasman, and it was first circumnavigated by James Cook in 1769. The late 18th Century saw an increase in European visitors and settlers, and by 1840 there were approximately 2,000 European settlers in New Zealand, compared to approximately 200,000 Maori. On February 6, 1840 Captain William Hobson, on behalf of Queen Victoria, entered into a Treaty with Maori chiefs, known as the Treaty of Waitangi. Approximately 45 chiefs signed on that day, and more than 500 later signed as officials travelled the country to meet with tribes.

The Treaty consists of a preamble and three articles. It is worth quoting the text of the English version here:

ARTICLE THE FIRST
The Chiefs of the Confederation of the United Tribes of New Zealand and the separate and independent Chiefs who have not become members of the Confederation cede to Her Majesty the Queen of England absolutely and without reservation all the rights and powers of Sovereignty which the said Confederation or Individual Chiefs respectively exercise or possess, or may be supposed to exercise or to possess, over their respective Territories as the sole Sovereigns thereof.

ARTICLE THE SECOND
Her Majesty the Queen of England confirms and guarantees to the Chiefs and Tribes of New Zealand and to the respective families and individuals thereof the full exclusive and undisturbed possession of their Lands and Estates Forests Fisheries and other properties which they may collectively or individually possess so long as it is their wish and desire to retain the same in their possession; but the Chiefs of the United Tribes and the individual Chiefs yield to Her Majesty the exclusive right of Preemption over such lands as the proprietors thereof may be disposed to alienate at such prices as may be agreed upon between the respective Proprietors and persons appointed by Her Majesty to treat with them in that behalf.

ARTICLE THE THIRD
In consideration thereof Her Majesty the Queen of England extends to the Natives of New Zealand Her royal protection and imparts to them all the Rights and Privileges of British Subjects.

The New Zealand Court of Appeal has summed up the Treaty as 'the Queen was to govern and the Maoris were to be her subjects; in return their chieftainships and possessions were to be protected, but sales of land to the Crown could be negotiated'. While this suffices as a basic summary, the devil lies in the details. Conflict has resulted from the fact that there are two versions of the Treaty: the English version shown above, and a Maori version. The Maori version was signed by over 500 chiefs, while 39 signed the English version and 30 signed both. Captain Hobson, on behalf of the Queen, signed both versions. The language chosen for the Maori version (and it seems deliberately chosen to send a specific message) suggests a different effect than the English version.

As an example of the differing wording, the English version in Article 1 cedes sovereignty to the Queen. In the Maori version, the equivalent word to 'sovereignty' is 'kawanatanga'. 'Kawana' is a transliteration of the word 'governor', and 'tanga' is the equivalent of '-ship', making the word 'governorship'. This is clearly not the same as 'sovereignty'. A better word to reflect sovereignty would be 'rangatiratanga', which interestingly appears in Article 2 to explain the rights remaining with the Maori. The Maori version could, therefore, be understood as giving a governorship role to the Crown (perhaps to allow it to deal with its settlers and the issues that were already arising) while leaving the sovereignty of the Maori people to the 'iwi', or tribes.

Another example can be found in Article 2, the provision relating to lands. The Maori are to retain 'full exclusive and undisturbed possession' of, or 'rangitiratanga' over, their lands, estates, forests and fisheries, but if they chose to sell, the Government had the right of first refusal. The possessory right granted by the English version and the sovereignty right granted by the Maori version are clearly different concepts.

Relying on the English version, any land that was not considered Maori land on February 6, 1840 became the property of the Government. This included any land which had already been purchased by settlers from Maori. It also, controversially, included land that the Government considered 'unused' land on the basis that it was not being used by Maori for living or farming. For the Maori people, however, this was not unused land. All of New Zealand was Maori land, claimed by one iwi or another.

The decades following the signing of the Treaty were troubled. Increasing numbers of European settlers arrived, seeking land. Conflict broke out between Maori, the settlers and the Government. Some of this conflict was due to the different understandings in relation to rights over land. Europeans saw land as property that could be bought and sold. Once bought, it belonged to the purchaser, who could onsell the land, or pass it on to others in his will. For Maori their relationship with land was different. It was not something that could be owned; instead they saw themselves as guardians of the land for future generations. The people and the land were one, and this was not something that could be permanently sold. They understood 'sales' of land as allowing the Europeans use of that land for a period of time, for mutual advantage. Other conflict was a consequence of a perceived unfairness of land confiscation, following fights between the Maori and the Government. When the Government (with its superior weaponry) prevailed over the Maori people, it confiscated lands in compensation or as retribution. These confiscated lands were often not the lands over which the fighting occurred, but were simply chosen for their farming potential.

In 1877, less than 40 years after the signing of the Treaty, the Chief Justice of New Zealand described it as a 'legal nullity'.[3] This was based on the fact that the Treaty, signed by the Maori and the British Government, had never been formally incorporated into New Zealand law and could not therefore bind the New Zealand government. This approach to the Treaty remained the position for almost one hundred years.[4]

The treaty of Waitangi act and the beginnings of the Waitangi Tribunal

1975 is recognized as the turning point for the role of the Treaty of Waitangi in New Zealand. The 1960s and 1970s saw increasing Maori activism over indigenous land rights, culminating in the 1975 Land March. Led by (now-Dame) Whina Cooper, a protest hikoi (march) began on 14 September 1975 in the far north of New Zealand. It consisted of 50 people bearing a petition to end the sale of Maori Land. By the time the hikoi reached Parliament in Wellington on 13 October, numbers had increased to 5,000 and the petition had been signed by over 60,000 people. The hikoi arrived shortly before the Government passed the Treaty of Waitangi Act 1975, which created the Waitangi Tribunal.

At first, the Waitangi Tribunal was simply a Commission of Inquiry, which could make recommendations on any acts or omissions of the Crown *from the signing of the Act in 1975 onwards*. This obviously made it of limited value in addressing grievances in relation to land. Richard Boast describes the early years of the Tribunal in blunt terms: 'the establishment of the Waitangi Tribunal passed unnoticed, and on the few occasions on which it was convened in the first seven years of its tenuous existence, it said and did little of interest, was ignored by the government of the day, and made no mark of any kind on national life'.[5] It existed 'in obscurity tempered by minor obliquity'[6] and published only two reports in its first seven years.

In 1983, one Waitangi Tribunal investigation changed the way the Tribunal was perceived. The Motonui Report[7] was a comprehensive and well-written document, and as a result made the Government pay attention to its recommendations. Further, and more interestingly for the Maori people, the investigative hearings took place on maraes (Maori communal meeting places) and followed Maori protocol. This change in approach to the Tribunal's investigation made the Tribunal appear more accessible to Maori, and not merely as another Governmental body. The true impact of this Report can be found in the fact that two years later an amendment was made to the Treaty of Waitangi Act substantially altering the Tribunal's jurisdiction. The Tribunal was now permitted to consider claims relating to acts or omissions of the Crown *dating back to 1840*. In 1987 a landmark Court of Appeal decision commented that the Treaty was 'perhaps as important for the future of our country as any that has come before a New Zealand court'.[8]

The Tribunal today consists of up to 16 members and a chairperson. Members can be Maori or Pakeha (non-Maori), and its members are multidisciplinary, chosen for their knowledge and expertise in relation to tikanga maori (Maori custom), law, historical geography, anthropology, history, agriculture, business and industry. Claims must be made by Maori, and can be classified as historical (past Crown actions), contemporary (current Crown actions) or conceptual ('ownership' of natural resources). Claims are heard on marae and in accordance with traditional customs, factors which encourage elders to speak freely. Boast describes the hearings: 'Claimants, the Tribunal, counsel and witnesses mingle freely and informally during tea breaks and lunch in the marae dining room.... Kaumatua and kuia, male and female elders, give evidence in Maori; the day's sessions are opened and closed by prayers in the Maori language, and the opening of a hearing is always commenced by a formal calling-on to the marae and classical Maori oratory, in which the Tribunal's own elders participate fully. These are not small and inconsequential things, and it can certainly be argued that the Tribunal's willingness to conduct its sittings on marae has contributed in no small measure to its success'.[9]

However, some legal aspects still remain. There are opening and closing statements, discussions of legal precedents, and cross examination of witnesses.

The Tribunal has jurisdiction to enquire into 'the meaning and effect of the Treaty of Waitangi', and whether the Crown has acted in accordance with this. To clarify its starting point, the Tribunal is expressly required to consider both language versions of the Treaty, and not to give priority to one version. It can make non-binding recommendations for settlement where appropriate. The Tribunal has clarified that such settlements are 'not to pay off for the past, even were that possible, but to take those steps necessary to remove outstanding prejudice and prevent similar prejudice from arising; for the only practical settlement between people is one that achieves a reconciliation in fact'.[10] A tribunal hearing was designed to be the first step in the settlement process, with the second step being direct negotiation with the Crown, through the Office of Treaty Settlements resulting in a subsequent Deed of Settlement if appropriate.

Examples of claims

The following section discusses some of the claims heard by the Waitangi Tribunal, the overall recommendations made, and the consequences of these for New Zealand society.

The Ngai Tahu claim

The first large claim heard by the Waitangi Tribunal following the extension of its jurisdiction was the Ngai Tahu claim.[11] From as early as 1849 Ngai Tahu, the principal South Island tribe, had been protesting the methods used to purchase their lands. By 1864, the Crown had purchased over 34 million acres of land (approximately 80 percent of the South Island), at a price of less than £15,000. This equated to a price of less than 1 penny per acre. As a result, Ngai Tahu was left with less than 36,000 acres. This was not enough land to hunt and farm, and by the early 1900s, less than 2,000 Ngai Tahu remained.

In 1986, the Ngai Tahu Maori Trust Board filed a claim with the Waitangi Tribunal. The claim was known as the 'Nine Tall Trees of Ngai Tahu' (eight trees each representing a different area of land purchased, and the ninth representing food resources). The claim was heard over a two-year period from 1987–1989, and the report released in 1991. It concluded that the Crown 'acted unconscionably and in repeated breach of the Treaty of Waitangi' and recommended substantial compensation. Ngai Tahu entered into settlement negotiations with the Crown, and in 1998 signed a Deed of Settlement. The settlement, valued at $170 million, consisted of monetary compensation but also non-monetary elements including confirmation of ownership of pounamu (greenstone), a role in managing conservation resources within tribal boundaries, and rights to sites of significance. Most important to Ngai Tahu, however, was the symbolic return of Aoraki/Mount Cook to the tribe (which was then gifted by Ngai Tahu back to the people of New Zealand), and an official apology from the Crown for the suffering and hardship caused as a result of not honouring their Treaty obligations. The apology, in which the Crown 'expressed its profound regret and apologises unreservedly' for its actions, was made in both English and in Maori. To some Maori, this was the most important part of the settlement, allowing for the Crown to atone for the injustices and for both parties to move forward with the healing process.

Ngai Tahu today is the second largest tribe in the country, comprising almost 56,000 people, or 8.4 percent of the Maori population in the 2013 census. The settlement money from the claim was invested in businesses, property and tourism throughout the country and its main business arm, Ngai Tahu Holdings, today has equity of over $1 billion. Census information indicates that a greater percentage of Ngai Tahu people have formal qualifications, are in the labour force, and have a higher median income than the average amongst Maori in New Zealand. Their power and influence in the business world, particularly in the South Island and Christchurch, is unmistakeable. It is often commented that in relation to business, nothing in Christchurch happens without Ngai Tahu approval and support. The Ngai Tahu settlement is generally considered to be a major Waitangi Tribunal success story – a thorough investigation and detailed report, leading to settlement negotiations in which Ngai Tahu accepted far less in compensation than they had lost, but that opened the door to a genuine apology by the

Crown for past injustices. The settlement deal, which included not only compensation but also management of conservation and the symbolic return of sacred sites, showed an understanding by the Crown of what is important to Maori and allowed both sides to move forward. The intelligent investment of the monetary compensation has made Ngai Tahu a major influence in New Zealand business and politics, and has given strength to its voice.

The foreshore and seabed claim[12]

In June 2003 a Court of Appeal decision, *Ngati Apa,* brought a long-running debate over the ownership of the foreshore and seabed to the attention of the New Zealand public. The 'foreshore' is the area of land between the high and low water marks on a beach (The Waitangi Tribunal helpfully describes it as 'the land... that is daily wet by the sea when the tide comes in'.) The 'seabed' is the land that extends from the low water mark out to sea. These are obviously English words, there being no consistently used Maori words to describe these areas.

In *Ngati Apa,* the Court of Appeal determined that if the Government wanted to extinguish rights and ownership of customary land (which included the foreshore and seabed), then it must do this expressly or specifically. This was a reversal of the approach taken in previous cases, including *Wi Parata*[13] and *Re Ninety Mile Beach,*[14] where it was thought that these rights in relation to the foreshore and seabed could be, and in fact had been, extinguished indirectly. Based on the earlier cases, the Government had assumed that it had ownership of the foreshore and seabed. As a result of *Ngati Apa,* this assumption was no longer valid. Then Prime Minister Helen Clark immediately responded to the Court of Appeal decision, stating that legislation would be introduced to 'preserve the status quo'[15] of Governmental ownership. When commentators suggested this might have been an 'off the cuff'[16] remark, it was clarified that legislation would be introduced to make it clear that the Crown owned the foreshore and seabed for the benefit of all New Zealanders. This position was immediately criticized by Maori and also by academics, both of whom saw the introduction of legislation as circumventing the legal process.[17] Within a couple of weeks a slight back-tracking was seen, with an announcement that the Government would attempt to negotiate a political settlement rather than introduce legislation.

In mid-December 2003 it was announced that legislation would be introduced which would recognize customary rights, but would also protect public access. Ownership of the foreshore and seabed would be clarified by placing title in the public domain. Shortly thereafter, the Waitangi Tribunal agreed to urgently hear a claim, scheduling it for the end of January 2004. The report was released in March. In essence, the Waitangi Tribunal found that the government breached the Treaty through its rushed development of policy.

When it became apparent that the legislation would proceed despite the Waitangi Tribunal Report, Maori organized a hikoi. Beginning on 27 April 2004 and ending on 5 May 2004 outside Parliament, this was the biggest hikoi since the Lands March in 1975, with over 200,000 people taking part.[18] The response from the Government was less than positive. On the day before the hikoi began then-Prime Minister Helen Clark commented to the newspapers that it wouldn't stop the legislation, but 'if anything, it drives it the other way because people had had a gutsful of the extreme language and the extreme rhetoric'.[19] Despite public support for the protest, she refused to meet the hikoi on its arrival at Parliament, labeling some of the participants as 'haters and wreckers'.[20]

The Foreshore and Seabed Act was passed by the New Zealand Parliament on 19 November 2004. Its key provision was section 13 which stated that 'the full legal and beneficial ownership of the public foreshore and seabed is vested in the Crown, so that the public foreshore and seabed is held by the Crown as its absolute property'. One Member of Parliament, Tariana Turia, referred to the legislative process as 'the death of democracy'[21] and commented that: 'We listen to members [of Parliament] desperately trying to convince themselves that this Government is proud of the ongoing fiduciary obligation they have with Tangata Whenua [the Maori people]. The basis of a fiduciary relationship is that of trust. Does anyone in this House honestly think Tangata Whenua will be fooled into thinking they can trust a Government which has sacrificed, extinguished, confiscated the last piece of customary land that we held by default?'[22]

The story, however, does not end there. Days before the first Parliamentary debate on the Foreshore and Seabed Bill Tariana Turia (the Associate Maori Affairs Minister) resigned stating that she could not support the Bill in light of overwhelming opposition in her electorate. She had been elected to represent Te Tai Hauauru, one of 7 Maori electorates in New Zealand created to ensure Maori representation in Parliament. At the same time as her resignation, she announced the formation of a new political party, the Maori Party. Her resignation forced a by-election, which she won as a Maori Party MP, receiving 92.7 percent of the vote. When the Foreshore and Seabed Act was passed, she commented that 'a movement was born from this Bill', referring to the new political party.

The Maori Party's primary objective was the repeal of the Foreshore and Seabed Act. In the November 2008 election, the party had its chance. The National Party won the election, and the Maori Party entered into a coalition agreement with National to vote with them on confidence and supply, in exchange for the introduction of legislation to repeal the Act. In June 2010, such legislation was announced (with the Maori Party commenting that it had fulfilled its promise to its people). The Marine Coastal Area (Takutai Moana) Act 2011 removes Crown ownership of the foreshore and seabed and replaces it with a 'no-ownership' regime. In addition, it restores any Maori interests removed by the Act, and further recognizes Maori interests through participation in conservation processes, customary use rights and title interests.

Although the Waitangi Tribunal Report had little impact on the outcome of the debate (and in all likelihood was well aware of this when it agreed to hear the claim as a matter of urgency), the Report is interesting in terms of language used, adopting a diplomatic approach to addressing a highly political issue. While it begins by clearly stating that Articles 2 and 3 of the Treaty were breached, the language from there becomes more subtle. It comments generally on the relationship between the Crown and the Maori, stating that the 'Crown's exercise of kawanatanga has to be qualified by respect for tino rangatiratanga', as defined above. The Tribunal has called this the principle of reciprocity, which is an "overarching principle" that guides the interpretation and application of other principles, such as partnership. The nature of the relationship between the Treaty partners is a 'reciprocal one, with obligations and mutual benefits flowing from it'. More specifically, in terms of the foreshore and seabed legislation, the Tribunal commented that: 'We accept that the Crown has the authority to develop a policy in respect of the foreshore and seabed. However, the principles of 'reciprocity and partnership require it to do so in a way that gives meaningful effect to te tino rangatiratanga, and balances the interests of both peoples in a fair and reasonable manner. We do not think that the Crown's policy meets this test'. Language of partnership, acting in good faith, honourable conduct, fair process, and recognition of each other's authority, occurs frequently throughout the Report. The Tribunal then subtly wonders if 'the Government may have misunderstood, or may not have been fully advised upon, the implications of its approach'.

In making its recommendations, the Tribunal makes one clear recommendation (to begin the discussion of ownership of the foreshore and seabed again, with proper consultation and exploration of options), but also provides what it refers to as 'a range of suggestions, so that whatever course the Government chooses, it is aware that there are opportunities to enhance its performance in Treaty terms'. The report concludes with a 'Final Word'. This identifies fundamental points of agreement, as opposed to the points of disagreement that had been so prevalent throughout the hikoi and protests. It concludes with a hope for an outcome 'that is faithful to the vision of the Treaty: two peoples living together in one nation, sharing authority and resources, with fundamental respect for each other'. While it likely knew that its Report would do little to halt the passage of legislation, the Tribunal found a way to indicate an approach to be used in future claims.

The Wai 262 claim[23]

The Wai 262 Report is the most substantial report of the Waitangi Tribunal, both in terms of length of investigation (21 years) and size of report (over 1,000 pages). Occasionally also known as the 'flora and fauna claim' or the

'Maori intellectual property claim', it addresses issues of Matauranga Maori. This phrase roughly translates to 'Maori traditional knowledge' and includes issues relating to language, science and technology, law, history, art and rituals.

One section of the Report addresses Maori traditional knowledge of plants, and in particular, the use of these plants for medical purposes. Maori consider themselves to have an obligation as kaitiaki (guardians) to protect and care for the land. Any use of the land, including its resources, must comply with tikanga (customs or behavioral guidelines) or this kaitiaki relationship may be damaged. The concern for Maori in the Wai 262 claim was bioprospecting: the practice of gathering biological material from flora and fauna and using this to create new products, often pharmaceuticals. Under the New Zealand patent system, a pharmaceutical company that observes or accesses inform-ation about Maori traditional use of a particular plant as a medicine and then creates an artificial version of that plant (in other words, converts it from a leaf or bark to a pill or tablet) is entitled to a monopoly over that product for 20 years. Article 2 of the Treaty guarantees to Maori the 'full exclusive and undisturbed possession of their Lands and Estates, Forests, Fisheries and other properties'. In the Maori version, this 'possession' is worded as 'rangitirat-anga' (sovereignty, or absolute authority) and 'other properties' is translated as 'taonga' (treasured items). The Maori claim therefore, is that the Treaty grants them control over flora and fauna, due to their Matauranga Maori being a taonga, and that effective exercise of this control is necessary to protect their kaitiaki relationship with the land. While bioprospecting might be acceptable in relation to some flora and fauna provided it is carried out in accordance with tikanga, in relation to other flora and fauna it could not be permitted at all as any use would damage their kaitiaki relationship with the land. In more legal terms, the argument was that the Treaty promises Maori the ability to control, use and develop these resources, and satisfaction of this requires that they are given a right to determine patent and other intellectual property rights in the knowledge and use of their taonga. The then-current patent law was inconsistent with this.

The Waitangi Tribunal made interesting recommendations in relation to reform of patent law. First, it recommended the creation of a Maori com-mittee to 'advise' the Commissioner of Patents about whether Matauranga Maori contributed to the invention, whether the proposed use is contrary to tikanga Maori and whether there are kaitiaki interests at risk. The second recommendation that the term 'advise' in the first recommendation was intended to have significant weight: 'the commissioner should be required to take formal advice from [the Maori Advisory Committee] and work with a member of the Maori committee when making patent decisions'.

These recommendations were partially adopted in the Patents Act 2013. A Maori Advisory Committee was created, as per the first recommendation. The second recommendation, however, was not adopted. The Act clarifies that the Commissioner 'must consider, but is not bound by, the advice given'.

There is also no requirement that the Commissioner seek the advice of the committee. Despite these limitations, it is interesting and encouraging for Maori that the government included such an innovative requirement into well-established patent laws.

Te Paparahi O Te Raki claim[24]

The most recent Waitangi Tribunal investigation concerns the Te Paparahi O Te Raki claim, relating to lands in the north of New Zealand (geographically, those lands north of Auckland). The Tribunal took a novel approach to this claim, separating it into two parts. The first, published in November 2014, addressed the 'meaning and effect' of the Treaty. The second, still under investigation, will consider the more specific issue of whether the Crown acted inconsistently with the principles of the Treaty in relation to the claimants' lands.

The conclusions reached in the first part quickly caught the public's attention. The Tribunal found that the chiefs who signed the Treaty 'did not cede sovereignty' to the Crown. Instead, 'the rangitira consented to the Treaty on the basis that they and the Governor were to be equals, though they were to have different roles and different spheres of influence'. Public reaction to this was one of confusion. The Treaty of Waitangi Negotiations Minister Chris Finlayson responded in a statement that 'there is no question that the Crown has sovereignty in New Zealand' even though the report does not explain how this sovereignty was acquired if not through the signing of the Treaty. A University of Auckland academic responded that the tribunal appeared to be re-writing history with little apparent regard for evidence.

Finding its place: the changing role of the tribunal

The above section has discussed some of the more significant claims to have been heard by the Waitangi Tribunal. These claims represent a reasonable sample of the types of claims heard, from the first claim after the extension of jurisdiction to the most recent, and from a straight confiscation or unfair expropriation of lands claim to a claim examining customary rights attaching to land and a claim considering whether 'land' extends into the foreshore and seabed. What is noticeable in these examples is the lack of a consistent approach. The 1986 Ngai Tahu report is careful, testing the waters of its new jurisdiction, but with a clear focus on bringing the country together. Much is made in the report of the acceptance by Ngai Tahu that it would not be appropriate (legally, socially or ethically) to address issues relating to specific land which has passed into individual ownership, and while Aoraki/Mt. Cook was symbolically returned to the tribe due to their historical connection to it, it was then gifted back to the New Zealand people in recognition of its position as a national treasure.

By 2004, at around the time of the foreshore and seabed claim, commentators like Byrne considered that reports have become 'increasingly politicised, moving from a reparatory discourse, born of rights and based on the concept of the Treaty as a contract, to one that fractures ideas of national unity and advances a vision of Aotearoa New Zealand where separate autonomous political entities exert their own sovereignty yet still partake in the sovereignty of the "nation" as a whole'.[25]

Day, writing five years later in 2009, suggested that 'Byrnes' findings are frozen in time'[26] and that the Tribunal had more recently displayed a much more conservative narrative. He references an early report, the Orakei Report, which used emotive language and portrayed a clear sympathy for the plight of the Maori. By the 2006 Kaipara report, however, Day observed a 'focus on proof and practicality', asking whether 'the Crown's action or inaction toward Maori [was] reasonable or unreasonable in the circumstances of the time'.

This practicality gave way in 2011 to idealism, with the Wai 262 report recommending innovative changes to the well-established patent system in order to give effect to Maori rights over intellectual property. Finally in 2014, we see a return to the approach described in Byrne, of a vision of separate autonomous political entities exerting their own sovereignty over New Zealand.

While the approaches above arguably fail to reflect a consistent approach, this could merely reflect the diverse nature of the issues raised in particular cases, or even the particular membership of the tribunal. Indeed, it may not be necessary or desirable to identify a consistent approach – this may be a western approach to evaluation that is not helpful when applied to Maori claims.

The Tribunal has been assigned a difficult, possibly unachievable, task. It must hear grievances in relation to the Treaty, knowing that most of these are in relation to land that is now in private ownership and therefore cannot be returned to the Maori without destroying well established New Zealand property law. It must hear emotional claims from Maori who legitimately feel that the Crown has not acted honorably in relation to the Treaty in the past, while being aware of the desirability of moving forward as one country. It is all too aware of the non-binding nature of its recommendations, meaning that any recommendations that are too politically charged will likely be ignored. Further, it is about to move into a new stage of its existence. It has now investigated claims relating to 90 percent of the country's land area, and plans to complete these types of claims by 2020. It has recently announced that its focus will then shift to kaupapa claims (thematic claims of language, culture and identity).

Arguably, the measure of the Tribunal's success is not in the direct outcome of its reports, or whether its recommendations are adopted. If this was the measure of success some claims, like the foreshore and seabed claim would have been doomed from the start, as both sides and the Tribunal itself were probably aware that there was almost no chance the government would change its position on ownership following the Report. The Tribunal's role in the debate was, however, highly significant. It gave the Maori people a voice, potentially preventing violent protests over a very emotionally charged issue. Creating a forum for discussion might in itself be the success of the Tribunal. There is a hint of this in the two part investigation of the most recent 2014 claim. The first part considers broad, bigger picture, issues and the second considers the specific land claim. This might suggest that the most important issues for the Maori people are not the specific claims but broader issues of the place of the Treaty in society and the understanding of its role in the future of New Zealand. It is therefore the discussion process and not necessarily the adoption of recommendations which is important and of real value.

It could be argued that the Tribunal's most important role is not in resolving conflict, but in acting as history keepers, or recorders of oral traditions. During the investigation of the claims, the Maori people tell the stories of their tribes, their histories and their relationships with the land. Without someone to record these stories they might be lost, or never heard by those outside the tribe. Waitangi Tribunal reports are now often used to teach New Zealand history in schools and universities, and their words increase the understanding between Maori and Pakeha. Perhaps it is this understanding that will result in the spirit of the Treaty being given effect to, and if so, the Waitangi Tribunal can surely count that as a success.

Notes

1   *Wi Parata v the Bishop of Wellington* (1877) 3 NZ Jur (NS) SC 72.
2   Per Hon Matiu Rata, quoted in *Ngati Kuri Deed of Settlement* (February 7 2014), 11.
3   *Wi Parata v The Bishop of Wellington* (1877) 3 NZ Jur (NS) SC 72.
4   In 1941 in *Hoani Te Heu Heu Tukino v Aotea Maori District Land Board* (1941) NZLR 590, the Privy Council backed away from the phrase 'legal nullity', stating that the Treaty of Waitangi was a valid Treaty of cession, but agreed that it was not enforceable in domestic law until it had been incorporated into the laws of New Zealand.
5   R. Boast, *The Waitangi Tribunal: 'Conscience of a Nation' or Just Another Court?* (1993) UNSWLJ 223, 226.
6   A. Sharp, *Justice and the Maori: Maori Claims in New Zealand Political Arguments in the 1980s* (1990), 75, quoted in Boast, above.
7   Wai 6: *Report of the Tribunal on the Motonui-Waitara Claim* (1983).
8   *New Zealand Maori Council v Attorney-General* (1987) 1 NZLR 641, 643.
9   R. Boast, *The Waitangi Tribunal: 'Conscience of a Nation' or Just Another Court?* (1993) UNSWLJ 223, 234.
10 Wai 143: *Taranaki Report- Kaupapa Tautahi*, at 12.3.10.
11 Wai 27: *Ngai Tahu Report* (1991).
12 Wai 1071: *Report of the Crown's Foreshore and Seabed Policy* (2004).
13 *Wi Parata v Bishop of Wellington* (1877) 3 NZ Jur (NS) SC 7.

14 (1963) NZLR 461.
15 'Foreshore Decision Narrow – PM' *NZ City News* (June 20 2003).
16 'Clark Disappoints Marlborough Iwi' *NZ City News* (June 21 2003).
17 The Court of Appeal had said that the Maori Land Court had jurisdiction to determine rights over the foreshore and seabed.
18 Interestingly, Transit New Zealand (the governmental body responsible for roading in New Zealand) publically stated its concerns that the number of people involved in the hikoi would cause substantial damage to the Auckland Harbour Bridge as they all crossed at once.
19 'Hikoi Will Make No Difference To Seabed Policy, Says Clark', *NZ Herald* (April 26 2004).
20 'Clark will not meet "wreckers"', *NZPA* May 4 2004. In an interesting, but perhaps politically unwise move, she met with a sheep named Shrek (who had achieved national attention for evading having its wool sheared for 6 years by hiding in caves) the day before the hikoi arrived. On being asked why she had found the time for this photo opportunity but not to meet the hikoi, she responded 'well, Shrek was good company'.
21 'Foreshore Bill Passes After Marathon Session', *NZ Herald* (November 19 2004).
22 NZ Parliamentary Debates, November 16 2004.
23 Wai 262: *Ko Aotearoa Tenei: Te Taumata Tuatahi – A Report into Claims Concerning New Zealand Law and Policy Affecting Maori Culture and Identity* (2011). Reports of the Waitangi Tribunal are assigned a Wai (tangi) number, based on the order of lodging the claim. While most are then referred to by the subject of the claim (for example the Ngai Tahu claim or the Foreshore and Seabed claim), this claim is commonly simply called Wai 262, due to the diversity of subject matter.
24 Wai 1040: Te Paparahi o Te Raki (2014).
25 Giselle Byrnes, *The Waitangi Tribunal and New Zealand History* (2004), 5.
26 Jessica Day, 'Waitangi Tribunal History: Interpretations and Counter-Facts' (2009) 15 *Auckland U L Rev* 205, 213.

7 The 'Pacific Way'

Customary land use, indigenous values and globalization in the South Pacific

Spike Boydell

Introduction

For some, mention of the South Pacific conjures dreams of idyllic palm strewn beaches and perfect holidays. For others, media images perhaps portray the recent tsunami in Samoa or reminders of coup d'état and political instability in countries like Fiji, Papua New Guinea, Vanuatu and the Solomon Islands. For many, there are perceptions that the prevailing land tenure traditions impact on, and prejudice, business ventures in the South Pacific. This chapter will challenge this reductionist perception. As I will explain in this chapter, the customary nature of land ownership and control in the Pacific, whilst acknowledged and respected, does not prevent the optimum use of the land for development (in its many forms). Influences of globalism and modernity are placing greater emphasis on individual economic wealth accumulation and related pressures to derive economic benefits from customary land. This westernisation means that at times decisions are made for personal gain rather than in the best interest of the land-owning group as a whole. There is a recognised clash between indigenous values and capitalism. Some commentators see this clash as an impediment to business development within the region. However, despite the influences of individualism, most indigenous people see their relationships as coming from the land rather than using it as a commodity. In this chapter, I will explore the tensions and contradictions between custom, tradition and the 'Pacific Way' and development in its many forms. Nowhere are the tensions and contradictions more evident than in dealing with land and access to land in the South Pacific region.

Twenty years ago, in the concluding page of their edited volume *Land, Custom and Practice in the South Pacific*, Hooper and Ward (1995, 264) flagged that 'in coming decades further changes will occur in the values to which Pacific Island peoples adhere (or ignore) when they organise their societies, arrange their settlement patterns, choose their political leaders, and decide how they use land'. They highlighted that in the early years of independence Pacific Islanders had 'a breathing space in which to ignore the contradictions between practice, custom and law in land tenure, and between the 'rhetoric of tradition' and what actually happens in villages, towns, squatter settlements and farms' (Hooper and Ward, 1995, 264). Central to this 'breathing space' is a realisation that current land tenure does not follow tradition, the Pacific way or custom. This is because, according to Overton (1992, 326), 'the processes of social change are complicated by the persistence of traditional or neo-traditional social relations and the uneven impact of capitalism'.

In the latter part of the last century and particularly through the process of independence, the leaders of most Pacific Island countries endorsed the ideology of development. However they did this whilst also emphasising 'the importance of 'culture' and 'tradition' as the basis of national identity and the integrity of national institutions' (Hooper and Ward, 1995, 250). Obviously these contradictions play out in different ways in different countries of the South Pacific, but there are a number of generic issues that are discussed in the next section. The third section elaborates on the contradictions between what is said to be customary and what is actually practised as customary land tenure. A similar plurality or duality applies to tradition.

The fourth section highlights the confusion between the Pacific way and the Western way, which I elaborate through what we call the plurality of registers. This plurality is in many ways central to the conflict between the development agenda and notions of tradition and/or neo-tradition. The fifth section provides a critique of the development discourse and what Sachs (1992, 1) highlights as the 'frame of reference for that mixture of generosity, bribery and oppression which has characterised policies towards the south'. Nowhere is the 'delusion and disappointment, failures and crimes that have been the steady companions of development' that Sachs describes more evident than in contemporary dealings with land across Melanesia.

The sixth section draws on the voices of Pacific Islanders and their reaction to the development agenda at a time of accelerated resource grab, and the associated ground swell of emotion that resulted in the 2009 establishment of the Melanesian Indigenous Land Defence Alliance (MILDA). Rather than accepting the evident stalemate, the concluding section responds to the criticisms of leasehold structures and development and asks what is needed to make land work for multiple stakeholders in the 21st-century Pacific.

The South Pacific in context

Before exploring the tensions between custom and reality in the region, it will help to contextualise Pacific Island Nations and their development challenges. The Pacific Island Countries and Territories (PICs) comprise 12 nations to 22 nations depending on the definition of various regional organisations.[1] The Pacific islands region is unique because of the combination of geographical, biological, sociological and economic characteristics (Miles, 1999). The region occupies a vast 30 million km^2 of the Pacific Ocean. The 22 countries and territories comprise some 550,000 km^2 of land with 7.5 million inhabitants. Notably, if the largest landmass, Papua New Guinea, is excluded from the summation, the remaining 21 nations comprise 87,587 km² with a total population of 2.7 million. The region comprises three sub regional groupings: Micronesia, Polynesia and Melanesia, with a diversity of people and cultures – over 2,000 different languages are spoken across the region.

The common characteristics of the region include remoteness and geographic isolation; environmental fragility; rapid population growth; limited land resources; poorly functioning and immature land markets; land access issues, with 83–100 per cent remaining vested in the indigenous owners; informal housing; dependency on marine resources; (relative) poverty; limited diversification; limited capacity; and, vulnerability to critical environmental, ecological, and economic risks (Boydell, 2004). Through colonisation, a broad range of external tenure influences have been brought into the region. In many Pacific Island countries, these influences result in a plural system whereby Western notions of freehold and leasehold operate alongside customary regimes. The influences can be summarised thus:

- United Kingdom: Fiji, Solomon Islands, Gilbert Ellice (Tuvalu) and partly New Hebrides;
- France: New Caledonia, French Polynesia, Wallis and Futuna and partly New Hebrides;
- Germany: (until 1914) for north-eastern New Guinea, Western Samoa, Nauru, Caroline and Marshall Islands;
- Netherlands: until 1962 for West New Guinea (now called Irian Jaya);
- Indonesia: (since 1963) for Irian Jaya;
- Australia: Papua (since 1906), north-east New Guinea (since 1914) and Nauru (1914 to 1968);
- New Zealand: Cook Islands and Niue (since 1901) and Tokelau Islands (since 1925) and Western Samoa (1914 to 1962);
- Spain: Guam, Mariana and Caroline Islands (until 1899);
- Japan: Mariana, Marshall and Caroline Islands (from 1914 to 1945);
- U.S.A.: Mariana and Caroline Islands (from 1945) and Hawaii;
- Chile: Easter Island.

Custom versus reality (or tradition versus neo-tradition)

Land – or more correctly the lack of clearly defined real property rights to land and resources associated with access arrangements – is commonly cited as a major cause of dispute and resultant instability. This situation is, of course, compounded when considered from outside by those familiar with a different set of institutional land arrangements than those that prevail in the South Pacific.

Whilst land is obviously important in all societies, it holds different relevance in the South Pacific in that the majority of land was not alienated under colonisation (with Tonga being the only Forum island nation that was not colonised). This is in stark contrast to its larger neighbour Australia, where 'the vast majority of aborigines have been violently dispossessed of their land, and all have been subjected to economic and political marginalisation and oppressive state control' (Strakosch, 2007, 246). As a result, in the Pacific, some 83 to 97 per cent of land remains vested in the stewardship of customary guardians (Boydell, 2008a). Customary land is 'owned' by groups, with different property rights defined by inheritance and social relationships held by individuals, families and groups. In traditional societies 'ownership' of land relates to the notion of custodianship, where individuals and wider society jointly have a responsibility and duty of care to both current and future generations, whilst respecting the spirits of their ancestors. This form of custodianship reflects genuine sustainability. For indigenous Pacific peoples, their ties to the land bring together the complexity of ecological, geophysical, social, spiritual and economic dimensions.

As Farran and Paterson (2004, 3) highlight, one of the difficulties with any approach that looks at property as rights in the South Pacific is that 'in English common law, the notion of property as rights is seen as the relationship between the individual – or legal person – and the thing'. A similar challenge is present in considering ownership from a Western and an indigenous perspective – the former being an individualistic paradigm, the latter often being grounded in communalism, prioritising the relationship between native peoples and the land.

A survey of the relationships between various native peoples and their land reveals that, typically, the relationship has two dimensions – spiritual (or metaphysical) and material (relating to the political economy of land) (Small, 1997). Philosophically and spiritually, there is a deep-rooted belief in the stewardship of land. The current generation has a responsibility in respect of the land that relates to the spirits of their ancestors along with the expectations of their descendants, in addition to the needs of the current generation. Descendants, as future members of the tribe, are regarded as having the same rights of access to land as those tribe members currently alive. For the same reasons, children cannot be charged for access to the land of their parents. Land is free for the use of current tribe members on the basis that it will be passed on, without degradation, for the use of future members. The communalism of the tribe, the timeless stewardship afforded the land and the idea of land as a common legacy are concepts often difficult for Westerners to appreciate (Boydell and Small, 2003). They differ from the standardised model of private exclusive ownership that has now been disseminated in most developed societies (Hann, 1998).

The financial importance of land is in its utilisation for the most economically productive activities. As land comes to be used in more economically productive ways, it has prompted changes to the traditional ways of dealing with land. These changes have also encouraged reconsideration of the economic balance within the customary communities (Boydell *et al.*, 2007).

So, why is there a perception that the land tenure traditions in the South Pacific prejudice business ventures in the region? The income potential that is available from new commercial land uses compared to traditional uses has distorted some aspects of customary life. There is a disjoint between the notions of familial or group 'ownership' in customary land tenure systems that prevail in the South Pacific, and the Western concept of individualised private property rights that are seen as fundamental to a modern market-based economy. This misalignment affects the use of customary land for commercial purposes and business ventures, particularly where customary landowners have not been formally recorded and where the superior property rights of communal/tribal groups or families are not accepted by Western financial institutions.

Customary landowners have had the tendency to under-optimise the financial return on their land when it has been leased for commercial activity. In these circumstances, when they have subsequently become aware of the real economic value of their land, conflicts have arisen. This has challenged their willingness to uphold contracts regarding their land. The principle of *caveat emptor* (let the buyer beware) is an accepted foundation of Western commerce – where the contractual obligation is paramount, regardless of the equity in the arrangement. In contrast, customary peoples place more importance on equity and respect for cultural traditions, making contractual obligations of secondary importance.

The plurality of registers

The disconnect that exists between indigenous values and capitalist interests goes beyond legal pluralism (for example, on legal pluralism see Hooker, 1975, Griffiths, 1986), and is part of the on-going polemic over land use in Melanesia, with much of the debate driven by special interest groups seeking access to customary land (Anderson, 2006, 138). Hughes (2003, 346) argues that modern constitutionalism clouds the issue of identity emphasised in indigenous values. The state cannot be merely conceived of in abstract institutional terms, as the assumption of uniformity under a coherent body of law is at odds with the social and cultural reality of PICs. However, I do share the view of the von Benda-Beckmanns (2006, 13) that 'along with many anthropologists, we think that the term *law* can be used as an analytical concept'. They go on to articulate law in both cognitive terms (how things are, and why they are) and normative terms (how things could or should be). My colleague Ulai Baya and I apply these interpretations to what we refer to as the *Plurality of Registers* (Boydell and Baya, 2012) when attempting to articulate disconnected worldviews between indigenous values and capitalist interests.

By taking a transdisciplinary approach, the *Plurality of Registers* highlights discrete conceptions of knowing and valuing, each with different social relationships, behaviour, permissibility, and consequences – some of which are categorical (typified general rules) and others ideological (more generalised). 'Law in this sense is a generic term that comprises a variety of social phenomena (concepts, rules, principles, procedures, regulations of different sorts, relationships, decisions) at different levels of social organisation' (von Benda-Beckmann and von Benda-Beckmann, 2006, 13). The customary value of land that is used for subsistence purposes and retains strong spiritual ties to the ancestors whilst providing sustainable stewardship for future generations is intangible. Yet, in Western neo-classical economic terms, which ground notions of value as economic rent or surplus of production, such customary subsistence land has no value. There is no problem with these plural worldviews... until they meet. Where they meet, the inalienable notions of land held by the customary stewards are very much at odds with the commodity view of the West that emphasises individual ownership. The reality is that there is some overlap between these extremes. It is this overlap between worldviews that we have to address if we are to seek equitable compensation when – supported by governments relying on their constitutional right to mineral resources (or not, in the case of PNG) – mining interests seek to exploit the resources in, on or under land held by customary owners.

Development discourse and contemporary resource grab

The actual financial management of land is key to integrating the interests of customary owners into the recognised need to make customary-owned land economically efficient. Some economists have argued that customary ownership is linked to poor economic performance with claims such as, 'communal ownership has not permitted any country to develop' (Gosarevski *et al.*, 2004). This claim deserves some attention because it implicitly leads to the elimination of customary ownership. This implication was made more explicit by the same authors when they identified private title with freehold (Gosarevski *et al.*, 2004). In doing so, they aligned themselves with mainstream neoclassical economics in general, and with the current missionary promoting that position into the developing world, Hernando de Soto (2000).

The objections raised by such authors use as premises several valid observations about the economic underperformance of customary-owned land and move to the stronger conclusion that customary-owned land cannot deliver effective economic outcomes. This view perpetuates concerns that customary land tenure traditions prejudice business ventures in the Pacific. Fingleton and others do not reject the premises, but merely recognise that there are more possibilities available than the insistence on land reform leading to freehold title (Fingleton, 2004; Fingleton, 2005; Fingleton, 2007; Lightfoot, 2005).

We need to step back to analyse the presumption that, of itself, individualised title (to land) and in particular freehold title reduces poverty and encourages development in the poorer regions of the world, such as the South Pacific. Francis Fukuyama (1992) revived the generally discredited sociological notion of *progress* when he argued that democratic capitalism, of the sort found in the US, represented the cultural/economic system at the end of history. In terms of property, this translates into the popular claim that no system of property can deliver the same benefits as freehold title in land property. He built on a succession of thought that was earlier expressed by Richard Weaver (1948), who claimed that private property of the US freehold type represented the 'last metaphysical right' of humanity, and was an absolute necessity for a free and prosperous society.

This claim is implicitly embedded within neo-classical market economics and can be found within any defence of that system. It means three things (Boydell *et al.*, 2007). Firstly, that development necessarily requires land reform leading to freehold title. Secondly, that general economic thought is written in a way that makes freehold private property the only effective system of land title. Thirdly, and most uncomfortably, it means that if another system of land property were to succeed economically and socially, then the fundamental economic foundations of the West would be challenged.

Without intending it, customary people in the South Pacific are advocating another alternative, one that is definitely not socialist, but revolves around a system of landownership and community relationships that is alien to modern Western thinking. The possibility of its success is beyond the scope of modern economics and the realisation of that success would force a major rethink of some of the cultural fundamentals of the Western system, even though customary peoples contemplated nothing of that sort. It is therefore important that criticisms of customary land based economic systems are understood in terms of both this wider understanding of the modern Western theory and the culture from which they originate.

Despite the on-going debate over privatisation of interests in customary communal, familial or tribal property (de Soto, 2000; Gosarevski *et al.*, 2004; Fingleton, 2004; Fingleton, 2005; Fingleton, 2007) the need for clarification of property rights with sensitivity to local needs and custom is well articulated in the current World Bank, Asian Development Bank, Pacific Island Forum Secretariat, and AusAID thinking on land policy (see, for example, ADB, 2004; AusAID, 2006; PIFS, 2005; PIFS, 2006; World Bank, 2003). Although the pro-privatisation literature correctly recognises problems with the quality of property rights in many developing countries, such as Pacific Island nations, its conclusion that privatisation and individualisation of title is the best, or only practical, alternative is largely an unproven claim. As Bromley (2009, 20) explains, 'if we are to understand the meaning of formalisation it requires that we first understand the crucial differences between possession (or use) of an asset and ownership of that asset'. Possession and use can be obtained through leasehold structures that do not detract from the customary ownership of the superior interest in the land.

Above, I highlighted that in the Pacific some 83 to 97 per cent of land remains 'vested in the stewardship of the customary guardians'. In Western parlance, this means that the customary guardians 'own' the superior (or highest) interest and ultimate property rights over the land. It can be argued that colonisation has resulted in the Western term 'ownership' being inappropriately adopted where land is held under customary, tribal, or familial arrangements. The problem raised by the confusion over 'ownership' is compounded because the economic importance of land is at the nexus of customary norms and the emergent aspirations of individualised materialism in these post-independence nations (Boydell and Holzknecht, 2003).

The economic interests of external parties are difficult to realise because they have to operate within land tenure systems that do not perform in a way that enables individualised land titles, with resultant transaction uncertainty and loan security limitations (de Soto, 2000). I support Bromley's (2009, 21) challenge to the myth that 'formalisation of tenure for the issuance of titles finds its primary justification in the beneficent economic results that are alleged to emanate from the issuance of titles'. As he highlights, the view from the World Bank's World Development Report (World Bank, 2006) that there are 'potentially large benefits from titling' appears largely unfounded. The reality is that 'holding collateral gives lenders profound control over borrowers' (Bromley, 2009, 22).

Perhaps the real issue is the continued perception of the donor community that the imposition of Western-style institutional conditions on to agrarian societies will mean that they too can become 'developed'. Such development ideas continue to gain immediate widespread currency, particularly from donors, as they are central to the power and stake relationship between developed and developing States in a neo-colonial context. Helen Hughes promoted this doctrine when she opined optimistically that freehold title would mean that customary people may lose their land but they would have access to jobs not currently possible in the Pacific (Gosarevski *et al.*, 2004). What is not specified in this scenario is the level of wages these landless indigenous people might expect, as history suggests it would not be equivalent to ongoing meaningful participation in the future prosperity of the economy as a whole. The Hawaiians are a stark example of what this means. Within a generation of establishing freehold title more than 75 per cent of their land was owned by foreigners and, despite finding employment, the indigenous people have only occupied the lowest strata of the island's economic and social hierarchy ever since (McGreggor, 1989).

There is, of course, ample evidence that customary peoples can achieve impressive economic outcomes using their land productively. The early colonial era, Maori enterprises in coastal shipping, milling and other businesses (Kingi, 2002) and the achievements of the people of the PNG Burum Valley (Mandan and Holzknecht, 2005) are documented instances of outstanding entrepreneurial performance. The Ahi people of Lae, PNG, appear to be currently reproducing similar outcomes (Boydell *et al.*, 2007), demonstrating that effective economic outcomes are possible. The current question is how to increase the prevalence of successes, specifically utilising customary-owned land, while remaining within authentic cultural boundaries:

the dual goal of balancing economic independence for Pacific people whilst ensuring intergenerational equity.

This goal can be achieved when Bromley's (2009) differentiation between possession (use rights) and ownership is understood within an overarching regime of financially authentic continuing *customary* ownership. Authenticity requires arrangements that are culturally acceptable and have the capacity to return economically acceptable outcomes. Solutions need to focus on the mechanics of leasehold tenure arrangements (as these are already in operation within the Pacific) and examine the conditions whereby they might provide the cultural and economic objectives of Pacific peoples.

Leasehold tenure is a system of property rights that enables possession (use) for a fixed period. It has considerable history and application in the West. Historically, it correlates with some of the most successful periods of Western history in terms of the double bottom line of economic growth and equity (Rogers, 1884, reprint 2001; Burnette and Mokyr, 1995; Grantham, 1995).

In recent times, leasehold arrangements have been aggressively pursued as a strategy for financial success, with many international and national corporations divesting themselves of property assets in order to free capital for their core business, in many cases leasing back the property assets they previously owned. Their success illustrates that not only is leasehold tenure capable of producing financial and economic business success for tenants, but in Western countries it is often the preferred tenure system for property users. Likewise, Archer (1974) has documented the many international examples where leasehold development has been successful.

This is not to claim that leasehold is the most attractive tenure system for encouraging foreign investment, or that getting the design right does not pose considerable challenges. In this regard my stance differs from the 'ideal' promoted by UN Habitat as the *continuum of rights* under their Global Land Tools Network (GLTN, 2009). Rather, this 'continuum' presents the Western ideal, where informal customary tenures are located at the lowest end of the spectrum and registered freehold is seen as the ideal, or optimal, land holding. Whilst this may be 'ideal' from a Western mind-set or donor perspective, it is wholly inappropriate to consider individualised freehold title as the ideal in the South Pacific region.

Part of achieving the optimum design is objectively setting performance criteria. In the Pacific, these criteria include cultural and economic objectives as well as financial ones (for an expanded analysis of current and recommended leasehold models for the South Pacific, which draws on specific residential lease case studies in Fiji and tourism leases in Samoa, see Boydell, 2008a). The question of equity is an important practical issue within the cultural dimension of the effective use of customary-owned land. It is closely linked to the practical genesis of land-related conflict, which is a major issue in the Pacific. The notion of equity is problematic within economic thought. This is partly because the market and utilitarianism are implicitly relied upon as the ultimate moral reference point (Small, 2000). It is also partly because economic thought is normally considered to be an entirely separate discipline to ethics (Boettke, 1998), and therefore questions of equity are beyond its scope. This highlights the need for good governance in dealing with land matters.

Reaction – the pendulum swings against capitalism

In my previous writings [see references], I have made the point that in general, Pacific Island countries retain the traditional belief that the superior interest in the land should not be sold, but retained to ensure intergenerational equity and connection to place. However, I wonder if it is really a contemporary belief rather than a traditional belief, given that as Ward (1995, 208) reminds us, the concept of inalienability was 'invented' in the 1870s in Fiji and became enshrined (that is, it became 'tradition') through an Ordinance in 1912. Whilst Ward offers an interesting contradiction to the accepted notion of contemporary tradition, there is no doubt that the issues surrounding alienability (or, for that matter, the creation of a subsidiary leasehold interest) give rise to on-going tensions.

These tensions have resulted in the establishment of the Melanesian Indigenous Land Defence Alliance (MILDA), as an advocacy collective for Pacific Islanders to question and challenge the imposition of the 'Western Way' over the 'Pacific Way'. The Alliance was formalised in 2009, and has gained traction internationally through speaking tours (supported by AidWATCH) of informed and respected Pacific Islanders who eloquently articulate the underlying ground swell of concern amongst grassroots islander communities. Below, I draw directly on the insights of two of the founders of MILDA, Joel Simo and Ralph Regenvanu – insights which attest to the challenges and concerns they confront in the face of development in its many forms.

The following transcript from Joel Simo, Director of the Land Desk at the Vanuatu Cultural Centre, is taken from his response to the question 'what is customary land?', posed at an AidWATCH meeting in Sydney on 14 November 2014, as part of the MILDA speaking tour.

> Customary tenure, why it's worth fighting for, to protect. It has a lot of meaning for us. At independence we struggled for that, we fought for it and then we got it. The main issue for us was that land had to return to the customary landowners. Our founding fathers ensured that land is enshrined in the constitution and belongs to the customary people. The roots of custom form the basis of ownership, not modern laws.
>
> So why we value traditional lands so much in Melanesia is because land belongs to every member of the family, or every member of the clan or every member of the tribe. It does not belong to an individual.

Land is 'our' land, not 'my' land. The concept of individual ownership is a new concept in the region and Melanesia. We do not own land. We have the right to look after land for the benefit of our children. Land is not a commodity. One of the big reasons that we have tried to defend this is because the large part of the population in Melanesia is rural-based – they live off the land. And everything that comes from the land sustains them.

The traditional economy, that is their gardens, their houses, their mats, their pigs, their chickens or whatever belongs to the community – which is what we call the traditional economy. This sustains them. If they do not have any money in their pockets they still survive – they have a roof over their head and they still have food on the table. These are things that are very important, and all these things are taken from the land – not cash.

…These are the reasons why in Vanuatu and Melanesia we talk a lot about land issues, because land is our life. Land is ours, not mine. When you put it into an individual realm it becomes saleable, transferable. You put it in a legal framework and it becomes transferable and you will never ever get it back to its traditional understanding where it is indivisible. Once it has gone, it's gone.[2]

Ralph Regenvanu (currently the Minister for Land in the Government of Vanuatu) speaking at the launch of the Melanesian Indigenous Land Defence Alliance in June 2009 (Regenvanu, 2009), highlights:

Development has become a very terrible word because it means, it can be used in a way that covers up so much hidden agendas and mainly agendas to do with recolonisation and people coming in. These days development means basically foreign investment. The kind of development that we need in Melanesia and in Vanuatu is locally controlled development, I mean locally controlled enhancement of our opportunities – better cash incomes, better education, better health outcomes, improved food security that kind of thing. It is only possible for landowners in that in Melanesia to get those types of outcomes if they retain control of the land. As soon as they engage with Western laws and land alienation, they are getting into deep water in terms of not understanding what these laws are and what their rights are in terms of these laws.

Wayfaring the 'Pacific Way' through good governance

The challenges to any kind of land reform in Melanesia, be they internally or externally driven, are significant. The commoditisation of land requires markets to be efficient, equitable, environmentally sustainable and compatible, grounded in efficient and updated land management systems that clearly indicate the property rights, obligations and responsibilities of all parties and beneficiaries. The following issues (Boydell, 2005) require consideration:

- *Complexity* – Land policy reform issues are complex, country-specific, long-term and often controversial in nature – challenging stakes in the status quo. Leaders thus need vision and wisdom that transcends party politicking and racial intransigence. No one solution is universally applicable, and there are no total solutions to land problems. It is an evolutionary process, requiring careful sequencing of reforms.
- *Supportive* – Land reform requires support at the highest levels to implement policy changes. Governments have been unable to improve the efficiency of land registration systems because of institutional, human, technical and economic constraints, and a lack of political will.
- *Accommodating* – Land reform needs to accommodate economic aspirations whilst respecting non-economic social, cultural, religious and environmental values. Where this is not managed carefully, there will be inevitable calls for the nationalisation of land, or demands for redress by returning land to its 'previous' customary owners. Such typical reactions to land policy reform cause concern to investors by increasing risk and uncertainty in the property sector, which can negate the anticipated economic growth potential in the short term.
- *There is no property in nature* – The caveat to land policy is the risk of envisioning an implicit end state that becomes the norm against which region-specific problems are diagnosed, with the risk that the diagnosis then provides the basis for a 'policy prescription'. Embedded in every policy prescription ('do this') is also a prediction ('and that will happen'). We must keep in mind that different societies and cultures see land differently. This means that land is not land is not land.... Land is only what people see in it and make of it. Just as there is no property in nature, it follows that from an economic and social perspective there is no such thing as land – there is only land tenure, and within land tenure, there are only property rights.
- *Political governance* issues are seen as a constraint – there is a perception that when it comes to policy change, political leaders often take the 'do no harm' policy line. This results in inaction in order to avoid conflict. Any legislative or policy changes will have impacts and there will be losers even where the greater good is being pursued.
- *Political will* – How do you build the political will and vision for long-term improvement in land tenure systems?
- *Need for different frameworks for different land uses* – Should we look at land issues through two 'windows' – land for sustainable livelihood in rural areas and land for economic development, which includes land for public use.

- *Sharing benefits fairly* (distributive justice) – Transparency and account-ability are essential at all levels to manage income distribution from selling or leasing land. This applies as much at village level as it does at national or urban level.
- *Process matters* – The process involves several steps: hold discussions to reach consensus, develop policy, develop legislation and implement it, then regularly monitor and evaluate how it is implemented.
- *Identification of correct priorities* – Run with pilot studies to test policy incrementally (adaptive strategy) rather than leading straight into sweeping structural reform.
- *Putting communities at the centre* – The priority is to see the community as the centre of development and labour supply, rather than as the recipient of it or as blocking development.
- *Education and information* – People at all levels need to be educated about what their existing property rights are and what any policy changes will mean.
- *Getting the balance right* – When land is the only source of security for some people there are still many issues to be resolved regarding its commodification versus its cultural value.
- *Assessing costs and benefits* – What will the social costs of change to land tenure arrangements be? Conversely, what are the social and economic costs of making no change?
- *Customary tenure and individual rights* – How can we harmonise customary tenure with individual rights? What would a system of formal and informal titles look like?
- *Quantity versus quality* – There are examples where some customary owners have a large quantity of land but it is not always quality land (for productive purposes).

The story so far

The work undertaken thus far supports the notion that *analytical tools*, rather than *historical rules*, should be developed to continually monitor land tenure conflict situations to identify when transformative intervention is likely to be accepted by the multiple parties often involved in the conflict situation. Such is the evolution of land tenure itself. Arguably, part of the reaction by groups like MILDA to the evolution of land tenure is that the commoditisation of land requires markets to be efficient, equitable, environ-mentally sustainable and compatible, grounded in efficient and updated land management systems that clearly indicate the property rights, obligations and responsibilities of all parties or beneficiaries.

There are too many examples, in both the developed as well as the developing world, where leases are drafted to benefit one party over another. In the developed world, we usually find that landlords hold most power, and the rights of tenants are weaker. Conversely in the Pacific, where prospective tenants often hold knowledge, money, key information and power (especially in resource, agricultural or tourism ventures), leases have been drafted to benefit tenants over the customary guardians of the land, the latter often being disenfranchised as lands are leased under terms which effectively result in perpetual alienation.

The way forward

Education is essential to overcome the lack of understanding (and acceptance) of various stakeholders' property rights, with their respective obligations and restrictions. It is essential to educate both lessors and lessees to create better understanding of lease terms, property rights, obligations and responsibilities – especially termination/reversion issues, and the need for equitable rental payments and reviews. The chain of property rights, and the protection of the State to ensure legal enforcement of these rights, is essential in allowing land to serve its economic goal whilst incorporating and respecting customary rights.

The influence of current research and fieldwork will potentially serve to minimise much of the conflict, which is often grounded in the misunderstandings of the rights, responsibilities, revenues, and relationships of, and between, the respective stakeholders. Thus, the issues and approaches offered in this chapter represent an important starting point in a much bigger process.

The good governance principles of legitimacy, accountability, effectiveness, participation, and fairness relating to land administration are now clearly on the international agenda of the World Bank, the United Nations Food and Agriculture Organisation and the International Federation of Surveyors (Zakout et al., 2009, Boydell, 2008b). These principles build on recent regional initiatives and plans that engage with land issues in the Pacific. These include USP Solutions (2001) Land Tenure and Land Conflict in the South Pacific (Boydell, 2001), FAO/USP/RICS Foundation South Pacific Land Tenure Conflict Symposium (2002), and the subsequent National Land Workshops/Summits (Fiji 2002, Solomon Islands/Melanesia 2005, PNG 2005 and 2006, Vanuatu 2006), and ADB Swimming Against the Tide (2004), Forum Secretariat Pacific Plan (2006), AusAID Pacific 2020 (2006). Most recently these initiatives on current land management thinking have engaged more fully with the principles of good governance (Rakai, 2008).

The South Pacific has not escaped the impacts of modernisation and globalisation, which have brought fundamental changes to Pacific societies and affected values, goals, and social norms. Whilst the vision is to strive for land reform (emphasising leasehold solutions) that is both based on and sensitive to the reality of continuing customary ownership, there is a need to explore and reach consensus on where the citizens of the South Pacific want to be located between the extremes of traditional customary ways and Western materialism (Boydell et al., 2002). A shift is occurring within Pacific communities, which is affecting egalitarian and communal lifestyles.

Influences of globalism and modernity are placing greater emphasis on individual economic wealth accumulation and related pressures to derive economic benefits from customary land. This Westernisation means that at times decisions are made for personal gain rather than necessarily being in the best interest of the land-owning group as a whole. There is a recognised clash between indigenous values and capitalism, which has been seen as an impediment to business development within the region. Despite the impact of individualism, most indigenous people see their relationships as coming from the land rather than using it as a commodity (Boydell *et al.*, 2002). As I have highlighted above, the customary nature of land ownership and control in the Pacific, whilst acknowledged and respected, does not prevent the optimum use of the land for development (in its many forms).

Nowhere has the complexity of the land tenure tradition and commerce in the South Pacific been more succinctly and poignantly articulated than in the late Savenaca Siwatibau's opening address at the FAO/USP/RICS Foundation South Pacific Land Tenure Conflict Symposium (Siwatibau, 2002):

> They say that land, like financial and human capital, is a factor of production, which helps drive economic and social development, generate national income, wealth, jobs and government revenue, combat poverty, improve the standard of living of all and ultimately entrench social and political stability in any country. As in all things, changes and solutions have to be made and formulated. Solutions must be formulated from within and must reflect national, family and individual needs and aspirations and the changing global, regional, national economic, social and political dynamics that determine our destiny.

Siwatibau raises many of the issues that remain unanswered in the questions posed by Hooper and Ward (1995) in the introduction to this chapter. Siwatibau's wisdom encompasses all the principles of good governance and highlights the need for donors and business ventures to work more collaboratively with Pacific Island nations, their leaders and the community to find solutions from within that respect the place of land in the region.

References

ADB 2004. *Swimming Against the Tide – An Assessment of the Private Sector in the Pacific*. Manila, Philippines: Asian Development Bank.

Anderson, T. 2006. 'On the Economic Value of Customary Land in Papua New Guinea'. *Pacific Economic Bulletin* 21, 138–52.

Archer, R. W. 1974. 'The Leasehold System of Urban Development: Land Tenure, Decision-Making and the Land Market in Urban Development and Land Use'. *Regional Studies: The Journal of the Regional Studies Association* 8, 225–38.

AusAID 2006. Pacific 2020: 'Challenges and Opportunities for Growth'. Canberra: Australian Agency for International Development (AusAID).

Boettke, P. J. 1998. 'Is Economics a Moral Science? A Response to Ricardo F. Crespo'. *Journal of Markets and Morality* 1, 212–19.

Boydell, S. 2001. 'Land Tenure and Land Conflict in the South Pacific' [background report for the 2002 FAO/USP/RICS Foundation South Pacific Land Tenure Conflict Symposium]. Suva, Fiji: Food and Agriculture Organization (FAO) of the United Nations.

Boydell, S. 'Alleviation of Poverty: The Role of Surveyors, Land Economists and Related Professions in the Pacific Islands'. Commonwealth Association of Surveying and Land Economy (CASLE) Technical Conference for Built Environment Professions: 2004 Danbury Park Conference Centre, Anglia Polytechnic University, Chelmsford, UK (21–24 April 2004). CASLE.

Boydell, S. 2005. 'Secure Land Tenure in the South Pacific Region – Developing the Toolkit'. In: Van Der Molen, P. (ed.) *Expert Group Meeting on secure land tenure: 'new legal frameworks and tools in Asia & Pacific', organised by FIG Commission 7, UN-HABITAT, The World Bank and UN Economic and Social Commission for Asia and the Pacific (UNESCAP).* Bangkok, Thailand: UNESCAP.

Boydell, S. 2008a. 'Finding Hybrid Solutions to the Financial Management of Customary Land from a Pacific Perspective'. *Australian Journal of Indigenous Education* Supplement to v.37, 56–64.

Boydell, S. 2008b. 'Institutions, Complexity, and the Land'. *Integrating Generations: FIG Working Week 2008.* Stockholm, Sweden.

Boydell, S. and Baya, U. 2012. 'Resource Development on Customary Land – Managing the Complexity through a Pro-Development Compensation Solution'. In: Deininger, K. (ed.) *Annual World Bank Land and Poverty Conference 2012.* The World Bank, Washington DC: The World Bank.

Boydell, S. and Holzknecht, H. 2003. 'Land – caught in the conflict between custom and commercialism'. *Land Use Policy* 20, 203–7.

Boydell, S. and Small, G. 'The Emerging Need for Regional Property Solutions – A Pacific Perspective'. Pacific Rim Real Estate Society (PRRES) Ninth Annual Conference, 19–22 January, 2003, 2003 Brisbane, Australia. UNISA.

Boydell, S., Small, G., Holzknecht, H. and Naidu, V. 2002. *Declaration and Resolutions of the FAO/USP/RICS Foundation South Pacific Land Tenure Conflict Symposium, Suva, Fiji, 10 - 12 April 2002* [Online]. Suva, Fiji: Land Management and Development, University of the South Pacific. Available online: www.usp.ac.fj/landmgmt/PDF/SPLTCDECLARATIONRESOLUTIONS.PDF (Accessed 15/06/02).

Boydell, S., Small, G. R. and Sheehan, J. B. 2007. 'Review of Financial Management of Customary and Other Land in the Pacific'. Suva, Fiji: Pacific Islands Forum Secretariat.

Bromley, D. W. 2009. 'Formalising Property Relations in the Developing World: The Wrong Prescription for the Wrong Malady'. *Land Use Policy* 26, 20–7.

Burnette, J. and Mokyr, J. 1995. 'The Standard of Living Through the Ages'. In: Simon, J. L. (ed.) *The State of Humanity.* Malden, Massachusetts: Blackwell Publishers Inc.

De Soto, H. 2000. *The mystery of capital: why capitalism triumphs in the West and fails everywhere else.* New York: Basic Books.

FAO/USP/RICS Foundation. 2002. *South Pacific Land Tenure Conflict (SPLTC) Symposium, 10–12 April, 2002* [Online]. Suva, Fiji. Available online: www.usp.ac.fj/landmgmt/SYMPOSIUM/ (Accessed 07/07/2002).

Farran, S. and Paterson, D. E. 2004. *South Pacific Property Law.* Sydney, Cavendish Publishing Limited.

Fingleton, J. 2004. 'Is Papua New Guinea Viable Without Customary Groups?' *Pacific Economic Bulletin* 19, 96–103.

Fingleton, J. (ed.) 2005. *Privatising Land in the Pacific – A defence of customary tenures.* Canberra: The Australia Institute.

Fingleton, J. 2007. 'Rethinking the Need for Land Reform in Papua New Guinea'. *Pacific Economic Bulletin* 22, 115–21.

Fukuyama, F. 1992. *The End of History and the Last Man.* London, Penguin.

GLTN. 2009. *About GLTN (Global Land Tools Network)* [Online]. Nairobi, Kenya: UN Habitat. Available online: www.gltn.net/index.php?option=com_content &task=view&id=9&Itemid=69 (Accessed 25/08/09 2009).

Gosarevski, S., Hughes, H. and Windybank, S. 2004. 'Is Papua New Guinea Viable with Customary Land Ownership?' *Pacific Economic Bulletin* 19, 133–6.

Grantham, G. W. 1995. 'Agricultural Productivity Before the Green Revolution'. In: Simon, J. L. (ed.) *The State of Humanity.* Malden, Massachusetts: Blackwell Publishers Inc.

Griffiths, J. 1986. 'What is Legal Pluralism?' *Journal of Legal Pluralism and Unofficial Law* 1, 1–56.

Hann, C. M. 1998. 'Introduction: The Embeddedness of Property'. In: Hann, C. M. (ed.) *Property Relations – Renewing the anthropological tradition.* Cambridge, UK: Cambridge University Press.

Hooker, M. B. 1975. *Legal Pluralism: An Introduction to Colonial and Neo-colonial Laws.* Oxford, Clarendon Press.

Hooper, A. and Ward, R. G. 1995. 'Beyond the Breathing Space'. In: Ward, R. G. and Kingdon, E. (eds) *Land, Custom and Practice in the South Pacific.* Cambridge, Massachusetts: Cambridge University Press.

Hughes, R. 2003. 'Legal Pluralism and the Problem of Identity'. In: Jowitt, A. and Cain, T. N. (eds) *Passage of change: Law, Society and Governance in the Pacific.* Canberra: Pandanus Books.

Kingi, T. 'Individualisation of Customary Tenure and Māori Agricultural Development'. In: Boydell, S. (ed.) FAO / USP / RICS Foundation South Pacific Land Tenure Conflict Symposium, 2002 Suva, Fiji. University of the South Pacific.

Lightfoot, C. 2005. 'Does Customary Land Ownership make Economic Sense?' In: Fingleton, J. (ed.) *Privatising Land in the Pacific: A defence of customary tenures.* Canberra: The Australia Institute.

Mandan, T. and Holzknecht, H. A. 2005. 'Nanak Mutuk: Development through Self-Reliance in the Burum Valley'. *Development Bulletin,* 33–6.

McGreggor, D. P. 1989. 'The Perpetuation of the Hawaiian People'. In: Howard, M. C. (ed.) *Ethnicity and Nation Building in the Pacific.* Tokyo: UN University.

Miles, G. 1999. *Pacific Islands Environment Outlook.* Apia, Samoa, Co-publication of SPREP, UNEP and EU.

Overton, J. 1992. 'The Limits to Accumulation: Changing Land Tenure in Fiji'. *The Journal of Peasant Studies* 19, 326–42.

PIFS 2005. 'The Pacific Plan for Strengthening Regional Cooperation and Integration'. Suva, Fiji: Pacific Islands Forum Secretariat (PIFS).

PIFS 2006. 'Land Management and Conflict Minimisation Project'. In: Secretariat, P. I. F. (ed.). Suva, Fiji: Pacific Islands Forum Secretariat (PIFS).

Rakai, M. E. T. 2008. *FAO / USP Regional Seminar on Good Governance in Land Tenure and Land Administration in the Pacific* [Online]. Suva, Fiji: USP. Available online: http://usp.ac.fj/index.php?id=6806 (Accessed 25/08/09).

Regenvanu, R. 2009. *Defending Melanesian Land – Documentary On Customary Land And Melanesian Indigenous Land Defence Alliance. Youtube.com*, Indigenous Peoples Issues and Resources. Available online: www.youtube.com/watch?feature=player_embedded&v=bmolHFFdNyc (Accessed 10/12/2014 2009).

Rogers, J. E. T. 1884. (reprint 2001). *Six Centuries of Work and Wages: The History of English Labour.* Kitchener, Ontario: Batoche Books.

Sachs, W. 1992. *The Development dictionary: a guide to knowledge as power.* London, New Jersey: Zed.

Siwatibau, S. 2002. *Welcome Address for the FAO/USP/RICS Foundation South Pacific Land Tenure Conflict Symposium, Suva, Fiji, 10 - 12 April, 2002* [Online]. Transcribed by Boydell, S. Available online: www.usp.ac.fj/landmgmt/webpapers/welcomeaddress.pdf (Accessed 07/07/2002).

Small, G. 1997. 'A Comparative Analysis of Contemporary Native and Ancient Western Cultural Attitudes to Land'. Pacific Rim Real Estate Society (PRRES) 1997 Annual Conference, Massey University, Palmerston North, New Zealand.

Small, G. 2000. 'Modern Economics as Social Psychology: Escaping the Moral Dilemma of the Invisible Hand'. *The Catholic Social Science Review* V.

Strakosch, E. 2007. 'Australia'. In: Stidsen, S. (ed.) *The Indigenous World 2007.* International Work Group for Indigenous Affairs (IWGIA).

Von Benda-Beckmann, F. and Von Benda-Beckmann, K. 2006. 'The Dynamics of Change and Continuity in Plural Legal Orders'. *Journal of Legal Pluralism and Unofficial Law* 53–4, 1–43.

Ward, R. G. 1995. 'Land, Law and Custom: Diverging Realities in Fiji'. In: Ward, R. G. and Kingdon, E. (eds) *Land, Custom and Practice in the South Pacific.* Cambridge, UK: Cambridge University Press.

Weaver, R. M. 1948. *Ideas have consequences.* Chicago: University of Chicago Press.

World Bank 2003. 'Land Policies for Growth and Poverty Reduction'. In: Deininger, K. (ed.) *World Bank Policy Research Report.* Washington, D.C.: Co-publication of the World Bank and Oxford University Press.

World Bank 2006. *Equity and Development: World Development Report.* Washington, D.C.: World Bank.

Zakout, W., Wehrmann, B. and Torhonen, M.P. 2009. *Good Government in Land Administration: Principles and Good Practices.* Rome: FAO / World Bank.

Notes

1   For example, the University of the South Pacific (USP) incorporates twelve Pacific Island Nations, the Pacific Islands Forum Secretariat (PIFS) incorporates 16 members including Australia and New Zealand, whereas the South Pacific Geoscience Commission (SOPAC) has a membership of 19 Pacific Island Countries/Territories. The South Pacific Games (SPG 2003) in Fiji included 22 countries, encompassing the full breadth of the Pacific Ocean, with an administrative responsibility for one-seventh of the earth's surface (i.e. double that of the US and almost triple that of Australia).

2   Between the fourth and the final paragraph presented above are the following paragraphs:

One of the things that I think GDP fails to understand is that GDP is in monetary terms only but ignores what the bulk of the population is living off in the region. These people are still living happily. There may not be any hospitals out in the community but people still have food, they still have the basics – what they need in life. That is why people are so attached to land. Land and people are one. They are inseparable. Land is life for us in Melanesia, especially where I come from in Vanuatu.

The other part of it is this idea of saying that we have to bring development into the community so that it can provide employment, it can provide jobs to people. For us, land is the biggest employer as despite the fact that you do not have a job or you are not educated, you still have some place to work, to sustain yourself.

With this, I think this is one of the main reasons that we have to defend what has been sustaining us for thousands of years. What we are seeing now is this idea that you have to free up land for development purposes. In order to do that we have to register those lands. And that is taking away the land from its traditional tenure to a new model of land that is 'ownership'. But land is 'our' land, not 'my' land. Once we take it out of traditional tenure to this new system it becomes my land, and no longer our land. That's where disputes arise. That's where conflicts arise. Because one person in the community gets the land title and becomes a land owner, so other members of the community will retaliate because they cannot survive without the land.

So these are the new things that are coming and that are gradually displacing people off their land. In Melanesia, specifically for the rural people, there is no landlessness. Everybody has somewhere to build a house. Everyone has somewhere to make a garden to survive. So that, in Melanesia land is our safety net. You take it away from us and you only have one option – to find a paid job. Good luck with finding that. And if you do, you have nowhere to go.

I guess that this is one of the main reasons that there is no real poverty, if I can put it that way, in the rural community. And there they have houses, they have food, they have water – maybe it's not coming from the tap, but still it's a running stream, it's everything. These things are life. If the land is taken away from these people it raises the question of survival. How are they going to survive, when they have not been taught how to survive in monetary terms. They are not taught how to be independent when using money. This has impacted on the community in many negative ways, when you put land into an individual realm – when it is no longer our land, it excludes others. You hold a lease, alienating the land and excluding others – excluding people from the land that has been part and parcel of their life for generations.

The model of registration is being pushed by states, it is being pushed by government, it is being pushed by aid donors, to free up land so that developments can come in. Then again this raises the question of development for whom? What do we mean when we talk about development in our communities – this is a question that needs to be addressed properly? With this sort of model of land registration the argument is that it will push development in the country. But if you look at this carefully, you have to displace people from the land so that these things can take place at the expense of the customary landowners so that others can benefit while the bulk of the population have been feeding off of land – and their land, not my land – are displaced.

8 Threats and challenges to the 'floating lives' of the Tonle Sap

Carl Grundy-Warr and Mak Sithirith

Introduction

Threats to the 'pulsing heart' of the Mekong and neak tonle

The Great Lake of Cambodia or Tonle Sap is intimately linked to the broader Mekong Basin via hydrological and ecological processes. To understand the current challenges confronting indigenous people of the Tonle Sap and river systems (*neak tonle* in Khmer) requires understanding of their central place within 'the pulsing heart' of Cambodia and the Mekong Basin as a whole, which is a hotspot for biodiversity, for inland fisheries, and for unique 'floating communities'. This chapter considers the *neak tonle* who are 'water-based' and 'land-water-based' communities dependent on the aquatic resources of the lake. We examine complex issues of resource governance, in particular the political-spatial complexity of the Lake and floodplain, and institutional arrangements relating to resource governance. The biggest challenges to human and ecological security for the indigenous river- and water-based people are primarily exogenous ones relating to long-term land-cover change, water diversions, hydropower dam developments, and climate change that are likely to impact upon the duration, timing and reliability of wet and dry seasons and the regulatory flood-pulse of the Mekong Basin.

Figure 8.1 shows the trans-boundary scale of the Tonle Sap within the Mekong Basin as a whole, plus the Tonle Sap Lake catchment area within Cambodia, and the lake and its associated floodplain. All these scales inter-relate, yet governance of the Tonle Sap is primarily driven by institutions at the national and Tonle Sap floodplain scales, which means that many potential threats and future conflicts are not being adequately addressed by the existing system of resource governance. In contrast to the relatively narrow river zone of the upper Mekong, the Tonle Sap Basin covers a huge area, about 42 per cent of Cambodia's territory (Starr, 2008), including 11 river basins flowing into the Tonle Sap Lake, an extended floodplain area in the wet season, 10 provinces and the municipality of Phnom Penh (Kestinen and Varis, 2012). There are 4.5 million people in the Tonle Sap Basin, excluding the capital city, in 65 districts, 526 communes, and around 4,245 villages, out of which 1.2 million living in the floodplain (Sokhem and

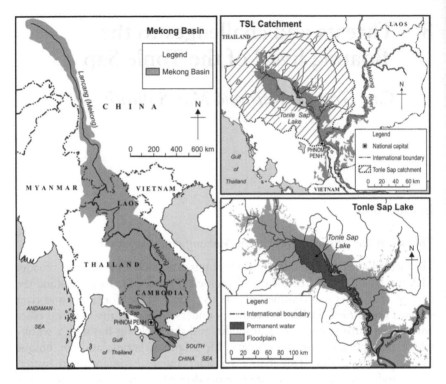

Figure 8.1 Mekong Basin, Tonle Sap catchment, lake and floodplain

Sunada, 2006). Thus, the Tonle Sap Basin incorporates jurisdictional, demographic and political complexity, with numerous sectors, stakeholders and boundaries to overcome.

Indigenous 'neak tonle' of the Tonle Sap

It is often said that youngsters learn to paddle before they can walk in the Tonle Sap. People living on or near this great lake of Cambodia have adopted their living according to the environment, particularly to the changes in the hydrological regime of the lake between the dry and wet seasons. The changing hydrological regime between the dry and wet season in the Tonle Sap induce several transformations to the physical-human environment, and indeed, transform the whole human landscape. People have developed a living system adapted to the lake's environment, and it is hard to think of their lives and livelihoods without reference to the seasonally changing waterscape, especially the annual rising waters which expand the Tonle Sap waterscape laterally over a very large flood plain. We include all the people, communes and villages of the Tonle Sap and its floodplain as 'indigenous' here, for they are all in some way *'neak tonle'* (Khmer meaning 'river people'), all living according to the rhythms and cycles of the hydrological regime and associated biophysical processes. As Figure 8.2 illustrates, there is an intensive settlement pattern around the lake consisting of mostly small villages. However, further distinctions are useful. Some people in the Cambodian context would be considered '*neak leu*' (uplanders) if they come mostly from landed settlements further away from the Tonle Sap and who travel to the lake to fish (Piseth, 2002), and the people who live permanently on land in predominantly farming communities are distinct from the *neak tonle* who live in the 'floating' and 'high-stilt' houses of the Tonle Sap perimeter.

Our view of the *neak tonle* as indigenous people inhabiting the lake and its associated wetlands is not justified in either ethnic or racial terms, because the Tonle Sap includes many Khmer, Vietnamese, and Cham (Cambodian Muslim) people who sometimes share the same communes and live in the same villages. Rather, we perceive long-term reliance upon aquatic spaces and resources of the Tonle Sap and the Lower Mekong system as providing specific *ways of life* and *water-based adaptations* which are genuinely *indigenous* (AFN, 2004). This fits with Berkes' (2012: 47) notion of 'traditional ecological knowledge' based around 'people who are dependent on local resources for their livelihood' and 'their time-tested, in-depth local knowledge' of their immediate environment and the services relating to it.

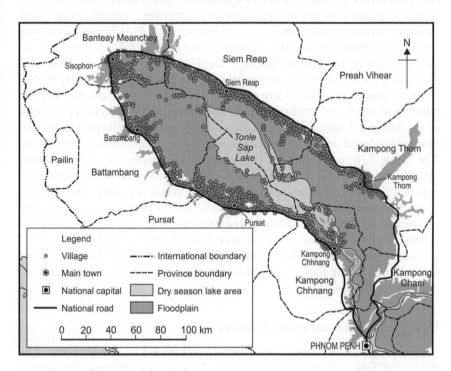

Figure 8.2 Settlements of the Tonle Sap

This is not to overly reify indigenous ways of knowing as being superior to or separate from other forms of knowledge, for there are examples of over-fishing, local environmental degradation, and lack of conservation ethnics that may be partly attributed to indigenous practices, excessive exploitation of resources, and poor local governance. Nevertheless, we observe that the *neak tonle* undoubtedly possess sophisticated understandings of their fluid and dynamic water world, and in order to understand conflicts, threats, challenges and adaptations within and relating to the Tonle Sap, we need to study indigenous ways of living within and relations with the ecosystem of which they are a part.

A sensitive eco-frontier and barometer of change

Human ecology in the Tonle Sap is influenced by the annual flood pulse and water levels. Nikula (2005) calls this the 'human-environment system' of Tonle Sap. Environment is linked to hydrology, biophysical parameters and ecosystem services, whilst human residents of the lake have many aquatic resource linked livelihoods, and associated socio-economic and cultural links to the lake's biophysical environment. Intense socio-ecology linkages make the Tonle Sap a fascinating arena for understanding long- and short-term transformations to the Mekong Basin's hydrology and ecosystem through energy policies (especially hydropower), rising urbani-zation, agribusiness transformations to land cover, infrastructures, and multiple forms of water utilization (Arias *et al.*, 2014; Baran, Starr and Kura, 2007; Piman *et al.*, 2013; Costa-Cabral *et al.*, 2007). As noted in our introduction, we tend to see the major conflicts and threats to the Tonle Sap as coming from exogenous and transnational processes of change. In this sense we perceive the Tonle Sap as a sort of eco-frontier of change, a space which is naturally interlinked with the hydrology and biophysical processes of the Mekong Basin, and is thus vulnerable to many developments, mostly humanly induced developmental changes, that are affecting those processes. The Tonle Sap in this regard is a gigantic barometer of environmental change for the whole Mekong Basin, or as an essential waterscape eco-frontier whereby indigenous vulnerability, resilience, and adaptability involve intense socio-ecological relationships. In other words, monitoring the health of the lake ecosystem requires not only research within that system, including resource governance systems involving the *neak tonle*, but also necessitates studies of multi-scale changes in the Mekong Basin that are influencing that system and impacting upon the life worlds and life changes of the *neak tonle*.

Flood pulse, ecosystem and fisheries

Life of people in the Tonle Sap is largely influenced by water as stated in Poole (2005:46)—*Tonle Sap: The Heart of Cambodia's Natural Heritage*:

While in the dry season the Tonle Sap Lake 'only' stretches for approximately 150 kilometers in length and averages around 20 kilometers in width, new radar satellite imagery has revealed the true extent of the lake's flood. At the peak of the wet season the Tonle Sap can expand to 250 kilometer long and in places more than 100 kilometers wide. The lake is shallow, measuring only 1–2 meters at its deepest in the dry season, rising to more than 10 meters in the wet season. As a result as it floods the total inundated area increases four-fold, from 2,500 square kilometers to over 13,000 square kilometers.

The water world of the Tonle Sap shapes and influences the livelihoods of people living in different fishing communities in the lake. Different fishing communities adapt differently to the fluctuation of the water level in the Tonle Sap between the wet and dry seasons. The water and the environment system and the human ability developed to cope with this water world creates the enormous cultural, social, environmental and economic values associated with the natural capital of the lake system, and particularly of the incredible biodiversity that lies within this important waterscape (Campbell *et al.*, 2006; Nikula, 2005).

The flood pulse causes oscillation between terrestrial and aquatic conditions on the floodplain. The growth of plants during the favorable phase and their decomposition during the less favorable condition intensifies the nutrient cycling, which is usually high in the floodplains, resulting in high productivity. The flood pulse also triggers certain fish migrations into and out of the Tonle Sap, and between the Tonle Sap and the Lower Mekong River and Basin (Baran and Myschowoda, 2009; Baird, 2011; Pech *et al.*, 2008). The Mekong River Commission (MRC) has also produced extensive scientific studies describing the flood pulse ecosystem of the Mekong basin. In this aspect, an understanding of how this ecosystem functions appears to fall along more 'natural' ecological boundaries, aligning itself closer to physiographic regions rather than to nation-states. In the flood pulse ecosystem process, exchanges of water, nutrients and organisms occur between terrestrial and aquatic environments (plant matter from the land to the water and water to the dry land) according to an annual flood-drought cycle driven by the river's hydrology that seasonally inundate floodplains (Lamberts, 2008). The flood pulse is intimately linked to the river's rich biological diversity and productive ecosystems (Nikula, 2008), and the water, ecosystems and wider terrestrial watershed is a highly integrated system (Sneddon and Fox, 2006; MRC, 2010). Scientific studies of the flood pulse often lead back to showing how the biological productivity of the flood pulse ecosystem is critical to constituting the natural resources that are relied upon by tens of thousands of communities in the Lower Mekong Basin.

The Mekong River is often cited to support the world's largest inland fishery, and its biodiversity, estimated to be at least 1,500 species, is second only to the Amazon River (Campbell *et al.*, 2006; Poole, 2005). Although basic migration patterns can vary by specific species and habitat, the importance of fish migrations between and within the region's wetlands and deep pools is well established, as is the dependence of millions of rural livelihoods upon them (MRC, 2002; Baran and Myschowoda, 2009). Whilst various fish migrations occur all year round, major fish migrations coincide with the Mekong River's monsoon-driven flood pulse (other triggers include water turbidity, and lunar cycles). Thus hydrological conditions affect the timing and pattern of fish migrations between the Tonle Sap and the Lower Mekong River system and its tributaries.

The Tonle Sap is connected to the broader hydrological regime of the Mekong Basin, which in turn has direct implications for multiple human-ecology interactions. The annual flood pulse is like the 'heartbeat' of the Lower Mekong system, which has supported biodiversity and a highly productive fishery of 'exceptional importance' to local people (Baran and Myschowoda, 2009: 227). Nutrient cycling and primary production are 'supporting ecosystem services', which are vital for the whole ecosystem functioning. Particular parts of the Tonle Sap ecosystem provide regulatory services beneficial for people. For example, a floodplain inundated forest helps regulate erosion and offers anchoring sites for floating villages. The forest also provides refuges, habitats and spawning sites for different fish species. People catch fish and collect non-timber forest products for food, medicines, and practical materials. Thus, the lives of *neak tonle* are closely tied to the functioning of various ecosystem services that are in turn affected by the annual flood pulse. In turn, the Tonle Sap supports livelihoods based on access to aquatic resources, fishing, and fishing-farming activities, and with few alternative forms of livelihood available, the lake is a large space of dependence for the *neak tonle*.

Within this waterscape there are distinctions between what we term 'aquatic', 'floodplain' and 'terrestrial' dimensions of the ecosystem. What is considered 'terrestrial' and what is 'aquatic' often depend on the timing of the flood pulse and geographical position in the lake and floodplain. The Mekong River Commission (2010: 12) utilizing numerous ecological and biodiversity surveys, identified '8 major sub-ecosystems: the permanent water body or Great Lake itself, rivers and streams, seasonally inundated shrublands, seasonally inundated grasslands, receding and floating rice-fields, seasonally flooded crop fields, and marshes and swamps'. These sub-ecosystems influence types of settlement and the life-worlds of the *neak tonle* in important ways. For instance, in seasonally inundated floodplain areas there are high-stilt villages which are vulnerable to very high water-levels in the monsoon period (late June to early October) and very-low water levels in the dry season (especially from February to June). Clearly these water-levels have significant impacts for livelihoods based upon access to fisheries, aquatic resources, and some farming. Totally 'terrestrial' areas, which flood a little in the wet season but are mostly landed communities, are not technically *neak tonle* except that in Cambodian rural society, villagers will still seek out fish in their rice paddies and ponds, and fishing supplements agriculture in so many ways. On the edges of the Tonle Sap are numerous 'floating villages' which are on water the whole year round, and they are somewhat mobile (vertically and laterally according to water-levels). These 'floating lives' are almost totally dependent on aquatic resources most of the year round, and they have adapted unique indigenous adaptations to their water world. There are also stilt-house villages, which have very distinctive dry and wet season ways of life. Whilst these villages do have access to land, the landscape literally becomes a waterscape during the wet season, thus livelihood adaptations to land and water are seasonally linked.

Typology of villages

There are six provinces around the lake, namely Kampong Chhnang, Pursat, Battambang, Banteay Meanchey, Siem Reap and Kampong Thom (see Figure 8.3), covering 60707 km^2. The Tonle Sap Lake is home to approximately four million people (Keskinen, 2003; NIS, 2008). Of the total population, about 1.4 million people live in the Tonle Sap floodplain between the National Road No. 5 and No. 6 in 1,158 villages within 160 communes (Sithirith, 2011; CNMC & NEDECO, 1998; Keskinen, 2003; Keskinen, 2006). Figure 8.3 distinguishes between what we term 'water-based', 'water-land-based' and 'land-based' villages. Put simply, settlement types reflect different indigenous adaptations to conditions in and around the lake. 'Water-based' villages are literally those that are on water the whole year around, and these villages have very little access to land, if at all. They also are somewhat mobile, although the degree of mobility they have is often restricted by administrative boundaries, environmental conditions, and neighboring community boundaries. 'Water-land-based' villages are built on the land, but usually with high stilts, so that when the areal extent of the Tonle Sap widens and water levels rise, these villages become literally water-based for several months, although they do not alter location. Finally, 'land-based' villages represent the majority of villages in the Lower Mekong Basin, and around the lake, which are typical farming-

Province	Water-based village	Water-land based village	Land-based village	Total
Battambang	10	2	117	129
Siem Reap	12	14	269	295
Kampong Thom	10	0	109	119
Kampong Chhnang	6	16	63	85
Pursat	15	1	238	254
Banteay Meanchey	0	3	152	155
Total	53	36	948	1037

Source: Sithirith, 2011

Figure 8.3 Typology of fishing villages by province in the Tonle Sap

fishing villages, whereby their livelihoods are certainly linked to and affected by seasonal changes and the flood-pulse, but these villages own and/or have access to land for rice cultivation and agriculture, and the primary occupation is often farming. Whilst these villages also experience annual flooding and fish are still very important as a form of revenue and component of the diets of people living there, for the purposes of this chapter we focus more on the *neak tonle* lives in the floating villages and land-water-based villages.

As noted earlier, people living around the lake have adapted to the natural ecosystem, hydrology, and developed their own human systems to use resources, improving their skills in fishing and processing of fish. Their cultural and social lives are uniquely and tightly reliant on fishing and on other resources the Tonle Sap provides, including uniquely adapted vegetation, aquatic plants and animals in the annually inundated forests, shrub-lands and grasslands around the lake proper (Campbell *et al.*, 2006). In the Lower Mekong Basin, inland wild capture fisheries have been estimated to generate a catch of 2.5 million tonnes of fish annually and an estimated economic value of US$1.4 to 1.9 billion (Van Zalinge *et al.*, 2004), and in the Tonle Sap there is an estimated annual catch of between 180,000 – 250,000 tonnes (Campbell *et al.*, 2006). The exceptional value of fisheries is linked to commercial fisheries, but there also exist a wide diversity of wetlands and farming-fishing cultures in the Lower Mekong, with fish being vital to the food security of the *neak tonle*.

In late October, communities around the lake eagerly anticipate the end of the floods and the beginning of a new cycle. At the height of the wet season, water covers half to two-thirds of the trees in the 'flooded forest'. Houses and huts are built on stilts; some as high as six meters, forming human-made island homes connected only by boats. So in the dry season when there is no water, these houses present an amazing sight as they are raised high up and need ladders to reach the houses. During the flood though, the water almost reaches even the highest houses' top doorsteps, and people require boats to navigate the waterways. Pagodas, schools and government buildings must be built in areas where there is dry land and during the floods these often provide the only refuge from high water levels.

Floating houses and shops made of bamboo, some with tiny aquaculture pens underneath floating homes. Such floating houses are located on water and move along the shoreline according to the water level. People living within floating houses literally move up and down according to the annual flood- pulse, and in some areas like in Kampong Loung in Pursat and Chong Kneas in Siem Reap Province, people move their houses at least 20 times per year in order to adjust to the water level fluctuations. Moving houses not only costs money but sometimes cause environmental damage as people obtain building materials from the flooded forest (CNMC and NEDECO, 1998). The *neak tonle* in floating villages have thus adapted their whole lifestyle according to hydrological and ecological processes, which represents a fascinating study in indigenous ways of living in wetland environments.

Floating villages and the complex political spaces of the lake

Many of these floating people are relatively poor. Marginalization is partly related to their relative lack of official recognition, because for some floating villages are not even included on official maps of the Tonle Sap settlements. Floating communities often have no sense of real 'ownership' over water space, although as communities they do have their own sense of 'communal space', but as they definitely have no legal property rights over land-based resources, access to water-space is absolutely critical to their cultural and livelihood survival. Floating communities have also been part of the Tonle Sap 'waterscape' for many generations, which means that they are deeply embedded communities in the rich cultural landscape of Cambodia as a whole. Nevertheless, as our research indicates, many of these floating communities lie at the razor's edge of cultural and economic survival within a rapidly transforming national economy and highly competitive fishery sector. Thus, empirical research is needed to better appreciate the lives and livelihoods of such communities, particularly as these people are the most dependent on fisheries, but the least represented in terms of fishery governance mechanisms and specialist knowledge(s) about the lake system.

In the Tonle Sap, there are two types of floating communities; first, some floating communities float vertically and move laterally as the water level of the lake rises up gradually; and second, however, some floating communities float up vertically, but do not move laterally. The rise and fall of waters in the Tonle Sap Lake between the wet and dry season induces the floating villages to move up and down in the lake. The mobility of the floating villages occurs within space that is often bounded or zones designated for other uses, such as fishing zones, fish sanctuaries, conservation areas and neighboring community fisheries. Thus, the floating village floats and moves, but this is not without restrictions, as they often have to define their own territorial space in accordance with other stakeholder zones. The unique forms of mobility, resource use and fishing practice adaptations, the design of homes and collective strategies they follow to ensure continued access to livelihood materials forms a very important component of my unfolding ideas about human-nature adaptations through human territoriality.

The lake space is an incredibly complex and hotly contested political space (Sithirith, 2011; Sithirithand& Grundy-Warr, 2011; Sithirith and Grundy-Warr, 2013). Superimposed on the waterscape are numerous limits and zones delineating areas for conservation, biosphere reserves, fishery lots, and community based resource management. To illustrate an aspect of this complex political territoriality we would like to focus on one floating village called Anlong Raing. Figure 8.3 reveals the location of this village in Pursat province, and how the whole village uses local creeks to move according to water-levels. In May, which is near the height of the dry season, water-levels are very low and the village locates near to an island in the lake proper. As water-levels rise, the village moves up a natural creek within an area of inundated forest, and is actually quite far inside the flooded forest zone by the end of the wet season in October.

Anlong Raing's human-nature relations have evolved over decades, but adaptive responses are additionally affected by more contemporary political economic changes and political geographies relating to state inspired alterations in lake governance for fishing revenues since the French colonial power introduced commercial fishing lots in the early 20th century (Degen *et al.*, 2000). Figure 8.3 shows a fishing conservation zone which limits the space of community fishery, and it also shows previous areas where privatised fishing lots prevailed. In the recent past there were numerous conflicts over fisheries in this area, and the privately auctioned fishing lots controlled by powerful absentee owners and guarded by armed security personnel, considerably restricted where the *neak tonle* from Anlong Raing could and could not fish. Frequently, villagers would complain about the bamboo and net fencing that were erected in the lake as a form of fishing lot boundary, preventing fish from entering into the spaces open to smaller scale fishing activity.

Some floating communities float, but they do not alter locations. For example, the floating villages of Peam Bang Commune used to be surrounded by a fishing lot. Peam Bang is subject to seasonal up and down

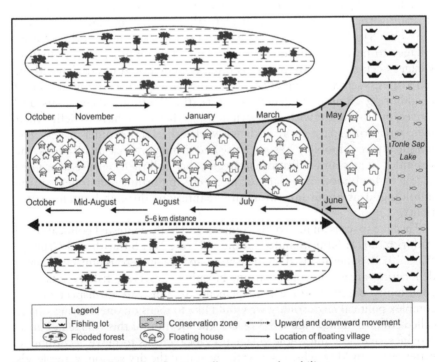

Figure 8.4 Diagram showing floating village seasonal mobility

vertical movement, but the houses remain within relatively fixed positions. The floating villages in Peam Bang float on water the year round, but the 'floating space' of these villages is unlike the other floating villages in the Tonle Sap, such as Anlong Raing and Kampong Luong. The 'floating space' of these villages was zone-locked by the existence of the 'fishing lots' and the 'Biosphere Reserves'. Thus, there existed little opportunity for the boat houses of Peam Bang to move laterally and plenty of scope for incursions, transgressions and poaching into their community space. The boundaries of the floating villages used to be demarcated in some areas by fishing lot boundaries placed in the water. The fishing lot owners erected bamboo fences around their fishing lot areas. During the open fishing season, from October to May, the fishing lot owners built fences around their fishing lots to protect property and maximize catches within the lot. Bamboo fences around the lots effectively create a large pen to catch fish. In this way, the territoriality generated conflicts between the *neak tonle* and commercial operators. Similarly, there are problems of encroachment by *neak tonle* from Peam Bang and neighboring areas into the designated Biosphere Reserve, which is further indication that the spatial organization of the lake is not necessarily effective in terms of managing either fisheries or biodiversity conservation needs.

Numerous privatized lots covered most of the most productive fishing areas of the lake, and by 2001 they accounted for about 60 per cent of the total fish catch of the Tonle Sap (Van Zalinge *et al.*, 2000). Since 2001, the State has encouraged the formation of Community Fishery zones within the lake; however, until recently, there were several instances of disputed borders between 'community' and 'fishing lot' areas. By leasing access to fish in the lots at certain times, the key beneficiaries were larger-scale fishers who could afford to pay rents to fish in these restricted access zones.

More recently, the Cambodian State has reviewed the threat of declining fisheries in the Tonle Sap, and in August 2011 Prime Minister Hun Sen announced the revoking of operational licenses from all 35 fishing lots in the Tonle Sap following widespread reports of use of illegal fishing traps (Ana, 2011). The implications of this for possible extensions of community fisheries are uncertain due to the continuing influence of the lot owners, complex webs of patrons and clients interfering with the implementation of fishery laws, and a lack of effective accountability within fishery governance at various scales (Un, 2011; Sithirith, 2014). Recent evidence from Anlong Raing suggests that the former fishing lots are now being fully utilized by the *neak tonle* albeit in competition with fishers moving in from neighboring zones and villages (Authors' fieldwork, September 2014). Furthermore, illegal fishing and commercial fishers still encroach into the spaces of dependence relied upon by the mostly smaller scale fishers of Anlong Raing, and there is growing pressure upon fisheries. At the scale of the lake fisheries, there remain numerous resource and boundary conflicts, which only add to the worries that the *neak tonle* have over their livelihood futures.

In other words, we should consider how both complex forms of 'territory' affect issues of access to common property resources, and how community-level institutions are nested within broader political-legal frameworks. It may be that we cannot conceive of the environmental and aquatic resources of the Tonle Sap without incorporating forms of bordering in an age when practically all the 'bundles of rights' associated with common property are territorialized (Peluso, 2005). However, the case of the *neak tonle* also reveals that socio-spatial relations in the Tonle Sap are inseparable from the rhythms and cycles of the 'pulsing ecosystem' (Junk, 1997) associated with the annual flood pulse (Lamberts, 2006). The vernacular cultural waterscape of the *neak tonle* may be entirely unique to the Tonle Sap, but the bio-physical processes, fish migrations, and ecosystem services are entirely trans-border in scope.

Institutional change and challenges

During the last decade a complex institutional governance structure has been emerging. These institutions include the Tonle Sap Biosphere Reserve (TSBR), which was established in 2001 mostly to strengthen coordination over the protection and sustainable management of the core conservation biosphere areas of the Tonle Sap under a Secretariat within the Ministry of Environment under the Cambodian National Mekong Committee. For a while another key institutional initiative was the Tonle Sap Basin Management Organization (TSBMO) set up by the Asian Development Bank to tackle socio-economic issues and environmental problems of the Basin (ADB, 2005). Finally, a Royal Decree in September 2007 established the Tonle Sap Basin Authority (TSBA) 'for coordination of management, conservation and development of the Tonle Sap Basin areas' (RGC, 2007: 1), which has at once made the State ministries and Government supreme in Basin affairs over and above 'external' bodies, such as the ADB, international NGOs and IOs with biodiversity and conservation interests, such as WWF and IUCN. The TSBA is also meant to coordinate the roles of relevant ministries, including the increasingly important Ministry of Water Resources and Meteorology, the Ministry of Agriculture, Forestry and Fisheries (including the Fisheries Administration), and the Ministry of Environment (Dore and Lebel, 2010; Kestinen and Sithirith, 2010; Kestinen and Varis, 2012).

Within the Tonle Sap Basin there already exists an institutional framework for addressing in complex hydrological, environmental and developmental problems. However, various observers have argued that even within the overarching TSBA, the institutional setting in the Tonle Sap remains sector based and overlapping, 'with different actors promoting their own agendas and interests, often at the expense of others' (Kestinen and Varis, 2012: 57). Whilst this Basin-wide institutional structure offers plenty of scope for both top-down and more 'organic' bottom-up approaches to be coordinated (Middleton and Tola, 2008), there is a strong tendency for the higher levels of management to focus primarily on big developmental plans affecting the Tonle Sap, with little influence on the 'external', 'trans-border' scale (such as hydropower projects on the Mekong River) and leaving micro-management to sub-provincial levels of organization.

All of this suggests that there is an institutional and policy mindset disconnect between Tonle Sap Basin and the rest of the Mekong Basin, and between *Basin-scales* and the composite *multiple localities* of the majority of the *neak phum* (village people), particularly *neak tonle*. Whilst some scholars discuss the need for a broadening of the 'spaces of engagement' for *neak tonle* (Sithirith, 2011), and for 'knowledge partnerships' incorporating diverse specialist knowledge and indigenous knowledge (Middleton and Tola, 2008), the current institutional arrangements seem to be encouraging centralized State and international organizational control over major developmental changes, leaving 'lower order' localized conflicts over management of space and resources to provincial level and sub-provincial authorities.

At multiple locality scales, particularly within the floodplain and lake area proper, there have also been institutional changes that are transforming the resource governance for *neak tonle* communities. Since 2001, the State has encouraged the development of Community Fisheries, which was formalized by the Sub-Decree on Community Fisheries Management in June 2005, permitting all Cambodian citizens the right to create Community Fisheries in their local areas on a voluntary basis. ADB loans also supported the development of 'over 160' Community Fishery Organizations (CFOs) in zones around the Tonle Sap Biosphere Reserve. Whilst the number of CFOs is growing, the evidence is patchy in terms of tackling fundamental issues of resource governance. Problems of illegal fishing (using very fine mesh nets, electric fishing, use of poisons, and encroaching conservation zones) still exist in many areas. Examples of relatively tight coordination do exist between local authorities, fisheries department officials, communes and CFO committees, but there are equally numerous cases where cooperation has been hindered by petty corruption, rivalries, lack of accountability, capacity and enforcement (Un, 2011). Similarly, the 'opening' of previously closed commercial fishing lots to many fishers does not necessarily mean a broadening scope for CFOs, for there are more areas of relatively unregulated open access that may be exploited more easily by capital intensive fishing operators (IUCN, March 2012). According to Sithirith (2011) only greater inter-CFO coordination and inter-CFO partnerships with relevant NGOs and authorities can generate conditions for more grounded resource governance approaches to emerge, which as Un (2011) has argued, would require much greater accountability, financial and technical support, as well as genuinely open alliances between CFOs, local authorities and relevant fishery officials.

The dragon apparent: hydro-power and the future socio-environmental security for the neak tonle

Hydropower dams have become the major 'drivers' of development in the Mekong region (Grumbine, Dore and Xu, 2012). However, major dams built on the mainstream and tributaries of the Mekong have raised concerns about trade-offs between hydropower led development and issues of food, livelihood and environmental security for communities who still rely a lot on wild capture fisheries, such as the *neak tonle* of the Tonle Sap. The total potential for feasible hydropower projects in the four Lower Mekong Basin countries is approximately 30,000 MW including 13,000 MW on the Mekong's mainstream, and the remaining tributaries' potential (13,000 MW in Lao PDR's tributaries, 2,200 MW in Cambodia and 2,000 MW in Vietnam) (ICEM, 2010).

Since the 1950s, nearly 6,000 large and small dams have been built in the Lower Mekong (FACT and EJF, 2001). Between 1965 and 2005, 22 major dams, both hydropower and irrigation were constructed in four Mekong countries; Thailand, Laos, Vietnam and China. About 40 per cent of these dams were built for irrigation and the rest for hydropower. The active storage capacity of these dams was estimated at about 15,328 mcm. At Kratie on the Mekong in Cambodia, the average annual flow is estimated to be 440,000 mcm/year. The total storage of dams in the Mekong is about 3.5 per cent of the average annual flow of the Mekong at Kratie.

China has moved forward with its own dams on the upper part of the river (called the Lancang) without consulting its downstream neighbors or sharing data about water flows. China has built six dams in the Mekong mainstream in China (Arias *et al.*, 2014). So far, the completed Lancang dams include the Dachaoshan (2003), Manwan (2007), Jinghong (2009), Xiaowan (2010), and Nuozhadu (2012). There is evidence that Chinese dams are changing the Lower Mekong River's natural flood-drought cycle, disruptions to floodplain habitats and their contribution to aquatic primary production, and fluctuations in the timing and amount of water, sediments, and nutrients that flow into the river basin and surrounding coastal areas that are affected by hydropower dam operations (Arias *et al.*, 2014). Scientists have yet to fully study the cumulative impacts of these dams, although useful modeling tools are being developed that reveal likely alterations to the annual flood pulse and its implications for the Lower Mekong Basin (Arias *et al.*, 2012, 2013; Kummu and Sarkkula, 2008; Baran and Myschowoda, 2009). One of the key limitations of environmental impact assessments commissioned for some of the existing and ongoing hydropower projects is that they have focused only on direct upstream and downstream impacts but not on the basin-wide implications, which are critical for assessing different future scenarios confronting the Tonle Sap Basin (Poff and Zimmerman, 2010; Arias *et al.*, 2014).

In the Lower Mekong Basin, 12 hydropower dams have been proposed in the mainstream of the Lower Mekong River that would displace 100,000 people, and 2.1 million others would be at risk of indirect negative impacts. Dams would turn more than half of the length of the main river into reservoir characterized by slow-moving water conditions, thereby increasing the risk of water-borne diseases (Grumbine, Dore and Xu, 2012). In November 2012, Laos and Thailand held a groundbreaking ceremony for the controversial Xayaburi Dam, which is largely financed by Thai banks and being constructed by a Thai company (Middleton, 2011). In fact, Laos and Thailand have been implementing the project since 2010, despite ongoing concerns from Cambodia and Vietnam about the dam's trans-boundary impacts. Recently in mid-2013, Laos announced the plan to move forward with implementation of the Don Sahong Dam near the Cambodian border, and it seems that Laos is determined to go ahead regardless of much international criticism (Baran and Ratner, 2007; Baird, 2011; International Rivers, n.d.). There is considerable concern about the impacts these dams will have on cross-border fish migrations in the Lower Mekong, including the Tonle Sap which has large numbers of long-distance white fish migratory species (Campbell *et al.*, 2006; Baran and Ratner, 2007; Baran and Myschowoda, 2009; Baird, 2011). According to Baran and Myschowoda (2009) there are already strong indications that ongoing hydropower projects are having adverse impacts on ecological inter-connectivity and alter natural 'hydrological triggers' for fish migrations. Any blurring of the timing and duration of the flood pulse is going to have major ecological, social, economic and environmental implications for the farmer-fishers of the Lower Mekong Basin and all of the *neak tonle* of the tributary rivers and Tonle Sap. All these exogenous hydro-ecological changes are taking place at a time when there are increasing pressures on the Tonle Sap fisheries and ecosystem from the intensification of agriculture and built infrastructures in the lake basin (Baran, Starr and Kura, 2007).

Other huge changes are also occurring in the 3S basin (Sesan, Srepok and Sekong Rivers on the borders of Vietnam, Laos and Cambodia); the second largest tributary of the Mekong, covering about 78,650 km^2 and home to about 2.5 million people, mostly ethnic groups; 42 dams are built and being built. Vietnam has built 13 dams and plans more dams on the Sesan and Srepok; Laos has built one dam on Sekong; five other dams are under construction, and 15 dams have been proposed, and Cambodia is building the Lower Sesan 2 dam and has planned to build another 6 dams (Arias *et al.*, 2014; MRC, 2003; Piman *et al.*, 2013). The continued dam building on the Mekong and its tributaries induces conflicts and a 'non-traditional security' situation, characterized by severe food shortages, the destruction of livelihoods and large, irregular movements of people, affecting livelihood security of communities living along the rivers (Baker, 2012). In addition, most private hydropower investors invested in the Mekong have limited commitment to environmental and livelihood security in areas distant from the projects (such as the Tonle Sap), and most of the energy produced is for export or to supply industry and predominantly urban areas in the region. Future changes to flood pulse hydrology, sediment load, water quality and fish migration patterns are going to affect human and environmental security of wetlands, floodplains, and impact negatively on the life worlds of the *neak tonle*.

Climate change, vulnerability and adaptation

In Cambodia, climate change is about any long term change in which sometimes in the year it will be too hot and too dry, causing drought and sometimes too much rain leading to unusual flooding events. As noted in this chapter, the annual floods are not really considered 'flooding' events by the *neak* tonle, and the flood pulse helps to regulate fishery migrations, brings much needed sediment, and is critical to flora and fauna, as well as socio-ecological adaptations over a long period of time (Arias *et al.*, 2013; Baran and Myschowoda, 2009; Campbell *et al.*, 2006; Lamberts, 2006; Nikula, 2008). However, a part from the flood pulse, in recent years, there are more frequent and severe floods and droughts, which have resulted in a significant number of fatalities and considerable economic losses (Ministry of Environment (MOE), 2006). Successions and combinations of droughts and floods have resulted in a significant number of fatalities and considerable economic losses. Losses arising from floods have been further exacerbated by deforestation. Floods have accounted for 70 per cent of rice production losses between 1998 and 2002, while drought accounted for 20 per cent of losses (MOE, 2006). For the Tonle Sap climate change could have major consequences on hydrology and water resources, agriculture and food security, terrestrial and freshwater ecosystems, coastal zones and marine ecosystems, and human health. Adverse impacts include increased flood and drought magnitude. As an agrarian country highly dependent on rice and fish culture, Cambodia is highly vulnerable to the impacts of climate change (NIS, 2008). Already facing considerable exogenous and internal changes in water and land-use, which are beginning to impact on inland fishery productivity and ecosystem services, long-term climate change will undoubtedly have the severest impacts on people whose rural livelihoods are still highly dependent on the terrestrial-aquatic resources (MOE and UNDP, 2011).

Provinces around the Tonle Sap are vulnerable to the flood and drought (MOE, 2006). Over a period of 18 years between 1984 and 2000, floods occurred 10 times, almost one every two years. However, after 2000, floods occurred almost every year (NCDM, 2002; MOE, 2006; UNDMT, 2007). Over this period (1982-2000), there were three times of severe floods in 1984, 1996 and 2000. Floods in Cambodia in 2000 were reportedly the worst in more than 70 years, but the flood in 2011 was even worse (UN News Centre, 2011). Such floods need to be distinguished from the annual flood pulse, which the *neak tonle* see as natural and seasonal rising and falling waters. Severe floods have resulted in a high number of casualties and destruction of infrastructures. The most severe floods, which occurred in 2000, killed some 350 people and caused US$150 million in damages to crops and infrastructures (NCDM, 2002). The worst flooding in a decade in September and October 2011 made Cambodia lose 10 per cent of their rice crops (UN News Centre, 2011). The most severe drought, which subsequently occurred in 2002, affected more than 2 million people and destroyed more than 100,000 ha of paddy fields. Floods have accounted for 70 per cent of rice production losses between 1998 and 2002, while drought accounted for 20per cent of losses (MOE, 2006).

About 270 communes out of 1,621 communes in Cambodia are prone to drought and 260 communes are prone to floods. The frequency and intensity of floods may increase with changing climate conditions, and cause severe damage to rice harvests. Seasonal floods occur along the Mekong River and the Tonle Sap Lake during the monsoon season from July to October (MOP/WFP, 2003). Communes around the Tonle Sap Lake and along the Mekong River, particularly in the southern provinces along the Cambodian-Vietnamese border, are the most vulnerable to flood (UNDMT, 2007). About 28 communes around the Tonle Sap are prone to the drought and other 92 communes are prone to unusual flooding events.

Neak tonle communities in the Tonle Sap have a high resilient capacity to the hydrological changes in the Tonle Sap. The adaptive capacity of communities in the Tonle Sap varies significantly, depending on the community type. The water-based community or the floating community has a high adaptive capacity to the change in the hydrology of the lake for they have developed rafted and floating housing that can move up and down as waters rise and fall. However, peak floods may make fishing difficult for small-fishers as they use small-scale fishing gears that are not suitable to fish in the deeper water. The higher water level, the longer flood duration and expanded flood areas will have serious impacts on small-fishers. Too much rain over a longer period will cause fishing difficulties and affect household food security for many *neak tonle*. Prolonged dry seasons will induce water pollution in a shallower lake, which is already subject to large amounts of chemicals from increasing agribusiness, pesticide use, household detergents, and effluent from humans and livestock in the lake communities. Thus, climate change is likely to feed sanitation problems, water-related diseases, and public health problems around the Tonle Sap.

Conclusion

During our fieldwork in one of the floating villages, a boy of 10 years took us in a boat from house to house, during the day he had to mend the engine, and later pick up his younger sister from a floating school. The girl, aged 8 years, later was seen rowing a smaller boat to meet some friends on the other side of the waterway. Earlier in the day, brother and sister helped their mother mend a fishing-net, and skin and dry some water snakes. Undoubtedly, these children were well versed in life-skills necessary to survive in a water world. When asked what he most wanted, the boy said some dry land to play football on with some of his friends, so floating life is far from idyllic! When we had finished our fieldwork we returned to Phnom Penh, which although close in terms of distance, seems a universe away from the water worlds of the Tonle Sap, with its rapid urban transformations and quick pace of life. Many urban-dwellers who have not migrated from around the Tonle Sap are quite remote from the lake and its environs in spite of the many resources and services it provides to their lives. Most of the freshwater fish, the *prahoc* (much loved fish-paste), and aquatic resources enjoyed by people in Phnom Penh come from the Tonle Sap. There are multiple daily flows that connect these seemingly detached life-worlds.

This chapter has focused on major human-induced transformations that are generating internal and exogenous threats social and ecological security of the lake and its inhabitants. Elsewhere the authors have argued that it is increasingly imperative to examine 'volumes, flows and fluidity across time and space' (Grundy-Warr, Sithirith and Yong, 2015), and to pay deep attention to vital human and physical interconnections of pulsing ecosystems that underlie social, livelihood and ecological security at multiple scales. In reality the lives of the *neak tonle* are intimately linked to socio-economic transformations throughout the Mekong Basin, particularly the urban centers, such as Phnom Penh. Once socio-ecological connections of the Tonle Sap are permanently disturbed and there is an unrecoverable loss of ecosystem services, massive livelihood and food insecurity are likely to adversely affect not only indigenous *neak tonle* but the whole country and beyond. Concern over the future of 'floating lives' is thus also one for our own.

References

ADB (2005). *Cambodia: Establishment of the Tonle Sap Basin Management Organization*. Final Report, Technical Assistance Consultant's Report, Prepared By H. Milner, S. Carson, T. Sopharith, and U. Sokco. Cambodian National Mekong Committee, The Asian Development Bank (ADB), Phnom Penh.

Ana, Phann (2011). 'Hun Sen establishes protected zone for Tonle Sap Floodplains'. *Cambodia Daily*, August 17, 2011, www.cambodiadaily.com/date/2011/08/ (accessed 25 March 2015).

Arias, M., Piman, T., Lauri, H., Cochrane, T., Kummu, M. (2014). 'Dams on Mekong tributaries as significant contributors of hydrological alterations to the Tonle Sap Floodplain in Cambodia'. *Hydrology and Earth System Sciences Discussions*, 11(2), 2177–2209.

Arias, M., Cochrane, T., Norton, D., Killeen, T., Khon, P. (2013). 'The flood pulse as the underlying driver of vegetation in the largest wetland and fishery of the Mekong Basin'. *AMBIO*, 42, 864–876.

Arias, M., Cochrane, T., Kummu, M., Killeen, T., Piman, T., Caruso, B. (2012). 'Quantifying changes in flooding and habitats in the Tonle Sap Lake (Cambodia) caused by water infrastructure development and climate change'. *Journal of Environmental Management*, 112, 53–66.

Asia Forest Network (AFN) 2004. *Flooded Forests, Fish and Fishing Villages, Tonle Sap, Cambodia*. Bohol: AFN Philippines.

Baird, I. (2011). 'The Don Sahong dam'. *Critical Asian Studies, 43*(2), 211–235.

Baker, C.G. (2012). *Dams, Power and Security in the Mekong: A Non-Traditional Security Assessment of Hydro-Development in the Mekong River Basin.* NTS-Asia Research Paper (8), Singapore: Consortium of Non-Traditional Security Studies in Asia (NTS-Asia), S. Rajaratnam School of International Studies (RSIS), Nanyang Technological University (NTU).

Baran, E. and Myschowoda, C. (2009). 'Dams and fisheries in the Mekong Basin'. *Aquatic Ecosystem Health and Management, 12*(3): 227–234.

Baran, E. and Ratner, B. (2007). 'The Don Sahong dam and Mekong fisheries'. *A Science Brief.* Phnom Penh: World Fish Center.

Baran, E., Starr, P. and Kura, Y. (2007). *Influence of Built Infrastructures on Tonle Sap Fisheries.* Phnom Penh: Cambodia National Mekong Committee and World Fish Center.

Berkes, F. (2012). *Sacred Ecology.* New York and London: Routledge.

CNMC (Cambodian National Mekong Committee) and Nedeco, 1998. *Natural Resource-Based Development Strategy for the Tonle Sap Area.* Cambodia. Final Report Volume 2, Part B: Sectoral Studies. Phnom Penh: MRC/UNDP.

Campbell, I., Poole, C., Giesen, W. and Valbo-Jorgensen, J. (2006). 'Species diversity and ecology of Tonle Sap Great Lake, Cambodia'. *Journal of Aquatic Science, 68*(3), 55–373.

Costa-Cabral, M.C., Richey, J.E., Goteti, G., Lettenmaier, D.P., Christoph Feldkotter, C. and Snidvongs, A. (2007). 'Landscape structure and use, climate, and water movement in the Mekong River Basin'. *Hydrological Process, 22,* 1731–1746.

Degen, P., Van Acker, F., Van Zalinge, N., Thouk, N. and Vuthy, L. (2000). *Taken for Granted: Conflict over Cambodia's Freshwater Fisheries Resources.* Written for the 8th IASCP Conference, Bloomington, Indiana, 31 May to 4 June, 2000. Phnom Penh: MRC, DoF and University of Antwerp, Belgium.

Dore, J. and Lebel, L. (2010). 'Deliberation and scale in Mekong Region water governance'. *Environmental Management, 46*(1): 60–80.

FACT, EJF (2001). *Feast or Famine? Solutions for Cambodia's fisheries conflicts.* London, UK.

Grumbine, E.R., Dore, J. and Xu, J. (2012). 'Mekong hydropower: Drivers of change and governance challenges'. *Frontiers in Ecology and Environment, 10*(2): 91–98.

Grundy-Warr, C., Sithirith, M. and Yong, M.L. (2015). 'Volumes, fluidity and flows: Rethinking the 'nature' of political geography'. Editorial, *Political Geography, 45,* 93–95.

International Center for Environmental Management (ICEM) (2010). *Strategic Environmental Assessment of Hydropower on the Mekong Mainstream. Summary of the Final Report,* prepared for the Mekong River Commission (MRC), Victoria, Australia: ICEM, October, 2010.

International Rivers (IR) (n.d.). www.internationalrivers.org/files/attached-files/ don_sahong_briefing_sheet_2.7.14.pdf (accessed 14 November 2014).

International Union of Conservation of Nature (IUCN) (2012) *Reference details to follow.*

Junk, W. (1997). 'The Central Amazon Floodplain: Ecology of a pulsing system'. *Ecological Studies, 126.* Springer Verlag: Heidelberg.

Keskinen, M. and Varis, O. (2012). 'Institutional cooperation at a Basin Level: For what, by whom? Lessons learned from Cambodia's Tonle Sap Lake'. *Nat. Res. Forum, 36,* 50–60.

Keskinen, M. and Sithirith, M. (2010). *Tonle Sap Lake and Its Management: The Diversity of Perspectives & Institutions.* Chiang Mai: M-Power.

Keskinen, M. (2006). 'The lake with floating villages: Socioeconomic analysis of the Tonle Sap Lake'. *Journal of Water Resources Development,* 22(3), 463–480.

Keskinen, M. (2003). *Socio-Economic Survey of the Tonle Sap Lake, Cambodia.* Master's Thesis. Helsinki University of Technology.

Kummu, M. and Sarkkula, J. (2008). 'Impact of the Mekong River flow alteration on the Tonle Sap flood pulse'. *Journal of Human Environment,* 37(3), 185–192.

Lamberts, D. (2008). 'Little impact, much damage: The consequences of Mekong River flow alterations for the Tonle Sap ecosystem'. In Kummu, M., Keskinen, M., Varis, O. (eds). *Modern Myths of the Mekong.* Helsinki University of Technology, 3–18.

Lamberts, D. (2006). 'The Tonle Sap Lake as a productive ecosystem'. *Water Resources Development,* 22(3): 481–495.

Mekong River Commission (MRC) (2010). *State of the Basin Report 2010.* Vientiane, Laos: MRC.

Mekong River Commission (MRC) (2002). *MRC Annual Report 2002. A Vision for the Mekong River Basin.* Vientiane: MRC.

Mekong River Commission (MRC) (2003). *State of the Basin Report. Executive Summary: Meeting the needs, keeping the balance.* Phnom Penh, Cambodia: MRC.

Middleton, C. (2011). 'Conflict, cooperation and the trans-border commons: The controversy of mainstream dams on the Mekong River'. The 3rd International Winter Symposium of the Global COE Program 'Reshaping Japan's Border Studies: Weaving the Borders Together-Network between Japan and the World', November 25–27, 2011, Slavic Research Center, Hokkaido University, Sapporo, Japan.

Middleton, C. and Tola, P. (2008). 'Community organizations for managing water resources around Tonle Sap Lake: A myth or reality?' In Kummu, M., Keskinen, M., Varis, O. (eds) *Modern Myths of the Mekong.* Helsinki University of Technology, 149–159.

Ministry of Environment (2006). *National Adaptation Programme of Action to Climate Change (NAPA).* Phnom Penh: MOE, Royal Government of Cambodia.

Ministry of Environment, UNDP (2011). *Building Resilience: The Future of Rural Livelihoods in the Face of Climate Change.* Phnom Penh: MOE, Royal Government of Cambodia.

Ministry of Planning (MOP), UN World Food Programme (WFP) (2003). *Poverty and Vulnerability Analysis Mapping in Cambodia,* Phnom Penh: MOP, Royal Government of Cambodia.

National Committee for Disaster Management (NCDM) (2002). *Disaster Management in Cambodia.* National Committee on Disaster Management (NCDM), Phnom Penh.

National Institute of Statistics (NIS) (2008). *Provisional Population Totals of Census 2008. Ministry of Planning, Royal Government of Cambodia.* Available Online At: www.nis.gov.kh/statistics/surveys/census2008/provincialpopulation-totals. (accessed 22 November 2009).

Nikula, J. (2008). 'Is harm and destruction all that floods bring?' in Kummu, M., Keskinen, M., Varis, O. (eds). *Modern Myths of the Mekong.* Helsinki University of Technology, 27–38.

Nikula, J. (2005). *The Lake and its People.* MSc Thesis. Helsinki University of Technology, Finland.

Pech, S., Sunada, K., Oishi, S., Miyazawa, N. and Tanaka, D. (2008). 'Trends of fish resources in the Tonle Sap Basin: Their correlation with the hydrological conditions of the Mekong River'. *International Journal of River Basin Management*, 6(3), 277–282.

Peluso, Nancy L. (2005). 'From common property resources to territorializations: Resource management in the Twenty-First Century'. In P. Cuasay and C. Vaddhanaphuti (eds) *Commonplaces and Comparisons: Remarking Eco-Political Space in Southeast Asia*. Chiang Mai: Regional Center for Social Science and Sustainable Development (RCSD), Faculty of Social Science, Chiang Mai University, 1–9.

Piman, T., Cochrane, T., Arias, M., Green, A. and Dat, N.A. (2013). 'Assessment of flow changes from hydropower development and operations in Sekong, Sesan, and Srepok Rivers of the Mekong Basin'. *Journal of Water Resources Planning and Management*, 139(6), 723–732.

Piseth, C. (2002). *Contested Legitimating of Access to Fisheries: A Case Study of Everyday Practices among Fishers in the Tonle Sap Lake, Cambodia*. (Unpublished master's thesis.) Chiang Mai: Chiang Mai University.

Poff, N. and Zimmerman, J. (2010). 'Ecological responses to altered flow regimes: A literature review to inform science and management of environmental flows'. *Freshwater Biology*, 55, 194–205.

Poole, C. (2005). *Tonle Sap: The Heart of Cambodia's Natural Heritage*. Phnom Penh: Bangkok: River Books (Photographs by Eleanor Briggs).

Royal Government of Cambodia (RGC) (2001). *Royal Degree on the Establishment and Management of the Tonle Sap Biosphere Reserve*. Translation by Neou Bonheur, Available online at: www.tsbred.org/docs/law_and_regulation/Royal_ Decree_On_creation_and_managemet_of_tsbr_Eng.pdf (accessed 22 July 2008).

Sithirith, M. (2014). 'The patron–client system and its effect on resources management in Cambodia: A case in the Tonle Sap Lake'. *Asian Politics & Policy*, 6(4), 595–609.

Sithirith, M. (2011). *Political Geography of the Tonle Sap: Power, Space and Resources*. (Unpublished doctoral dissertation.) Singapore: National University of Singapore.

Sithirith, M. and Grundy-Warr, C. (2013). *Floating lives of the Tonle Sap*. Regional Center for Sustainable Development (RCSD), Chiang Mai University, Chiang Mai, Thailand.

Sithirith, M. and Grundy-Warr, C. (2011). 'Representations and contestations of space'. in C. Vaddanaputi and Amphorn Jirattikorn (eds). *Spatial Politics and Economic Development in the Mekong Sub-region*. Chiang Mai: Chiang Mai University, 144–189.

Sneddon, C. and Fox, C. (2006). 'Rethinking transboundary waters: A critical hydro-politics of the Mekong basin'. *Political Geography* 25(2), 181–202.

Sokhem, P. and Sunada, K. (2006). 'The Governance of the Tonle Sap Lake, Cambodia: Integration of Local, National and International Levels'. *International Journal of Water Resource Development*, 22(3), 399–416.

Starr, P. (2008). 'The Tonle Sap Authority takes shape'. *Catch & Culture*, Mekong River Commission, Vientiane, Laos, PDR, 14(3), 31–34.

Un, B. (2011). 'Impact of Cambodian decentralization policy in fishery management on human security of fishers around the Tonle Sap Lake'. *The 4th International Conference on Human Rights & Human Development. Critical Connections: Human Rights, Human Development and Human Security*. Bangkok: Chulalongkorn University.

UNDMT (2007). *Cambodia Disaster Preparedness and Response Plan 2007*. Phnom Penh: UN Disaster Management Team.

UN News Centre (4 November 2011). 'Cambodia: UN stepping up emergency response to severe floods', *UN News Centre*, www.un.org/apps/news/story.asp?NewsID=40310#.VRI_hfnF-NA (accessed 24 March 2015).

Van Zalinge, N., Degen, P., Pongsri, C., Nuov, S., Jensen, J. G., Van Hao, N. and Choulamany, X. (2004). *The Mekong River System*. Contribution to the Second International Symposium on the management of large rivers for fisheries Phnom Penh, 11–14 February 2003.

Van Zalinge, N., Nao, T., Touch, T. S. and Deap, L. (2000). 'Where there is water, there is fish? Cambodian fisheries issues in a Lower Mekong Basin perspective'. M. Ahmed and P. Hirsch (eds), *Common Property in the Mekong: Issues of Sustainability and Subsistence, ICLARM Studies and Reviews* 26, 36–67.

9 Long road to justice

Addressing indigenous land claims in Kenya

Darren Kew and Abra Lyman

Like many countries in Africa, land dispossession of indigenous peoples in Kenya began in the colonial era, but was expanded upon by post-independence governments seeking to solidify their national sovereignty and a state-based model of economic development. Indigenous attempts to seek redress through legal or political means have been systematically stymied by the state, until recently. After the inter-ethnic violence of the 2007 presidential elections, which was largely rooted in land disputes, Kenya adopted a new constitution, its first national land policy, and a series of land laws that provide a solid legal foundation through which indigenous rights could potentially be recognized and protected for the first time in the region. An examination of Maasai and Ogiek case studies illustrates how the conflict over land has persisted throughout Kenyan history, how the national and regional legal landscapes have changed over the past five years, and how this and similar conflicts across the region might thus be resolved in the future.

Introduction

The plight of indigenous peoples in Kenya is emblematic of the conflicts that indigenous peoples face across Africa. Although driven partly by widespread poverty and competition for control over finite resources, these disputes are tied to deeper issues of identity, cultural survival, and self-determination. Fundamentally, however, indigenous legal claims strike at the heart of the state system in Africa, questioning the fragile sovereignty that African governments have sought to build over the last fifty years. Consequently, every African government perceives a measure of common interest in quashing indigenous claims, and few of these claims are likely to be addressed unless a mutually acceptable solution is found. Unfortunately for indigenous communities, the balance of power has been tipped heavily in favor of governments, who can afford to allow the situation to fester.

The roots of Kenyan government intransigence run deep. When Kenya gained its independence in 1963, the new government made the same decision that nearly every other young African government made – namely, to work within the artificial colonial borders to consolidate its authority. The first prime minister of Ghana, Kwame Nkrumah, spearheaded the notion of a pan-African state, but the Charter of the Organization of African Unity (OAU) signed in 1963 pointedly accepted colonial borders and sovereignties, opting to solidify local controls and promising not to interfere in one another's internal affairs. Most of these governments soon saw their concern for internal consolidation drift into paranoia, leading to the collapse of the early democracies and the onset of a long authoritarian period into the 1990s. Internal opposition was barely tolerated, sparking civil wars in several states.

For most of this period, governments largely viewed dissenting indigenous peoples as internal opposition and a threat to the regime, to be dealt with accordingly. Although indigenous claims did not typically seek to remove regimes in power, they questioned the limits of the sovereignty of African states by supporting local control of resources and maintaining allegiance with tribal members across national borders. With many states already divided along ethnic lines, legal, political, or economic concessions to indigenous peoples were often viewed as a slippery slope, encouraging rival ethnic groups to secede. Unsurprisingly, neither the 1963 OAU Charter nor the 1981 African Charter on Human and Peoples' Rights make mention of indigenous peoples. By the time authoritarian governments collapsed across Africa in the 1990s and the early twenty-first century, many of the new democracies inherited these fears that any reduction in sovereignty could unravel the semi-stable, multiethnic arrangements built over the last half-century.[1]

As we discuss below, the experience of the Maasai and Ogiek in Kenya mirrors this historical shift across Africa from intolerance toward the promise of negotiated legal solutions that offer indigenous peoples greater self-determination without compromising state sovereignty. As Kenya underscores, however, this recent shift toward greater openness on the part of some African states is still tentative and requires further action to attain real security for indigenous communities as well as national security for the state.

Colonial dispossession

The Maasai

The Maasai are an indigenous pastoral tribe of the East African savannah, world-renowned for the maintenance of their traditional warrior culture. The semi-nomadic peoples occupied much of the Rift Valley region of Kenya and northern Tanzania when British colonialists first arrived in the late 19th century. Because Maasai subsistence traditionally depends solely on herding, and cattle are the central measure of Maasai wealth and power, control over grazing lands has always been of vital importance. Prior to colonialism, Maasai considered land inalienable, so that neither the individuals nor the community at large have the right to sell, rent or lease it.[2] Land was held communally under Maasai customary law, and individuals within the community were obligated to protect and manage it with limited rights to use all natural resources. After establishing Kenya as an East African Protectorate in 1895, the British implemented a policy of displacing indigenous communities from the most fertile areas of the Kenyan highlands for the benefit of European settlers. In 1904, the first Anglo-Maasai Agreement transferred the Maasai community from 500,000 acres of prime grazing land to a smaller northern reserve in Laikipia and a southern reserve along the Tanzanian border for 'as long as the Maasai as a race shall exist'.[3] Several years later, British authorities reneged on this agreement and forcibly relocated the northern Maasai from Laikipia into an already cramped and arid southern reserve per a newly negotiated 1911 Anglo-Maasai Agreement. Through these two moves, the Maasai lost up to 75 per cent of their traditional lands and were confined to an arid region infested with tsetse flies, drought, and disease, which killed off a large number of their youth and half of their livestock within the first several years.[4]

In 1913, representatives of the Maasai community became some of the first indigenous Kenyans to challenge the British in court when they filed suit against the Attorney General of the British East African Protectorate for breaking the 1904 Anglo-Maasai Agreement. The community sought full restitution of Laikipia, compensation for their losses, and a determination that the 1911 Agreement was invalid due to fraud and duress. Among other claims, the elders argued that the leases were invalid because the Maasai signatory to the lease was not a traditional Maasai leader and did not have authority from the community to represent their interests. The case was dismissed and appealed to the East African Appeals Court, where it was also dismissed without reaching the merits of the Maasai claims. Instead the Court stated that the leases were international treaties between two sovereign states, and therefore outside the local court's jurisdiction.[5] The irony behind this decision was clear to all involved: the colonizer obstructs the colonized from seeking its sole legal remedy in regaining its appropriated land by labeling them a sovereign state. The only jurisdiction in which to appeal this decision was the British Privy Council in England, but the Maasai were unable to raise the necessary funding to bring the case to Europe.

The Anglo-Maasai Agreements have had long lasting repercussions on the Maasai community. Marginalized on arid reserves far from urban centers, the community has become increasingly impoverished and underdeveloped on overgrazed, drought-prone lands that are less and less able to sustain a growing population of pastoralists. Yet one hundred years after the original Anglo-Maasai agreements were signed, the Kenyan government refused to honor the end of this contract in 2004, dismissing indigenous claims with an arbitrary proclamation that the Anglo-Maasai lease officially terminates after 999 rather than 99 years.[6]

The Ogiek

Another indigenous community that remains dispossessed by the Anglo-Maasai leases is the hunter-gatherer Ogiek tribe that traditionally resides in the Mau Forest complex of central Kenya. The Ogiek are known to be descendants of the earliest inhabitants of East Africa, and reportedly have lived in the Mau escarpment since at least the 18th century.[7] They are an egalitarian, clan-based society, who practice sustainable harvesting of wild honeybees and other forest-based natural resources. The name Ogiek means 'caretakers of all animals and plants', and their collective cultural identity is intricately linked to conservation of their ancestral forest homelands.[8]

Prior to British colonization, the Maasai and Ogiek communities were engaged in warfare over much of the forested portions of the highlands. Both tribes are semi-nomadic and seasonally inhabited overlapping areas. The 1904 Anglo-Maasai lease not only transferred much of this disputed land to European settlers but also effectively dispossessed the Ogiek of any claim to land whatsoever, as the British did not consider them politically important enough to include in the negotiation process. The transaction resulted in forced relocations of Ogiek communities to the newly established Maasai reserves, where they were compelled to surrender their belongings, give up their language and customs, and assimilate into the culture of dominant tribes.

Like the Maasai, the Ogiek community attempted to reclaim their lands through colonial legal institutions without success. In 1932 the British administration appointed the Morris Carter Land Commission to investigate native Kenyan grievances that were threatening to erupt into violence. Recommendations by native law experts to include Africans on the commission panel were rejected, so the three-person Commission was ultimately composed of two European settlers and the same judge who had previously ruled against the Maasai in 1913 and later devised the segregationist land settlement policy in then-Rhodesia (Zimbabwe), Sir William Morris Carter.[9] By failing to create a more representative and objective panel, the British lost out on a timely opportunity to recommend an equitable land settlement proposal in Kenya, a failure that would eventually result in the violent Mau Mau uprising and bloody independence wars of the 1950s.[10]

Along with many other tribal leaders, Ogiek elders were invited to testify before this Commission to argue for the right to remain on their ancestral lands. In its final report, the Commission supported the administration's policies, stating that the Ogiek were a primitive tribe that was 'possibly dying', and recommending that rather than have their own land reserves, they should be assimilated further into larger tribes.[11,12] These recommendations solidified the policy of legitimized Ogiek ethnocide and dispossession that have persisted to this day. After the Commission failed to recognize their rights, many Ogiek community members chose to return to their customary homes in the Mau Forest, where they have endured continual harassment and forcible evictions by the Kenyan government and powerful logging interests.[13]

Post-independence dispossession

Land dispossession only worsened for indigenous communities under Kenyan leaders after independence. During constitutional negotiations between the British government and Kenyan nationalists leading up to independence, the British had agreed to finance land resettlement programs whereby many areas occupied by European settlers would be repurchased and divided amongst landless Kenyans. However, the nationalist movement that gained control over the country through this transition was dominated by Kenya's majority ethnic group, and like many other post-colonial governments in Africa, the loyalties of the new political leaders ran largely along ethnic lines. Rather than returning repurchased lands to the original landowners, the new government instead distributed these lands to families from majority ethnic groups and those that had been allied to the nationalist movement during Independence struggles. An estimated one million Kenyans gained land in this way during the first five years of independence, but very few were members of minority tribes such as the Maasai and Ogiek.[14]

Several decades later, public lands had become the primary source of political patronage, and corruption in land allocations was the rule. Because indigenous peoples tend to practice traditional methods of subsistence that are dependent on maintaining a healthy ecosystem, their lands are often targeted by outsiders as rare preserves of valuable natural resources and wildlife. In the past twenty years alone, the Kenyan government is estimated to have appropriated over 1 million acres of what was left of Maasai grazing lands through both legalized and highly irregular land-grabbing schemes.[15] In the Mau forest, government officials and well-connected individuals have claimed huge sections of pristine land for settlement, logging, and cash-cropping purposes.[16] Additionally, once Kenya's tourism industry became a substantial source of foreign income, the government further targeted indigenous lands for environmental conservation efforts, carving out large holdings for national parks, wild game reserves, and protected forest zones. Indigenous peoples of contemporary Kenya are thus struggling to survive and maintain their traditional livelihoods on ever diminishing landholdings.

Former domestic legal barriers to indigenous rights

During the first four decades of post-colonial rule in Kenya, the national courts and land laws were aligned decidedly with state over indigenous interests, as the new government adopted much of the colonial regime's legislation favoring European settlers and individualized ownership over collective indigenous ownership. All lands that were not privately owned and registered were considered either public land owned by the government, or trust land to be managed by county councils for the use and benefit of local communities[17] In actuality, the President had vast powers over all of these lands and could dispose of them at will through the Ministry of Lands. This already weak system was further undermined in 1968 with the advent of two land laws that provided for the dissolution of any trust land upon individual or governmental registration.[18] The unfortunate result of this legislation was that local officials appointed as trust land custodians were now able to extinguish indigenous land tenure by registering large tracts of community land for their own personal use, a practice that independent land commissions later reported to be widespread and commonplace throughout Kenya over the next several decades.[19]

Indigenous peoples faced tremendous difficulties in fighting these backhanded acquisitions in court, because the Kenyan judiciary protected the rights of registered landowners over all other claims, regardless of how or why the lands were registered.[20] Additionally, the judiciary was itself replete with corruption, so the majority of indigenous lawsuits targeting irregular land transfers were either dismissed on technicalities or left eternally pending.[21] The few indigenous land cases decided on their merits during this time were very unfavorable to indigenous groups.

The most prominent of these was *Kemai & Others v. The Attorney General*, argued at the High Court of Kenya in March 2000. In this case an Ogiek community from the Tinet Forest in the Eastern Mau filed suit for the return of ancestral lands the government had evicted them from in 1997. The Court determined that the evictions were justified for conservation purposes, because, having traded their traditional thatched dwellings for semipermanent houses with corrugated tin roofs, the community no longer lived in harmony with their ancestral homeland. Additionally the Court found that the Ogiek were no longer dependent on their natural environment for survival, as they supplemented hunting and gathering practices with limited herding and farming, and wild honey no longer constituted 'more than one fifth of their diet'.[22] Although the Court appeared to wrestle with the complex issue of potential conflict between environmental preservation and traditional subsistence, its arguments seemed disingenuous in light of the fact that Kenya's largest logging companies continued to hold active licenses in the Mau Forest throughout the case and thereafter.[23]

Another indigenous land claim filed in the same year at the High Court of Kenya in Nakuru concerned the eviction of the pastoral Endorois tribe from their traditional lands at Lake Bogoria. In this case the Court did not attempt to justify its decision with extrajudicial rhetoric, stating simply that Kenyan law does not protect group land rights on the basis of historical occupation and culture. The case was dismissed in 2002.[24]

International law as an alternative strategy

In this environment of sanctioned corruption by legal and political systems hostile to their concerns, indigenous communities in Kenya faced the same choice indigenous peoples worldwide have faced: to turn to international law for the realization of their basic rights. Over the past several decades, indigenous legal standards and instruments promoting indigenous rights have proliferated worldwide. Many of these new standard-bearing instruments have addressed the issue of land appropriation explicitly, as the relationship of indigenous communities to their traditional lands is a central theme across the world. The following conventions and declarations are some of the most applicable international instruments to the land-related issues faced by the Maasai and Ogiek.

International instruments of indigenous rights

The International Labor Organization's Convention (hereafter ILO No. 169) concerning Indigenous and Tribal Peoples and the more recently adopted UN Declaration on the Rights of Indigenous Peoples (hereafter UNDRIP) provide the most comprehensive treatment of indigenous issues. Both instruments contain multiple provisions requiring governments to recognize indigenous peoples' rights under pre-colonial customary law to own the natural resources and lands they have traditionally used and occupied. UNDRIP goes further, however, specifying that governments must establish impartial mechanisms for the recognition and adjudication of indigenous land claims through an inclusive, collaborative process.[25] This process should provide either full restitution or just compensation for any unfairly confiscated lands, where full restitution is impossible.[26]

Several international human rights entities provide support for this approach. Regional treaties such as the African Charter and the American Convention on Human Rights require lawful recovery and compensation for all dispossessed peoples.[27] The UN Committee for the Elimination of Racial Discrimination (CERD) issued a general recommendation regarding the treatment of indigenous peoples, in which it instructs states 'to recognize and protect the rights of indigenous peoples to own, develop, control and use their communal lands, territories and resources and, where they have been deprived of their lands and territories traditionally owned or otherwise inhabited or used without their free and informed consent, to take steps to return those lands and territories'.[28]

A general comment issued by the Human Rights Committee emphasized that Article 27 of the International Covenant on Civil and Political Rights (ICCPR), which protects the rights of minorities to practice their cultures, should be interpreted as also protecting the rights of indigenous peoples to carry out traditional subsistence activities associated with particular land resources.[29] The Committee's reasoning is that without having access to these specific activities, the central component of the community's culture ceases to exist. This interpretation is an important development for indigenous peoples, as the ICCPR is one of the most widely accepted human rights instruments in the world.

These international legal standards could be used by the Maasai and Ogiek communities to fight their land claims in several ways. First, as part of their overall litigation strategy in domestic court, indigenous plaintiffs theoretically could claim direct violations of international legal instruments of which Kenya is a party. Plaintiffs could also use positive indigenous rights decisions from other jurisdictions as persuasive authority to reinforce their arguments in domestic courts. Failing domestic options, indigenous Kenyans can litigate their land claims in international tribunals. Each of these options presents its own set of challenges for indigenous claimants to overcome.

Direct application of international law

Until recently, indigenous peoples faced nearly insurmountable obstacles in attempting to directly apply international indigenous rights law in Kenyan courts. First, Kenya has been a dualist state since independence, meaning that Parliament was required to create enabling legislation before ratified international treaties could be applied within the domestic legal system. Thus although Kenya has ratified the ICCPR and ICERD, the domesticating legislation was never created to make their provisions applicable in domestic court, so their provisions have no binding authority over the Kenyan legal system. Secondly, Kenya has not ratified ILO No.169, and was one of only eleven countries in the United Nations General Assembly that abstained from voting to adopt UNDRIP in 2007.[30]

An abstention may not necessarily defeat indigenous claimants' use of UNDRIP's provisions in Kenyan courts, however. Despite the fact that international declarations are considered to be 'soft law' that are meant to guide behavior rather than bind its parties to explicit provisions, some have argued that the norms embodied in UNDRIP may eventually be understood as representing customary international law, which is itself binding on all states. The process of creating customary international law develops as states and other international law-making entities increasingly accept the principles within the declaration (which are also echoed in other international human rights instruments), as the expectation of what conforming state behavior concerning indigenous rights should be.[31] In this way soft law may eventually become binding law within the international community through state practice and general consensus, even without the participation of states like Kenya. However, this process develops over time.

International jurisprudence

In addition to or in support of the options above, indigenous rights principles encompassed within jurisprudence from other parts of the world may also be used to support Maasai and Ogiek land rights arguments in Kenyan court. Over the past fifteen years, courts around the world have issued countless judgments in favor of indigenous plaintiffs with parallel land dispossession issues, particularly in Latin America.[32] Although case law from other jurisdictions do not necessarily serve as binding precedent over domestic courts, Kenyan judges may consider these decisions to be persuasive authority in their deliberations. In the Ogiek case in 2000, for example, the High Court analyzed the *Mabo v Queensland* decision, a breakthrough Australian case that conferred native title to Aboriginal communities in 1992 for the first time.[33] *Mabo* was finally dismissed by the Kenyan court, not because the decision was not authoritative but because of mere inconsistencies between the factual details of the two cases, leaving open the possibility that a different foreign case with more factual similarities might be accepted by the courts as persuasive authority. This is indeed what has happened in more recent cases.

Decisions from the British Privy Council may also be looked to for persuasive authority. Although the Council no longer has appeals jurisdiction over Kenya, many local legal practitioners believe their decisions still influence Kenyan courts.[34] This could be another useful instrument for the Maasai and Ogiek to consider in drafting their legal arguments, as the Privy Council has recognized pre-colonial land rights in Nigeria as surviving the transfer of sovereignty at independence.[35]

International tribunals

Barring the option of successfully arguing their international law-based claims in Kenyan courts, indigenous Kenyans could potentially bring their land claims to international tribunals as well. Several international human rights conventions include mechanisms whereby victims can file petitions at the corresponding international tribunal for violations of its provisions. Limiting factors include whether the tribunal has jurisdiction over the state party and whether the petitioners are able to meet admissibility requirements.

In order for an international tribunal to obtain jurisdiction over a state party named in a complaint, the state must have ratified the corresponding convention and acquiesced separately to the jurisdiction of the mechanism by which individual complaints are submitted. Thus the Maasai and Ogiek could otherwise file a petition to the Human Rights Committee regarding violations of Articles 1 and 27 of the ICCPR, as dispossessed Canadian and New Zealand tribes have done, except that Kenya has never ratified the Optional Protocol necessary for the Human Rights Committee to establish jurisdiction over such claims. Likewise, a petition to the Committee on the Elimination of Racial Discrimination would fail because Kenya has not made the necessary declaration under ICERD's Article 14 to accept the Committee's jurisdiction over individual complaints.

Indigenous claimants may have more success on the regional level, in petitioning the African Commission on Human and People's Rights (ACHPR) for violations of several provisions of the African Charter. The ACHPR does have jurisdiction over Kenya, and although the Commission's reports and recommendations are not legally binding in themselves, they may become binding through adoption by the African Union at its annual assembly. Additionally, the Commission is able to refer important cases to the new

African Court of Human and Peoples Rights, whose decisions are automatically mandatory on all state parties.

Because African heads of states themselves elect the ACHPR commissioners, however, the Commission has only begun to show a constructive interest in indigenous rights over the past few years. Aside from the obvious bias in supporting their own state governments over concerns of indigenous groups, part of the problem in this regard was that African states did not recognize the concept of indigenous peoples as distinct from other African citizens until recently. Once colonizing European powers were defeated by African nationalists, independent heads of state considered all native populations to be indigenous, in that they are originally African rather than European.

The notion of indigenous peoples as a subset of Africans requiring specific protections was not seriously considered by the ACHPR until 2001, when, in response to ongoing abuses across the continent, non-governmental organizations successfully pushed for the establishment of a Working Group on Indigenous Populations (WGIP) as a Special Mechanism of the ACHPR. WGIP produced its first comprehensive report on the concept of African indigenous peoples in 2003, distinguishing them from dominant populations by factors such as maintaining an enduring physical and spiritual connection to their traditional lands, striving to maintain their collective cultural identities, and experiencing a historic pattern of marginalization, discrimination and/or exploitation within state political and economic structures.[36] The report also presented in detail the situations of various indigenous communities suffering from dispossession and human rights abuses across the continent. Following the adoption of this report by the ACHPR, WGIP's mandate was expanded to undertake regular site visits to individual African countries and report annually on human rights violations carried out against indigenous communities. Two recent decisions out of the ACHPR may illustrate the result of this positive change in attitude towards indigenous issues in the African region.

Endorois case

The landmark case of the *Centre for Minority Rights Development and Minority Rights Group International on behalf of Endorois Welfare Council v. Kenya* of 2009 was the first land rights claim within the regional African court system to favor a dispossessed indigenous group over the state government. The Endorois are a pastoralist group in Kenya that traditionally occupied the fertile Lake Bogoria area of Rift Valley Province. Like all community land in Kenya, the area was pronounced Crown land during the colonial era, and converted into trust lands upon Independence, to be held by local county councils on behalf of the Endorois community. The Endorois continued to use and occupy their ancestral lands without interruption until 1973, when the state designated the area a game reserve and evicted all community members without prior consultation or compensation. After unsuccessfully seeking restitution through legal and political channels in Kenya, the community brought their case before the ACHPR in 2003. Two international attorneys pieced together a convincing argument based largely on successful indigenous rights decisions from the Inter-American Court of Human Rights, and citing UNDRIP provisions and human rights case law from the European Court of Human Rights and the African Commission for support.

In an unprecedented decision, the ACHPR found that the Endorois are indeed a distinct tribal people whose traditional use and occupation of ancestral lands equates a collective property right that the state has a duty to protect.[37] The Commission went further to state that special measures were owed to safeguard the property rights of indigenous and tribal communities, due to the close link between their lands and their cultural and physical survival, and that the trust lands system instituted by Kenya to govern tribal lands was insufficient to serve this purpose.[38] Additionally, although 'encroachment' by the state is permissible in limited public interest circumstances, the standard is higher to meet on indigenous lands than on private property, and the governmental action taken should be the least restrictive alternative possible and in line with both domestic and international laws. In this case the Commission found that international law provides indigenous groups with both the right of participatory consultation prior to a governmental encroachment, and the right to adequate compensation following an encroachment, both of which the Kenyan government failed to do.[39] Therefore the appropriation was deemed an impermissible encroachment of the community's land, in violation of six articles of the African Charter, including the rights to property, culture, free disposition of natural resources, development, and freedom of religion.

Kenya was instructed to allow the Endorois to return to their ancestral lands with full, unrestricted access, to grant the community registration and title to their territory in order to permanently safeguard their collective property rights, to pay compensation payments for the community's losses, and to ensure royalty payments to the community from existing tourism and mining activities undertaken on their lands.[40] The African Union (AU) endorsed the decision in February 2010, making it legally binding. Noncompliance with the recommendations could therefore result in AU sanctions against Kenya.

This decision was a tremendous win for indigenous peoples throughout Africa. Of particular relevance to the land claims of Maasai and Ogiek communities, in its dictum the Commission had also echoed the opinions of the Inter-American Court on how to address cases in which the indigenous group has been unwillingly dispossessed of ancestral lands which were then transferred to a third party. The Commission proposed that in this situation the indigenous group would maintain its full property rights, unless the third party was innocent and the transfer occurred in good faith. In the latter case, the indigenous party is entitled either to restitution or to substituted land of equal quality and value.[41]

Exhaustion of domestic remedies requirement

In considering how the Maasai and Ogiek might bring their own land claims before the ACHPR, it is first necessary to address how they would meet one of the more challenging admissibility criteria required for a case to be considered by the Commission, the exhaustion of domestic remedies.[42] The exhaustion requirement means that prior to submitting their case to the ACHPR, claimants must have attempted to first resolve their claim through all available State legal and administrative processes.[43] The Commission has recognized several exceptions to the exhaustion requirement, however, where domestic remedies are unavailable, ineffective, insufficient, or unreasonably delayed by the State respondent.[44]

In the *Endorois* case, admissibility to the African Commission was met for several reasons. First, as mentioned above, the Endorois had initially filed their case in Kenyan court in 2000, where it was dismissed. An earlier attempt to try the case had been thrown out on procedural grounds, and the community's efforts to seek administrative relief by lobbying the President were equally unfruitful. In addition, the Kenyan government did not provide admissibility arguments to counter the petitioners' claims within the time limit required, so the Commission did not examine other potential issues involved. Otherwise, the Endorois probably could have also successfully argued that no domestic remedy yet existed under Kenyan law to protect collective land rights. Additionally, as the community had been evicted thirty years prior without remedy, the Endorois could have argued that the Kenyan government had unreasonably delayed in providing resolution of the issue. Indigenous petitioners to the Inter-American Commission and Court have been successful with similar arguments.

Several of these arguments may be more difficult for the Maasai and Ogiek to prove, however. First, the argument that no domestic remedy exists to protect indigenous land rights under Kenyan law could potentially be defeated, because, since the *Endorois* decision, Kenya has instituted massive legal reforms which provide new protections for community land rights. Secondly, a newly reformed justice system has spurred multiple indigenous land claims in domestic court over the past several years, some of which involve lands covered by the Anglo-Maasai Agreements and most of which remain unresolved. Unless the courts unreasonably delay in deciding these cases, the ACHPR could decide not to review issues that are already tied up in domestic courts. However, another perspective is that because the Maasai and Ogiek communities have continuously lobbied for their land rights for 80 plus years without resolution, admissibility could be granted via the undue delay exception regardless of the current status of court cases. It is also too early to tell whether the legal and judicial reforms can provide indigenous communities with a resolution that is sufficient and effective.

Implementation of international decisions

In addition to the issue of admissibility, decisions from international tribunals are only useful to the extent that States actually comply with them. For this reason, as novel and progressive as the *Endorois* decision was, it has been only partially successful in resolving the community's dispossession issues thus far. Six years after the landmark ruling, the Kenyan government has failed to provide land title, compensation, or benefit-sharing royalties to the Endorois community, despite the potential threat of AU sanctions for non-compliance. In fact, to date Kenya has only fully implemented one of the seven final recommendations in the Commission's decision, by permitting the representative body of the Endorois community to register as an official association. During Kenya's Universal Periodic Review in 2010, the UN Human Rights Council publicly called on the government to implement the decision, as did both the Human Rights Committee and CERD in the concluding observations of their country reports in 2011 and 2012. The African Commission itself issued a second resolution in November 2013 directing the Kenyan government to comply with its original order.[45] Finally, momentum appears to be slowly building. Nine months after the ACHPR's second resolution, the President of Kenya has created a task force to investigate and submit recommendations on implementation of the ACHPR decision within one year. However, because the task force consists solely of government representatives and possesses a mandate that does not require consultation with the Endorois, the community is concerned that the Commission's full recommendations still may not be met.[46]

Domestic legal reform since 2008

International legal avenues may thus offer one important channel for Kenya's indigenous peoples to gain leverage against the Kenyan government. Ultimately, however, with no mechanism to enforce the final decisions and recommendations of international tribunals, the State maintains control of implementation. Therefore, the best hope for effecting real change on the ground may still be through direct engagement with governmental processes. For Maasai and Ogiek communities, new hope for this process is emerging as Kenya begins to reform its legal and political institutions.

For the past several decades Kenya was engaged in a complex and controversial constitutional review process to revitalize its legal system. The process was stalled by political stalemate until the presidential elections of 2007 erupted into widespread inter-ethnic violence. Because the conflict was fueled by minority groups frustrated by years of exclusion from effective political participation and land dispossession, the post-conflict coalition government negotiated by Kofi Annan took major steps to address inter-ethnic issues with a completely revamped legal and political framework. Some of the changes include a progressive new Constitution, the establishment of a comprehensive National Land Policy, a National Land Commission, a new Environment and Land Court, several new land laws, the enforcement of multiple judicial reforms, including the appointment of a progressive new Chief Justice and the establishment of a Truth, Justice and Reconciliation Commission to address human rights violations perpetrated by the State since Independence.

New constitution, national land policy and land legislation

At the start of the new millennium, indigenous community leaders began to organize themselves extensively to participate in the constitutional review process, both by engaging in civic education within their communities, and by collecting historical data and community views in order to present strong collective positions before the Constitutional Review Commission. This participation resulted in a new Constitution, adopted by national referendum in 2010, that attempts for the first time to address longstanding indigenous concerns. For example, multiple provisions include special protections for marginalized communities and groups, with 'communities' defined in Section 260 as indigenous hunter-gatherers, pastoralists, or traditional communities resisting assimilation, and 'groups' defined as groups historically disadvantaged by government discrimination on the basis of culture, race, ethnicity, sex, etc. Article 56 calls on the state to enact affirmative action programs to ensure that minorities and marginalized groups are able to develop their cultures and languages, have reasonable access to water, health services and other infrastructure, and participate in governance. Article 100 directs the State to enact legislation providing for the representation of minorities and marginalized communities in Parliament. An entire chapter of the Constitution is devoted to the necessity of devolving governmental powers to local county levels, with the stated purpose of 'promot[ing] the interests and rights of minorities and marginalized communities'.[47]

Perhaps most significantly for the Maasai and Ogiek, the new Constitution also institutes broad land reforms to support community land rights. Many of these reforms incorporated principles set out in the government's new comprehensive National Land Policy (NLP), adopted by Parliament in 2009. This policy itself was the product of decades of investigations into the country's land inequity issues, integrating information from earlier initiatives such as the 2002 Presidential Commission of Inquiry into the Land Law Systems in Kenya (Njonjo Land Commission) and the 2003 Presidential Commission of Inquiry into the Illegal/Irregular Allocation of Public Land (Ndungu Land Commission). The NLP represents the first nationwide land policy since the colonial era, and is a major statement of support for indigenous rights in Kenya.

A key principle of the NLP is the official recognition of customary rights to land. The introductory section affirms that existing land laws have long protected private land rights at the expense of indigenous group land rights, and the policy lays out a plan to reform this trend and other inequities.[48] These reforms include:

- Repealing the Trust Lands Act through which community lands were controlled by county governments.
- Replacing the Trust Lands Act with community land law that documents, recognizes, protects, and registers customary rights of communities to land and associated natural resources.
- Officially recognizing pastoralism as a legitimate and sustainable land use system, and providing for a legislative framework to register pastoral land rights in order to 'maintain their unique land systems and livelihoods'.
- Legislating to secure the individual and collective rights of minority forest communities, including a restitution framework for any loss of cultural habitat, and the facilitation of their resource management systems to secure the most sustainable use of natural resources.
- Instituting a benefit-sharing system, whereby legal mechanisms ensure communities' equitable participation in receiving compensation where natural resources on community land are managed by the government for public interest purposes.
- Creating a National Land Commission to redress historical land griev-ances, and a National Land Titles Tribunal to address rightful ownership of former public or trust lands appropriated through illegal land allocations.

The National Land Policy thus sets out one of the most progressive plans for addressing indigenous land concerns on the African continent. However, like all policy documents, the extent to which it can bring results on the ground depends on how closely the implementing legislation follows its principles.

The 2010 Constitution incorporated key aspects of the policy in its chapter on land and environment. Where the former Constitution did not recognize collective property rights at all, the current Constitution replaced the trust lands regime with a specific category for community land tenure, alongside private and public land tenure. Community lands are identified as former trust lands held on behalf of communities, as well as lands traditionally occupied by hunter-gatherers and lands lawfully used by specific communities as grazing areas or community forests. Unlike the former trust lands regime, these lands are meant to vest in and be held by the communities occupying them, rather than by governmental agents.

Although this provision officially recognizes collective customary land rights for the first time in Kenya, there are several loopholes that may diminish its effect somewhat. First, community land that is unregistered remains under trusteeship by county councils. No guidance is provided on how communities in this position can transition the status of their lands in order to regain control from local governments; thus they remain subject to the same threats of corruption and land insecurity as they did prior to the new land laws. Secondly, a prohibition on the external use or disposal of community land may be defeated by conflicting legislation, so far as the legislation clarifies the rights of all occupants. This provision seemingly would not obstruct Parliament from issuing any manner of legislation to divest control of community lands from the communities, as long as the law is clear on what rights will be taken away. Third, the definition of public land was expanded to include game reserves and leased lands, which will now encompass much of the Maasai communities' ancestral lands. These lands will be under exclusive control of the government, which is clearly the opposite of what the Maasai are advocating for, and again no process is provided for transitioning this land to community ownership. Finally, the Constitution requires Parliament to enact legislation to specify and expand upon the concept of community land tenure. This future legislation could potentially resolve some of the issues above by clarifying the processes for community land conversion and disposal, but the most recent draft of the Community Land Bill has languished in Parliament for over a year. Additionally, the Bill is apparently rife with contention, as communities fear it does not go far enough to protect their rights.

National land commission

Aside from the official recognition and protection of community land tenure, another key NLP proposal embraced by the new Constitution was the establishment of an independent National Land Commission (NLC) to resolve current and historic issues of land appropriation. Although appointed by the President and allocated funding by Parliament, NLC commissioners are subject only to the Constitution itself and not the control or direction of any official or branch of government. This is an extremely important development because the agency previously responsible for addressing land issues was the Ministry of Lands, which was controlled by the President and has allegedly been involved with many corrupt land transfers throughout Kenyan history. An independent mechanism is greatly needed in order for Kenyan society to regain faith in governmental processes regarding land dispute resolution.

Parliament passed legislation enabling formulation of the NLC in 2012, enumerating its twelve functions to include the management of all public lands and unregistered community lands, the development of alternative dispute resolution mechanisms to address land conflicts, and the recommendation to Parliament of legislation to address the investigation and adjudication processes of historical land grievances within two years of appointing NLC commissioners. The Constitution had provided a broad mandate for the NLC that included these functions, plus any prescribed by national legislation. The Land Act of 2012 later created 35 additional functions for the NLC. Many of these duties were previously fulfilled by employees of the Ministry of Lands, who will now answer to the NLC until a vetting process has been established to review the competence and integrity of each individual.

Although the NLC has potential to become the best avenue for resolving indigenous land claims in Kenya, the process of getting the Commission up and running has been slow and marred by controversy. Setbacks are due primarily to lack of political will from an executive branch unwilling to cede its previously uncontested powers to allocate land or to address the consequences of its previous involvement in corrupt land transfers. For example, nine Commissioners were appointed and approved by Parliament within several months of the Commission's formulation, but the former President stalled on officially swearing them in for six additional months, until the High Court finally ordered him to do so within one week. County Land Management Boards appointed to implement NLC functions at the local level have yet to take on any cases. Adding to the delays and rising public confusion, the Lands Ministry has challenged every aspect of the NLC's powers as the commissioners attempt to fulfill their mandate, from the appointment of land officers to the signing of land titles, at one point even going so far as refusing them office space to work in.[49]

The NLC finally filed for an advisory opinion on the extent of its mandate at the High Court of Kenya, which resulted in court-ordered peace talks and the public signing of an agreement between the heads of both agencies to work together cooperatively.[50] The Commission's efforts continue to be undermined by low political will, however, as Parliament designated only four per cent of the funds the NLC needed to function in 2014.[51] Even so, the Commission appointed a Task Force in May 2014 to create legislation on how to move forward with the investigations and adjudications of historical land grievances, and it is obligated to deliver draft legislation by March 2015.

Judiciary reforms and contemporary wins

That the High Court of Kenya was able to render impartial judgments regarding the above disputes was possible only because of strenuous judiciary reforms undertaken since the adoption of the new Constitution. In its section addressing the judiciary, the Constitution distanced the Chief Justice position from executive control, called for the dispersal of judicial power through the establishment of three new superior courts presided over by elected judges, and expanded representation and transparency for the Judicial Service Commission. Six months after the Constitution came into effect, a progressive new Chief Justice was appointed to fight corruption within the justice system. He has since put into place a five-year plan to completely restructure the judiciary in order to create a more independent and accountable institution. All existing and future judges are required to pass stringent vetting procedures to determine their competence, and several highly placed judges have been terminated already for failing to meet new standards. New magistrates and judiciary staff hired to address a 30-year backlog of court cases throughout Kenya have also undergone the lengthy vetting process. Other reforms include intense training of all personnel, the creation of new oversight agencies, regularization of personnel payment, financial investment in court infrastructure, and greater inclusion of the media and public participation in judicial procedures. Finally, in order to address the tremendous backlog of land-related claims and disputes, an Environment and Land Court was established in 2012 with exclusive jurisdiction over land issues.

The public has responded to these changes with a strong show of support, and fresh claims have flooded the already overburdened court system. Nevertheless Kenyan courts are issuing decisions faster than ever before, and public opinion polls report that the majority of decisions are fair and corruption within the system appears low. Newly confident indigenous communities have filed dozens of new land claims, some of which include lands within the original Anglo-Maasai lease agreements. For the first time in Kenyan history, there have even been several promising wins for indigenous claimants.

Second Ogiek case

Fourteen years after the High Court's decision in *Kemai*, the Kenyan justice system had the opportunity to address the displacement of Ogiek from their Mau homelands anew this year. Where the Court's approach to indigenous rights law had previously been anachronistic, and the judgment rife with stereotypes about indigenous peoples, the decision in this year's *Joseph Letuya & 21 others v Attorney General* is well versed in the language of the contemporary indigenous rights movement.

The specifics of the case were very similar to those in *Kemai*, and originated in the same time period during the 1990s. They involved the displacement of an Ogiek community from the Mariashoni portion of the Mau Reserve, in an attempt by a former Rift Valley Province Commissioner to settle landless non-Ogiek families there instead. 22 Ogiek representatives filed suit in 1997 to stop the evictions and remove the outsiders from their ancestral homelands. The Court found that despite the fact that the suit was filed when the original Constitution was in place, the current Constitution is applicable because the issues are ongoing.[52]

In regards to whether the Ogiek community has recognizable rights arising from their traditional occupation of the Mau Forest, the Court cited to the 2010 Constitution, the 2009 National Land Policy, the 2009 Report of the Government Task Force on the Conservation of the Mau Forest Complex, and numerous instruments of international law, including ILO No. 169 and the Universal Declaration of Human Rights. The claimants were able to use international indigenous rights law in their arguments because the new

Constitution provides that ratified international conventions are directly applicable to Kenyan law without requiring further enabling legislation, essentially transitioning Kenya from a dualist to a monist state.

The Court found that the Ogiek community has special rights and protections as an indigenous community under both Kenyan and international law, and that preventing the Ogiek from fulfilling their livelihoods in accordance with their culture in the forest amounts to violations of both their rights to life and to freedom from non-discriminatory government action. The Court also found that the settlement of non-Ogiek in the forest was not legal, and that Ogiek should be given priority regarding any allocation of land in the Mau, due both to their reliance on the land and to their sustainable management of forest resources. However, the Court did not find that the Ogiek community's customary occupation of the Mau arose to the level of property rights. Instead, the Court referred the issue of property rights to the National Land Commission to resolve in line with provisions of the Community Land Bill.

As far as providing remedies for the Ogiek, the Court determined that the NLC should implement the recommendations of the 2009 Mau Task Force by registering Ogiek community members who were designated land in the 1990s, and within one year ensuring that they receive plots of land within the Mau but outside of environmentally sensitive water catchment areas. The Court also stated that the NLC is the only institution Constitutionally-mandated to determine how to handle the issue of landless non-Ogiek families previously settled or seeking to be settled in the Mau.

Although the Court in *Letuya* chose not to protect the full range of indigenous rights recognized by international law, the positive change in attitude and approach toward indigenous claimants in this case was tremendous. It remains to be seen whether the Community Land Bill will close the remaining gap by finally equating the customary occupation of ancestral lands with fully recognizable property rights, as called for by the National Land Policy. Regardless of this, the fact that resolution of the *Letuya* case was ultimately referred to the NLC is perhaps a problematic harbinger for indigenous land claims to come. The NLC remains drastically under-funded and over-burdened. If there continues to be low political will to support these mechanisms, all the hard-won reforms will be powerless to make meaningful change.

Negotiating forward

Resolving the Anglo-Maasai Lease debacle will be challenging, whatever approach is chosen. For the Maasai, it may be an even more difficult prospect than for the Ogiek, because while Ogiek forests have largely been reserved as government land since the colonial era, the lands the Maasai historically claim have changed hands many times over the past century, often for large sums and by very powerful hands. This will make it complicated to determine who legitimately owns the land, how to address innocent third parties who bought this land in good faith, and how to approach powerful individuals who either broke the law to acquire the land or changed the law to meet their needs. This is an especially delicate issue because many of these powerful families are still involved or influential in contemporary Kenyan politics.

Further complicating matters is the fact that most of the northern lands claimed by the Maasai are increasingly desirable as commercial safari destinations and large-scale farming regions. The Laikipia area, in particular, has recently seen a tremendous increase in land sales to foreign corporations by absentee landlords of lands on which Maasai have been herding for decades.[53] This trend is aggravated by escalating drought throughout the region, which forces small-scale farmers and herders out of neighboring districts into fertile, well-watered Laikipia. All of these competing interests are issues that the Government would rather avoid dealing with. Any resolution will require an intricate mix of restitution, reparations, and compensation that is bound to be expensive for the Government, and could easily dissolve into physical conflict by any dispossessed party.

So while legal avenues may thus offer important channels for indigenous peoples to gain leverage against the Kenyan government, especially in light of the growing credibility of Kenyan courts – without the political will necessary to implement judicial decisions or to fund the newly created adjudicating bodies like the NLC, progress through legal strategies alone may remain somewhat limited. A negotiated agreement between indigenous groups and the Kenyan government may offer an alternative or complementary solution. If such a deal were to be brokered, it would have to address the existential fears of the African state writ large that any limitations on its sovereignty over indigenous peoples will not reverse the tenuous gains of state consolidation in recent decades. Kenya's recent election crises, in which conflict along ethnic lines was narrowly averted through extensive local and international mediation efforts, clearly demonstrated this state fragility.

Two levels of bargaining are evident. The first is within Kenya itself, where the Maasai are currently engaged in discussions with the government, though with little progress thus far. Ultimately, the Maasai and Ogiek want the state to implement key provisions of the National Land Policy, including the establishment of mechanisms to resolve their historical land claims. The government has put these mechanisms in place, including a suitable legal and administrative framework to help delineate and protect customary group rights to ancestral lands and to safeguard their rights to practice their traditional livelihoods and customs. At the same time, however, the Kenyan government has so far refused to provide sufficient funds to allow these instruments to work to their full effect, and in some instances has refused to allow more powerful agencies to cooperate with them. Serious political will to fund and allow them to operate fully would likely provide indigenous communities with at least partial restitution in land, as well as reparations and compensation for other physical and economic losses. If these concerns were met alongside actively implemented legislation protecting their properties from non-indigenous encroachment by development and agricultural operations, most indigenous groups would probably agree to certain environmental use restrictions of the land.

Although these items provide ample negotiating room for the government, underlying them are the more difficult politics of the Kenyan government having to put a stop to corruption-ridden development schemes and other land-related contracts. Pervasive government corruption has so far been the primary obstacle to reaching an agreement, since Kenyan politicians are deeply involved in lucrative contracts in indigenous lands and wish to protect similar benefits of power. Reparation payments may also be a stumbling block in that regard, as they may prove very expensive.

A partial solution to the government's problems may be found in the fact that the British committed the original Maasai-Ogiek land seizures. Consequently, the Kenyan government could seek to pass the reparations tab – as well as some of the legal machinery costs – to the British, who may be amenable to providing some financial assistance if it is part of a larger settlement package and does not require them to agree to any universal legal obligations to colonial-era wrongs. If the British refuse – which is likely, given their historical position that all responsibility for domestic affairs rests with the sovereign Kenyan government, to which they returned white settler properties at independence – the Maasai and Ogiek could agree to have the Kenyan government bring the matter to a global adjudication body such as the UN Human Rights Council.

British involvement points to a second level of bargaining integral to resolving the dispute between Kenya and its indigenous peoples: the engagement of African states across the region. This is necessary in order to address the shared fears of African states regarding the possibility of indigenous claims leading to territorial dismemberment and loss of sovereignty, which was exacerbated somewhat by the 2007 UN Declaration on the Rights of Indigenous Peoples. A region-wide effort to address this concern may help, if it can provide African governments with additional legal guarantees of their sovereignty over indigenous peoples and lands, and if it can provide an alternative to the UN human and indigenous rights mechanisms, over which African states have less control. The active role that the ACHPR has played regionally in addressing a number of indigenous disputes, in addition to the leverage African states possess within it, may make it the appropriate vehicle.

The Maasai and Ogiek may request, for example, that the ACHPR's recently appointed Working Group on Indigenous Populations of Africa develop an African Treaty or Declaration on Indigenous Rights, as the Inter-American system has done. Such a legal instrument could: first, clearly delineate what state recognition of indigenous rights entails throughout Africa and clarify what the tradeoffs between indigenous land controls and environmental protections may be; second, reassert the historical responsibilities of the European powers to pay for reparations and other land claims; and third, set up an international tribunal to hear cross-border disputes and domestic cases that do not get a fair hearing or are hindered by government corruption. Most importantly for state governments, this Charter could reaffirm the inviolability of current borders and the sovereignty of states over the indigenous territories within these borders, making the ACHPR the primary mechanism for managing African indigenous peoples' international legal claims. In addition, Maasai and Ogiek representatives could request that the UN Special Rapporteur on Indigenous Rights act as a mediator/facilitator for both the Kenyan negotiations as well as this proposed regional process.

The Kenyan government is likely to be a reluctant partner to any of the negotiations proposed above, especially since international involvement may expose government corruption. However, the Maasai and Ogiek's creative engagement of international instruments, alongside their willingness to compromise on the extent of their control over ancestral territories, should convince the Kenyan government that it has more to gain from such a grand bargain than from the status quo. This is particularly true if the ACHPR is involved, given the control that African governments exert over their regional organizations. These initiatives could assuage African states' shared concerns about indigenous matters by giving their governments greater management roles in international legal claims, which may help to contribute to the resolution of indigenous conflicts across the continent.

If the Kenyan government is invited to be a central actor in such a regional grand bargain, it may increase the chances that it will also implement the much-overdo domestic legislation to make ACHPR enforceable law in Kenya. In the least, the government will need to ensure that the Community Land Law passed by Parliament is in line with the stated purposes of the NLP and sufficiently respects the rights of customary landholders. It will also need to fund the NLC to ensure it can perform its functions adequately. International stakeholders can put pressure on the Kenyan government to respect this institution, although the US and other governments are wary about getting involved, despite the development potential of a lasting settlement. Lastly, the NLC should appoint a Task Force to investigate and find resolutions for the Anglo-Maasai Lease issues. Together, this combination of local and regional action could result in a more comprehensive system for the proper management of indigenous rights and interests in a manner that strengthens Kenya's sovereignty and makes it a world leader in protecting cultural diversity.

Notes

1   Eghosa E. Osaghae, *The Crippled Giant: Nigeria Since Independence* (Indiana University Press, 1998); and Pierre Englebert and Denis M. Tull, 'Postconflict Resolution in Africa: Flawed Ideas about Failed States', *International Security* 32, no. 4 (Spring 2008): 106–139.

2 Nasieku Tarayia, 'The Legal Perspectives of the Maasai Culture, Customs and Traditions', *Arizona Journal of International and Comparative Law* 21, no. 1 (2004): 183, 205–206.

3 Lotte Hughes, *Moving the Maasai: A Colonial Misadventure* (Palgrave MacMillan, 2006), 5.

4 Joseph Ole Simel, 'The Anglo-Maasai Agreements/Treaties: A Case of Historical Injustice and the Dispossession of the Maasai Natural Resources (Land) and the Legal Perspectives', report prepared for the Office of the United Nations High Commissioner for Human Rights Expert Seminar on Treaties, Agreements and Other Constructive Agreements between Governments and Indigenous Peoples, UN Doc. HR/GENEVA/TSIP/SEM/2003/BP.7 (Geneva: 2003), 4.

5 *Ole Njogo v Attorney General*, Case No. 91 of 1912, (5 E.A.L.R. 70). (1914) 5 EALR 70.

6 Stephen Mburu, 'Land Pacts Were Signed Under Duress', *The Daily Nation*, August 29, 2005.

7 Joseph Markus, 'Hunters or Hunted? The Ogiek of the Mau Forest', *Social Justice First*, August 14, 2012, http://socialjusticefirst.com/2012/08/14/hunters-or-hunted-the-ogiek-of-the-mau-forest (accessed June 9, 2015).

8 Towett J. Kimaiyo, 'Ogiek Land Cases and Historical Injustices, 1902–2004', Chapter 2, *Free Africa*, http://freeafrica.tripod.com/ogiekland/book.htm#Hist Injust (accessed September 15, 2009).

9 Hansard HL Deb, 'Kenya Land Commission', 84 (May 4, 1932) 305-320, http://hansard.millbanksystems.com/lords/1932/may/04/kenya-land-commission (accessed October 29, 2014).

10 Michael S. Coray, 'The Kenya Land Commission and the Kikuyu of Kiambu', *Agricultural History* 52, no.1 (1978): 179–193.

11 www.scribd.com/doc/74835533/CAB-24-248-The-Kenya-Land-Commission-Report-1934#scribd https://sites.google.com/a/ogiekpeople.org/www/Home/ogiek-memorandum (accessed June 9, 2015).

12 Nyang'ori Ohenjo, 'Kenya's Castaways: The Ogiek and National Development Processes', *Minority Rights Group International*, (March 7, 2003), www.minorityrights.org/download.php@id=91 (accessed June 9, 2015).

13 Kimaiyo, supra fn. 7, Chapter 5.

14 Paul Ndung'u, 'Tackling Land Corruption in Kenya, Presidential Commission on Illegal & Irregular Allocation of Public Land in Kenya', *World Bank* (November 2006), 3, http://siteresources.worldbank.org/RPDLPROGRAM/Resources/459596-1161903702549/S2_Ndungu.pdf (accessed November 10, 2014).

15 Meitamei Olol-Dapash, 'Maasai Autonomy and Sovereignty in Kenya and Tanzania', *Cultural Survival Quarterly* (April 30, 2001).

16 'Kenya: Government Destroys the Ogiek's Forest', *Survival International*, November 30, 2001, www.survival-international.org/news/86 (accessed September 15, 2009).

17 Kenya Trust Land Act, Cap 288 (1939); George Wachira, 'Vindicating Indigenous Peoples' Land Rights in Kenya' (LLD diss. University of Pretoria, 2008), 65.

18 Trust Lands Act and Land Adjudication Act of 1968, Kenya.

19 Roger Southall, 'The Ndungu Report: Land and Graft in Kenya', *Review of African Political Economy* 103 (2005): 142–151.

20 Wachira, supra fn. 17, 7–8.

21 Ruth Jansen, 'Background to the Ogiek Case', *Ogiek.org*, www.ogiek.org/indepth/back-ogiek-case.htm (accessed September 15, 2009); Joseph Towett, 'Kenya's Ogiek Face Displacement from the Mau Forest', *Cultural Survival Voices*, July 10, 2008.

22 Civil Case No. 238/1999, 4.

23 Kanyinke Sena, 'Mau Forest: Killing the Goose but Still Wanting the Golden Eggs', *International Affairs*, 4 (IWGIA: 2006), 30-35.

24 *William Yatich Sitetalia, William Arap Ngasia et al. v. Baringo County Council*, High Court of Kenya in Nakuru, Judgment of 19 April 2002, Civil Case No. 183 of 2000, 6.

25 United Nations Declaration on the Rights of Indigenous Peoples, 111-12, UN Document. E/CN.4/Sub.2/1994/56, para. 26; International Labour Organization Convention on Indigenous and Tribal Peoples No. 169 (1989) para.14.3.

26 UN Declaration, Paragraph 27, UN Document, E/CN.4/2006/79.

27 African Charter on Human and Peoples' Rights, adopted June 27, 1981, entered into force October 21, 1986, 1520 U.N.T.S. 217, art. 21.1; American Convention on Human Rights, adopted July 18, 1978, 1144 U.N.T.S. 123, art. 21.2.

28 Committee on the Elimination of All Forms of Racial Discrimination, General Comment XXIII on Indigenous Peoples, U.N. Doc A/52/18, Annex V, (1997) para. 4 (d).

29 Martin Scheinin, *Indigenous Peoples' Land Rights Under the International Covenant on Civil and Political Rights* (Norwegian Center for Human Rights: 2004).

30 144 voted for while 4 voted against, including the U.S.

31 James Anaya, *International Human Rights and Indigenous Peoples* (Aspen Publishers, 2009) 80.

32 Inter-American Commission on Human Rights, 'Authorities and Precedents in International and Domestic Law for the Proposed American Declaration on the Rights of Indigenous Peoples', IACHR Doc. OEA/Ser.L/V/II.110 (March 1, 2001), art. 18; Albert Barume, 'Constitutional Protection and Aboriginal Title in Commonwealth African Countries', report for the Commonwealth Project Africa Regional Expert Meeting (October 2002); Gumisai Mutume, 'Indigenous People Fight for Inclusion', *African Renewal Online* (April 2007)www.un.org/africarenewal/magazine/april-2007/%E2%80%98indigenous%E2%80%99-people-fight-inclusion (accessed June 9, 2015).

33 *Kemai & Others v. The Attorney General*, supra n. 22 at 2–3.

34 Barume, at fn. 33.

35 *Amodu Tijani v Sec of Nigeria*, Privy Council (1921).

36 'Report of the African Commission's Working Group of Experts on Indigenous Populations/Communities', ACHPR Doc OS (XXXIV)/345, (2003) para.4.2, www.achpr.org/files/special-mechanisms/indigenous-populations/expert_report_on_indigenous_communities.pdf (accessed June 9, 2015).

37 African Commission on Human and Peoples' Rights (ACHPR), *Centre for Minority Rights Development and Minority Rights Group International on behalf of Endorois Welfare Council v. Kenya*, ACHPR Communication 276/2003 (2009), www.achpr.org/files/sessions/46th/comunications/276.03/achpr46_276_03_eng.pdf (last accessed June 9, 2015).

38 African Commission on Human and Peoples' Rights (ACHPR), *Centre for Minority Rights Development and Minority Rights Group International on*

behalf of Endorois Welfare Council v. Kenya, ACHPR Communication 276/2003 (2009), para. 197-205, www.achpr.org/files/sessions/46th/comunications/276.03/achpr46_276_03_eng.pdf.

39 African Commission on Human and Peoples' Rights (ACHPR), *Centre for Minority Rights Development and Minority Rights Group International on behalf of Endorois Welfare Council v. Kenya*, ACHPR Communication 276/2003 (2009), para. 214-234, www.achpr.org/files/sessions/46th/comunications/276.03/achpr46_276_03_eng.pdf.

40 African Commission on Human and Peoples' Rights (ACHPR), *Centre for Minority Rights Development and Minority Rights Group International on behalf of Endorois Welfare Council v. Kenya*, ACHPR Communication 276/2003 (2009), para. 206, www.achpr.org/files/sessions/46th/comunications/276.03/achpr46_276_03_eng.pdf.

41 African Commission on Human and Peoples' Rights (ACHPR), *Centre for Minority Rights Development and Minority Rights Group International on behalf of Endorois Welfare Council v. Kenya*, ACHPR Communication 276/2003 (2009), para. 209, www.achpr.org/files/sessions/46th/comunications/276.03/achpr46_276_03_eng.pdf.

42 In order for the ACHPR to consider a case on its merits, the claimant must have met seven criteria for admissibility, as stated in Article 56 of the African Charter.

43 African Charter supra at fn. 27, art. 56.

44 *Sir Dawda K. Jawara v. The Gambia*, ACHPR Comm. No. 147/95, (2000) 31–32.

45 ACHPR Resolution 257, *Resolution Calling on the Republic of Kenya to Implement the Endorois Decision* (November 5, 2013), www.achpr.org/sessions/54th/resolutions/257/ (accessed June 10, 2015).

46 'Kenyan Task Force Formed to Implement the 2010 Endorois Ruling', *Minority Rights Group International*, September 29, 2014, www.minorityrights.org/12695/press-releases/kenyan-task-force-formed-to-implement-the-2010-endorois-ruling.html (accessed June 10, 2015).

47 Proposed Constitution of Kenya (May 2010), Chapter 11, Section 174 (e).

48 Sessional Paper No. 3 of 2009 on National Land Policy, Section 53.

49 Ibrahim Oruko, 'Kenya: Ngilu Now Recalls Land Officers From NLC', *The Star*, March 24, 2014, http://allafrica.com/stories/201403240710.html (accessed October 29, 2014).

50 Kazungu Chai, 'Swazuri and Ngilu Sign Agreement to Work Together', Official Website of the President (November 10, 2014), www.president.go.ke/swazuri-and-ngilu-sign-agreement-to-work-together/ (accessed November 15, 2014).

51 Rajab Ramah, 'Under-Funding Kenyan Land Commission Could Set Back Reforms', *Sabahi*, May 30, 2013, http://sabahionline.com/en_GB/articles/hoa/articles/features/2013/05/30/feature-01 (accessed October 29, 2014).

52 *Joseph Letuya and Others v. The Attorney General and Others*, Civil Application No. 635 (1997).

53 John Letai, 'Land Deals in Kenya: The Genesis of Land Deals in Kenya and its Implication on Pastoral Livelihoods – A Case Study of Laikipia District', report for Oxfam Kenya (2011), http://landportal.info/sites/default/files/land_deals_in_kenya-initial_report_for_laikipia_district2.pdf (accessed June 10, 2015).

10 Indigenous land rights and conflict in Darfur

The case of the Fur tribe

Jon Unruh

Introduction

Land rights in Darfur operate as a central feature of the conflict. Widely regarded as being at the heart of the war, land rights for the different indigenous groups involved in the conflict are complex, confused, sensitive, and volatile (e.g., Abdhalla, 2010; Flint and De Waal, 2008; Abdul-Jalil, 2007; Suiliman, 2011; Concordis, 2007). Of the six recognized and agreed upon 'root causes' of the war mentioned in the 2011 peace accord between the government and one set of the rebel factions, three dealt explicitly with land rights issues (Draft Dafur Peace Document (DDPD), 2011). In one of the most acute manifestations of the land rights problem, certain Arab pastoralists of northern Darfur were easily recruited into the *Janjaweed* for two primary reasons, land and money (Flint, 2009).

This chapter[1] examines the land rights of the *Fur* indigenous group in Darfur and how these have interacted with those of other indigenous groups in the region and the state's approach to land rights, to become highly contentious. Subsequent to a description of how the *Fur* indigenous land tenure system functions in the region and how it came about, the chapter looks at how indigenous land tenure has intersected with formal statutory tenure and Islamic law, and then focuses on the role and functioning of land rights in the conflict itself. This is done by exploring, 1) the stress, exclusion and resistance involving the indigenous tenure system; 2) the intrusion and confrontation of the statutory system, and; 3) the role of Islamic law regarding land rights.

Land rights in Darfur

Indigenous customary tenure in Darfur

Land in Darfur is divided up into tribal homelands known as *Dar*. As a general rule the *Dar* belongs to (or more specifically is named after or associated with) a major tribe or clan. Such a tribe initially obtained land rights as a result of earlier occupation dating from the pre-Sultanate period. During the Sultanate period the sultan merely recognized the fact of land occupation and control, and reconfirmed the position of the group's leader. The main advantage of this arrangement for the major tribe is that it gave it a monopoly over the land – political nexus as well as leadership and revenue collection. Thus Darfur is known historically as the *Dar* or homeland of the *Fur* tribe in recognition of its historical role in establishing what was at the time a thriving state. Thus while the *Fur* tribe did not occupy the entirety of what is today called Darfur the naming of the region as associated with the *Fur* follows a long history of state formation by the tribe even though other tribes and *Dars* are included within Darfur (O'Fahey and Salim, 2003).

Historically, when Darfur was annexed to Sudan in 1916 the colonial authorities changed very little of the land administration system. The tribal homeland policy of indirect rule adopted by the British in Darfur favored the larger tribes, in that their leaders were confirmed as Paramount Chiefs (otherwise known as *Nazir*, *Shartay*, or *Sultan*) to be responsible for managing large areas of land as well as the people within a given boundary (Abdul-Jalil *et al.*, 2007). This minimized the colonial oversight that would have been needed to interact with many smaller tribes. It also meant that small tribal groupings and their chiefs came under the administration of the larger tribal chiefdoms with or without their consent.

Thus many of the smaller tribes have struggled for their own tribal identity and land for some time. Currently the claim for independent *Dars* by the smaller tribes is linked to their desire for their own 'Native Administration' operating within broader customary law. Such an administration includes formal leadership positions in local and regional state institutions, including local councils and state advisory bodies. The claim for separate *Dars* by minority tribes was and is usually resisted by the majority tribes because it would lead to the fragmentation of the overall *Dar* and a diffusion of authority away from the larger tribes. This has been a major source of tribal conflict in the region, as illustrated by the *Ma'alyia* – *Rizeigat* conflict in 1968 (Abdul-Jalil *et al.*, 2007).

While all *Dars* are connected to a specific group, a parallel issue of critical importance to the current conflict, is that not all groups have *Dars*. This is particularly the case for the camel Arab pastoralist (*abbala*) indigenous groups of northern Darfur such as the northern *Rizeigat* who have historically roamed regions of the Sahara to the north of Darfur and who migrated into Darfur seasonally (Mohammed, 2004). This lack of *Dars* among some groups was partially because the granting of tribal *Dars* in the Sultanate era also favored the larger sedentary tribes as British colonial policy did, but also because in the past such permanent claims to land were not an important issue for Arab pastoralists, who instead depended on transient rights of land access (Abdul-Jalil, 2008; Babiker, 2001).

Thus Darfur's tribes can be classified into land-holding and non-land-holding groups. The first category includes all the sedentary groups plus the cattle-herding tribes of southern Darfur. The second includes the Arab camel nomads of the north and west (including into the Sahara) plus new-comers from neighboring Chad and elsewhere who were either driven by drought and political instability or drawn by opportunity to seek permanent residence in Darfur; or who migrated into Darfur as part of seasonal grazing patterns.

The *Dars* are further subdivided into *hakura*. While use of the term varies, essentially *hakura* are forms of land grants or titles given by the *Fur* sultans to chiefly families, religious figures, or court appointees. The *hakura* granted were of two types; an administrative *hakura,* which gave limited rights of taxation over people occupying a certain territory, and a more exclusive *hakura* of privilege that gave the title holder all rights for taxes and religious dues within the area. The first type was usually granted to tribal leaders. The *hakura* of privilege (which was relatively smaller) rewarded individuals for services rendered to the state and had more limited administrative implications. Both types of estates were managed through stewards acting on behalf of the title-holder (Abdul-Jalil, 2009; O'Fahey and Salim, 2003).

The implications of the distinction between land-holding and non-landholding groups for the current civil war is of fundamental importance. In this regard primary narrative is that many Arab pastoralists of the north justify their participation in the current conflict as part of a 250 year-old quest for land that was provided to others but denied to them. This perspective, while not well aligned with actual history, is so acute that 'hakura has become a battle-cry of the Janjaweed' (O'Fahey, 2008).

While a *hakura* exists as a document describing the land grant (including precise boundary definition) and had the Sultan's seal above the text, the term also refers to the land itself, which often comprise significantly large areas (O'Fahey and Salim, 2003). The *hakura* vary in size, and O'Fahey's (2008) research into Dar Aba Diima revealed the existence of about 200 *hakura* in an area of approximately 1500 miles square, resulting in an average *hakura* size of approximately 70 miles square. But *hakura* is also taken to mean as 'tribal land ownership', meaning that the *hakura* became attached to the area originally occupied by a tribal group. In actuality however the tribe of the original *hakura* owner (*hakura* being hereditary) gathered to the area and came to occupy and consolidate itself within the *hakura* (Flint and De Waal, 2008). The rights of the *hakura* owner were more akin to a feudal jurisdiction, with rights to collect taxes of various kinds, as opposed to a form of freehold (Flint and De Waal, 2008). Currently there is considerable confusion over the term and concept of *hakura*. Some see it as synonymous with *Dar*, others view it as a land tenure system belonging to the *Fur* only, and still others see it as simply a land management system that can be changed or replaced. The various confusing understandings associated with *hakura* are important to Darfur's current conflict, and will be elaborated upon further below.

Islamic law is fused with customary law in Darfur, as it is throughout the Muslim world (Flint and De Waal, 2008). The historical land documents granting the *hakura* to their original holders in the Sultanate era (the earliest dating from approximately 1700) refer to Allah, the Qur'an, Islamic law, and Islamic precepts throughout (O'Fahey and Salim, 2003). Some of the land titles (also referred to as deeds or charters) were actual *waqf*-granting documents (*waqf* being a form of Islamic land trust), while many other *hakura* grants were '*waqf*-like' to varying degrees in that they were given to Islamic religious figures and were intended to be continuously held by their descendants. The deeds given to such figures invoked and used religious phrases and words to different extents (O'Fahey and Salim, 2003). As a result a particular *hakura* deed with a significant amount of, or more powerful religious phrasing, would be considered more *waqf*-like than others which had less religious phrasing. Thus a certain 'argument' in a legal sense, could be made that a particular *hakura* should be seen as more *waqf*-like given its phrasing, or its mention of certain religious aspects, or the religious figure it was initially given to. Still other land deeds were charters granted to various holy clans (O'Fahey and Abu Salim, 2003). Such religious actors were then a primary factor in the further spread of Islam in Darfur (O'Fahey, 2008).

At the village and household level within the *hakura* system, customary rights over land were seldomly exclusive, hence there was no real 'ownership' of land in the Western legal sense. The basic principle was that there existed a form of land access whereby every adult male in the village was entitled to a piece of land on which to build a hut and establish an enclosure for animals, in addition to access to farmland outside the village. However there were communal rights that overrode individual user rights on such land. These included access to water for humans and animals; access to livestock routes (for agricultural, transhumant and nomadic animal movements); access to grazing and hunting areas; and the gathering of fodder, wild foods, firewood, and building materials; as well as access to ceremonial and ritual sites (Abdul-Jalil, 2006). Although these rights were in principle enjoyed by all, more localized sets of normative rules defined how access and claim in reality occurred. For example, rain-fed farmland (*talique*) had a specific set of rights because it was put under use for only part of the year and left fallow after harvest. There was a Darfur-wide custom with local variations that stipulated unfettered access to *talique* after harvest so that livestock belonging to pastoralists could graze on the remains of harvested crops. Accordingly, the farmer would not allow his own animals to graze while denying access to animals belonging to others. Management of *talique* was communal and access to it was decided by the local Native Administrators concerned.

A significant aspect of customary tenure is the 'Native Administration'. Under the colonial policy of indirect rule, tribal leaders were confirmed as part of a Native Administration system and were deemed to be custodians of land belonging to their tribes. Paramount Chiefs, who continue to represent the highest authority in the Native Administration system, performed their duties through a medium level leadership position (*Omda*), and the latter through the lower level leadership of a village headman (*Sheik*). The Paramount Chief was also responsible for allocating land for settlement and cultivation. Any disputes regarding land rights or natural resources first needed to pass through the village *Sheik* who then communicated with the upper level of the Native Administration to resolve it. Thus the Native Administration provided a system of local governance which managed the use of land and natural resources. Native Administrators were (and still are) entrusted with the role of implementing land rights and resource allocation decisions, and regulating the grazing activities of different tribes and outsiders so as to avert conflicts between farmers and pastoralists. This included the enforcement of boundaries that demarcated grazing and farming areas, regulation of the seasonal movement of pastoralists in terms of timing, the routes taken from their dry season grazing areas to wet season areas, containment and resolution of tribal disputes in the grazing areas, and the opening and closing of water points (Abdul-Jalil, 2007). It was unfortunate then that the Sudanese government dissolved the Native Administration in 1971, creating a precarious institutional vacuum; then re-instituted it later but with members selected by government instead of local constituencies. The result is that the Native Administration is now highly distrusted and largely ineffective (Elmekki, 2009). This has crippled much of the functionality of the customary tenure system, and did away with the primary way for the customary and statutory tenure systems to interact.

Prior to the current war nomadic pastoralists were provided with negotiated transient rights within indigenous sedentary customary tenure, and these were operationalized through special corridors that passed through the tribal lands of sedentary groups. These corridors were established by arrangements made between the traditional leaders of nomadic and sedentary groups, with the customary rights of each group respected. There also existed an arrangement prior to the war whereby if pastoralist groups wanted to cross from Chad or points north into Darfur they would be linked to a local 'advocate' or sponsor known to the local population, or someone from the incoming pastoralist group that was known locally. Such an advocate would be able to speak for and attest to the good intentions and behavior of the group in question. In this way the pastoralist group would be allowed to stay and negotiate grazing. But benefits from such an arrangement would flow both ways. Because livestock were one of the few ways to store capital, herders were desired by *hakura* members (O'Fahey, 2008).

As a general rule all *Dars* allowed settlement of newcomers both as individuals and groups, provided that they adhered to the relevant existing customary regulations. Farming, grazing, hunting and forest use were included in such arrangements. Historically it was advantageous for a Paramount Chief or *hakura* holder to attract newcomers, in order to till the land and provide taxes to the *hakura* holder (O'Fahey, 2008). Agriculturalist newcomers from outside the *Dar* who wished to farm were usually accommodated within uncultivated 'waste-land' areas or fallow-land, according to local customary norms. If the newcomer was an individual or a few families, they would join an existing village and come under the administrative jurisdiction of its *Sheik*. However, if the number of newcomers was large enough to constitute a separate village, they were allowed to have their own village and choose their own *Sheik* who would then be accountable to the *Omda* of the area. In such a case the new *Sheik* would not have jurisdiction over land and so was called *Sheikh Anfar* (*Sheik* of people) as opposed to the more powerful and prestigious office of *Sheikh Al-Ard* (*Sheik* of the land) which was open only to natives of the Dar.

Indigenous and statutory land law interaction in Darfur

The legal environment in Darfur comprising statutory, customary, and Islamic law has evolved over the course of history in Darfur and Sudan, from different sources and historical developments. While there is overlap between the three approaches to legality in land rights, this involves forms of congruence, as well as forms of co-option and opposition. But there are also fundamental incompatibilities. The priority of customary law is social stability, saving face and reconciliation of disputes outside of a winner – loser context. Thus customary law in Darfur is about obscuring individual culpability in favour of one's group compensating another or compensating an individual. Formal law on the other hand is concerned with finding and punishing an individual wrongdoer so as to achieve justice. The issue of evidence is also a fundamental problem for law in Darfur – with statutory law depending on the document and customary law allowing robust use of testimonial and landscape-based evidence. Islamic law as practiced in Darfur allows for yet a different avenue for evidence. In this context a claimant can ask an Islamic judge to have the person suspected of committing the act in question (i.e., damage to land, land and property disputes, etc.), swear on a Qur'an that he is innocent. If the Qur'an is a mass produced printed copy then the exercise is much less powerful than if the Qur'an is old, hand written, has a long religious history attached to it, was written from memory by a famous religious person known in history or who made the Haj, and is kept in a mosque. The reason the latter is more powerful is because to lie while swearing an oath on such a Qur'an is thought to bring calamity. Thus within these three legal domains, overlapping laws belonging to the different legal regimes actively work at cross purposes, creating significant confusion.

Most statutory land laws in Sudan that are relevant to Darfur were initially derived to serve areas in and around towns and on development schemes along the Nile valley, and were not intended for the wider rural areas of the country. Nevertheless such laws were passed as national legislation applicable to the entire country. In practice for much of the history of this legislation (Runger, 1987; Gordon, 1986) the government did not interfere in the administration of customary rights in many rural areas of the country, and these laws caused little initial concern or problems for the inhabitants of Darfur. However they came to be applied to Darfur when it became advantageous for those from outside the region and/or those not belonging to the customary *hakura* tenure system to do so. Most notable in this regard is the

1970 Unregistered Land Act, which stipulated that all land not registered with the government by the date of its enactment, became by default government land. In addition two other statutory laws were also problematic. The first was the Emirate Act of 1995 (GOS, 1995), passed by the state of West Darfur as part of a larger effort to make the Native Administration more responsive to Arab pastoralists. One result of this law was the division of a large area known as '*Dar Masalit*' into 13 estates, five for the native *Masalit* farmers and eight for the Arab camel herders (who in this area are part of the northern *Rezeigat* tribe). Prior to this division all the land in *Dar Masalit* was claimed by the *Masalit* tribe. The *Masalit* viewed the division as a way for the Sudanese government to downgrade or abolish their long-standing customary claims to the land (Abdul-Jalil and Abdal-Kareem, 2011). The Act and the resulting division of *Dar Masalit* are thought to have played a major role in the armed conflict in 1997 between the *Masalit* and Arab pastoralists in the area. The recruitment of *Masalit* youth into the present rebel militias can be linked to the problems over land that the Emirate Act brought about (Abdul-Jalil and Abdal-Kareem, 2011). The second law was the Investment Act of 1998 (GOS, 1998), which opened the door for the allocation of large tracts of land by central decision-making at the federal and state levels, without consultation with local inhabitants or recognition of their rights. This law built upon the 1970 Unregistered Land Act by allocating land for investment which was claimed by government under the 1970 law.

Conflict and Fur indigenous land rights

The indigenous Hakura tenure system: stress, exclusion and resistance

The *hakura* land system, while historically serving the *Fur* well, has proved to be exclusionary in important ways for those not native to a *Dar* that practices the system. This exclusion is partial, but ultimately quite significant and is a fundamental ingredient in the perpetuation of the current conflict. While the system does allow 'outsiders' to enjoy land access, and pursue various production systems, their representation in the political system is limited to the '*Sheik* of the people' and at the most the mid-level position of *Omda*, with both the much coveted '*Sheik* of the land' and the higher and more politically powerful position of *Nazir* (Paramount Chief) unattainable. The ultimate problem with this partial participation in the *hakura* system is that control over land and political participation are inseparable in Darfur. As well, alliances, loyalties, political gains and the power structures that support these have historically been formed around land (Egemi, 2009). As a result political participation is kept away from the growing communities of migrants, such as the *Zaghawa* and the Arab pastoralists – whose populace and in many cases wealth (especially for the *Zaghawa*) have grown considerably over the years. In reaction to the inability of their growing numbers, wealth, and aspirations to politically participate in the areas in which they resided, the communities of newcomers began to demand their own Native Administration, Paramount Chief, and importantly their own *hakura*. For example, arrivals from Chad were given locations in which to live, but as their numbers increased they wanted their own land, and for it to be administered by them. This became a problem because such land would need to be taken permanently away from the original *hakura* holders. This kind of aspiration became such a widespread issue, that a local conference convened by those native to the *hakura* system determined that land cannot be given to outsiders if it is to be taken from those native to the area. And since all land in Darfur is claimed in some way by individuals and groups native to the *hakura* system, it essentially meant that no land would be available under this construct.

With such partial political participation for the non-natives over time, land tenure insecurity became a serious problem, with the result being that fears about losing land access then drove the search for alternatives to the *hakura* system – such as statutory law, Islamic law, and forms of resistance and armed confrontation. Widespread pursuit of these alternatives within *hakura* administered areas then eventually degraded the *hakura* system itself, so that it began to have trouble functioning in a cohesive manner. Not surprisingly those native to the *hakura* system resisted this degradation, also in a confrontational way. Thus what began as a fairly benevolent approach towards 'guests' by those native to the *hakura* system, changed into a severe problem that has become widely recognized as a primary factor contributing to the persistence of the current armed conflict. The United Nations Office for the Coordination of Humanitarian Affairs in Darfur notes that the *hakura* system is one of the major stumbling blocks to the peace process, 'due in large part because the landless camel herders and to some extent the landless *Zaghawa* are always against customary law' (author's field notes). In this regard the original *hakura* granting documents became a target for destruction by the *Janjaweed*, in an attempt to reduce the customary legal basis for *hakura* claims. These documents, once only of historical interest, 'today they are weapons of war' (O'Fahey, 2008). Thus from their perspective, the Arab pastoralists saw an opportunity to correct a long-standing injustice of landlessness caused by the indigenous sedentary tenure system together with the colonial and independence era statutory legal land regimes, by pursuing their acutely felt need for land and hence greater political participation in Darfur.

The failure to adapt to newly emerging realities on the part of *hakura* indigenous law also has had repercussions and points of confrontation with statutory law – which itself has failed to adapt to *hakura* law. This mutual incompatibility has led to further problems regarding outside investment and the development this has the potential to bring. With no way for such investment (and the needed tenure security for large land areas that this requires) to occur within the *hakura* system, together with the inability of the statutory system to effectively connect with the *hakura* system, exclusively statutory approaches were and continue to be pursued in a 'forced' manner instead, because this is what outside investors and government have access to. One study notes that large allocations of land in Darfur have gone to investors from Jordan, Egypt, China, and the Gulf States, as well as Sudanese investors from outside Darfur in this manner (Pantuliano, 2007). With the appearance of such outsiders claiming land access via statutory law to large areas within *hakura* administered lands, significant resistance and animosity has emerged on the part of those operating within the *hakura* system.

A related issue regarding outsiders and land is the role of *hakura* law in any potential peace process. In this regard a hypothetical scenario was put to a local Paramount Chief during the fieldwork – 'if the problem outsiders now acting as secondary occupants were de-militarized, and promised to abide by local rules, would they be allowed to stay on unused land according to the old rules of allowing guests onto land?' The answer was an emphatic 'no', under no circumstances would such an arrangement be allowed. This is because good relations are critically important to obtaining land access in the *hakura* system as an outsider. And since the initial intention of the outsiders was belligerent, such a proposal would not be acceptable under *hakura* law. The Paramount Chief noted that even within the old *hakura* title documents it is stated 'do no harm to neighbors', and 'with good neighborly relations', and that such statements are still taken very seriously. Thus arriving in an area in an aggressive manner is the opposite of what is needed to access land. The Paramount Chief noted further that even when an individual or group arrives with good intentions, it usually takes three years of good behavior to obtain firm land rights as guests.

A compounding problem with *hakura* tenure, is that in the decades prior to the war the increasing importance of cash in order to purchase food and consumer goods turned some indigenous *Fur* land into a commodity even though the legal status of such land was not clear. Those who were not able to cultivate their land year-around, found they could sell or lease it as individuals on a cash or share-cropping basis. This appeared to occur without engaging any customary process or practice that transferred land rights from *hakura*-based holdings to individual holdings. This was a relatively new phenomenon for Darfur, which did not exist prior to the 1970s except in very limited occasions involving outsiders who wanted to establish gardens on land near small towns. But the practice has since grown considerably over time, and has spread to a number of larger areas, angering those who adhere to traditional *hakura* tenure and its authorities and structures. Currently, in areas where land purchase is now common, there is a good deal of resistance by some to going back to the old ways of *hakura* land tenure. Such that those who try to invoke the *hakura* system in order to evict others or solve problems, can be severely opposed.

The statutory tenure system: intrusion and confrontation

The land registration problem

In a significant change in the state's approach to land tenure, the government of Jafar Numeiri enacted the 1970 Unregistered Land Act, bringing into government ownership all land not registered by that date. The Act paved the way for subsequent developments to take place regarding land tenure in Darfur which have since contributed significantly to the current conflict. Most importantly, migrants from northern Darfur who settled further south, began to claim land rights under the Act, ignoring the *hakura* approach to guest accommodation for migrants. Instead they argued that such land now belonged to the government, and so could be given to them by the government. Such claims would have been impossible in the past when newcomers were expected to remain as 'guests' of the host tribe and abide by local customary rules regarding land rights.

When non-native interests (individual, group, and commercial) sought to gain access to lands in Darfur via the 1970 law instead of the *hakura* system, it became clear that there was never any real opportunity to register land in Darfur according to the 1925 Land Settlement and Registration Act, due to the lack of services for surveying and institutions for registration. Nevertheless in 1970 all unregistered land in Darfur became state land for the state to allocate. Thus the 1970 law asserted government ownership over lands already claimed by the *hakura* system. The potential for using 'guiding principles' within the 1970 Act for recognizing customary land rights acquired through occupation, were rendered meaningless by court decisions and thus a significant opportunity for statutory and customary law to become mutually accommodating was missed.

A number of large-scale mechanized agricultural projects, which required large tracts of land with statutory tenure arrangements, have been introduced in southern Darfur (mainly in *Um Ajaj*) using the 1970 Act. With the 1970 Act the government was also able to distribute large plots of farmland to urban merchant elites from outside Darfur (primarily from central and riverine Sudan). This process of land allocation by the state caused considerable animosity among many within the Darfur population. The customary user of unregistered land became completely subjected to the government who could exercise its legal rights at will, thus significantly undermining the ability and authority of indigenous customary tenure structures, and decreasing tenure security over indigenous *Fur* land. And while some local inhabitants now want to register their land to protect it from being reallocated by the state, the government indicates that it is too late, and that they should have registered their land earlier by the time the Unregistered Land Act was enacted.

The lack of opportunity to register land in Darfur according to the Act was not the only problem with the law. Even if there was the possibility of registering land between the 1925 and 1970 Acts and many individuals had done so, it would not have alleviated the animosity that would have emerged when the government moved to officially own and allocate the remaining unoccupied and hence unregistered areas of *hakura* and *Dars*. As well, if the farmers would have had the opportunity to register their occupied land and did, it would have been interpreted as acknowledgement that they concurred with the law that all unoccupied *Dar* land should rightly go to the government; thus there would still have been considerable resistance to the Act. And because under customary law lands are not regarded as property (i.e., a commodity), but are instead a form of homeland, engaging in survey, demarcation and registration based on occupation would have had the effect of converting them to property, allowing government to locate and transact them, thus further creating discord. As a result any remedies based on this law, with the presumption that the primary problem was lack of an opportunity to register, would still not have resolved the broader nature of the problem regarding the Act, which is essentially that all land in Darfur is already indigenously claimed. In this context those encountered during the fieldwork noted that it is the flexibility and ambiguity of customary tenure, not clarity, that allows for the elasticity needed in the tenure system to accommodate livestock migrations, pursue options in drought years, and importantly allow for local derivation of 'on the spot' solutions to tenure problems as they emerge. All of these are constrained by registration, demarcation and government imposition of statutory laws.

A further disruptive aspect of the law involved the Arab pastoralists and *Zaghawa* newcomers who sought to claim land under the law that was not already physically occupied. Historically they respected local customs regarding being 'guests' on others' land, including paying the local *Sheik* one-third of any crop they cultivated. But in reaction to the growing prominence of the Unregistered Land Act over time, they started to reason that if the government actually owns the land, why should they pay the local *Sheik* in order to acknowledge that the land belongs to the *hakura* system? Further aggravating the situation was a widely known case whereby a Darfur state governor (appointed by Khartoum) allowed, on his own initiative, an Arab pastoralist group headed by their own *Omda* to have their own land with no consultation with the local agriculturalist natives, because presumably the government owned the land through the 1970 Act. This has now set a form of precedent, with other nomad groups asking for similar arrangements. The many conflicts that the resettled *Zaghawa* have had with the *Fur* in the eastern *goz* (areas of stabilized sand dunes that are preferred for agriculture), south of El-Fasher in the mid-1980s, were due to the repercussions of the 1970 law. Thus the law asserted government ownership over lands already claimed by the *hakura* system, allowing outsiders to gain control (in a highly contested manner) over significantly large areas. To this day the legacy of the law's interaction with the *hakura* system facilitates confrontation between the *Fur*, the *Zaghawa*, Arab pastoralists and government.

Land disputes, Native administration and the 'land sheik'

A primary manifestation of the legal incompatibility regarding land in Darfur was the inability to resolve land disputes, and the subsequent aggravation of these over time into violent trends. When the major droughts hit the region in the 1970s (Leroy, 2009) and pastoral groups started to move south into the Jebel Mara area, serious land conflicts with the local sedentary groups emerged. While the Native Administration was traditionally responsible for dispute resolution, the abolishment of official government recognition of the Native Administration in 1971 caused significant problems. The institutional vacuum created had a direct effect on land disputes, particularly between tribes and between pastoralist vs. agriculturalist groups. Land conflicts became acute and irresolvable in the absence of the Native Administration's dispute resolution mechanisms, particularly with the inability of the government to replace these with viable, legitimate mechanisms based on statutory law. As a result claimants resorted to violence to deal with disputes. While in-group dispute resolution mechanisms such as the *judiya* (a mix of arbitration and mediation supervised by respected persons), and dispute resolution through local *Sheiks* by and large were able to continue to work on their own – attesting to their resilience – this occurred (and continues) only at the local level between those of the same tribal affiliation. But this was not the case when the dispute involved people over larger areas or between tribes, or pastoralist vs. agriculturalist groups. Such larger-scale disputes became irresolvable in the absence of an effective Native Administration, and turned severe, feeding into the developing narratives of injustice, victimization, and retribution which aligned with different sides in the current conflict. In place of such mechanisms many groups and individuals attempted to pursue (apart from violence) dispute resolution within various statutory laws, and different interpretations of Islamic law. However these suffer from interpretation, enforcement, compatibility and personnel problems, and in the case of statutory law, legitimacy problems. This led to a situation of 'forum shopping' for land dispute resolution mechanisms among the incompatible sets of law. While such forum shopping could be beneficial for disputants who agree on a single forum, for the more volatile group-based disputes, attachment to different fora became part of the larger tribal political problem.

An additional important cause of land disputes has resulted from a change in the duties of the 'land *sheik*'. The land *sheiks* were particularly important in the rain-fed areas and had a number of responsibilities, including negotiation with nomads regarding the timing of the use of livestock migration corridors which ran through cultivated areas. But perhaps the most important issue for the land *Sheiks* was to manage the timing and use of the post-harvest fields for grazing while livestock were progressing through the migration routes. Historically the land *sheik* would inform local farmers of the date by which they needed to have their harvested crops and possessions out of their fields, otherwise they could not complain about any livestock damage that might occur. This was an important role because in different years and in different areas, crops would be harvested at different times. However in 1990 the government bypassed the land *Sheiks*, and simply announced the date by which livestock would be allowed into rain fed crop areas Darfur-wide. This occurred without negotiation between farmers and herders, or an appreciation of the variation in harvest times across space and time or the role of the land *Sheiks*. The position of the land *Sheik* was thus undermined significantly. In many areas this meant that livestock entered cultivated areas prior to harvest and destroyed crops. The reason for the government intervention appears to have been that in years of drought some areas were congested with livestock waiting to enter post-harvest fields, and pastoralists asked farmers to harvest quickly so as to allow grazing. Some pastoralists complained to government about the timing and access problem, and also claimed that farmers were expanding their cultivated areas. As a result the government decided on its own calendar as to when pastoralists could enter cropped lands, instead of supporting the negotiated approach of the land *Sheiks*. This weakened the flexibility of indigenous tenure and its ability to manage relationships in a stable manner between agriculturalist and pastoral groups. The farmers reacted to this government intervention and the large increase in crop damage, especially near Jebel Mara where rain-fed crops are harvested later (and where the war began), by burning the bush grazing areas around their crops so as to discourage entry into the overall area by pastoralists. The nomads then reacted by taking their herds directly into the unharvested standing crops to graze, and burning farming villages. The farmers then reacted to this by killing livestock.

Cases of crop damage in the past had the nomad and farmer in question going to a Native Court headed by a Paramount Chief to negotiate damage payment. But with the new government calendar the nomads no longer felt obliged to go to these courts or negotiate for damage payments, further undermining the customary tenure system and aggravating relations between the two groups. This meant that if a farmer wanted to get damage payment for his crops he would need to go to a statutory court, which was expensive, and where statutory law meant that a different burden of proof was needed. Farmers regarded such courts as pro-Arab pastoralist and so did not engage them. With no widely legitimate institutional way to resolve such problems, farmers instead began to burn more grazing areas, arm themselves, and take matters into their own hands. The pastoralists then armed themselves in response.

The role of land-related islamic law in the conflict

As noted above, Islamic law is used in three distinct ways to justify claims to land for three different sectors of society – government, the *Fur* indigenous group (*hakura*), and the indigenous Arab pastoralists together with the *Zaghawa*. Although Islamic scholars agree that according to Islamic law the state can hold land in trust for the universal Muslim community, irrespective of national boundary, it applies only to 'plain land' (in its natural state) as opposed to land that is clearly occupied and used (Sait and Lim, 2006). However a primary effect, if not purpose, behind the Sudanese state's use of Islamic law, is to relieve other forms of claim – tribal, autochthonous, private, and even that based on customary law fused with Islamic law. According to the view of some in Darfur, the purpose of the Ministry of Religious Affairs and *Waqf* is in fact to co-opt Islamic law and take control of lands away from local people.

Alternatively the Arab pastoralist/*Zaghawa* use of Islamic law to gain land access facilitated dislocating people from lands that were clearly already claimed and used by other Muslims. Both approaches are at odds with lands designated as *waqf or waqf*-like by the *hakura* granting deeds. And both approaches seek to discount the establishment of such *waqf* – the state by no longer honoring the *hakura* deeds as it once did, and the *Janjaweed* by attempting to destroy the deeds. Such selectivity regarding use of Islamic law is not new to the conflict. O'Fahey (2008) reports that in 2003 and 2004 the *Janjaweed* burned mosques, desecrated Qur'ans and killed Imams in an apparent attempt at creating a divide regarding Islam between themselves and the agriculturalists. Thus these three uses of Islamic law (*hakura*, state, Arab pastoralist/*Zaghawa*) became set against one another, justifying claims in different ways to separate sets of people.

Conclusion

The case of indigenous land rights and conflict in Darfur illustrates two distinctions from the usual state vs. indigenous land rights scenario. The first is that one set of indigenous rights can become opposed to a neighboring set of indigenous rights. In this case the land rights system of the *Fur* group became opposed to the land rights (and aspirations) of the northern nomadic pastoralists. This was (and continues to be) a lingering confrontation which was exploited by the state for their own political objectives. Second, while the state is often the focus of recommendations regarding the need to adapt to and/or accommodate indigenous land rights, indigenous tenure systems also need to find ways to accommodate the rights of other indigenous groups, as well as those of the state, if they are to maintain or enhance their role in protecting and administering indigenous lands. In the Darfur case the inability of the indigenous *hakura* tenure system to allow full participation by nomadic pastoralists, significantly aggravated the divisions between the two indigenous groups, and allowed these divisions to be exploited by the government in the creation of the *Janjaweed*. Such a lack of adaptation on the part of indigenous land-related law to other indigenous groups' laws and state law is not unique to Darfur. Unruh (2008) observes a similar situation among local chieftaincies in Sierra Leone. While a valuable feature of any land-related law, such adaptation is particularly difficult in cases where armed conflict has prevailed for some time, causing indigenous groups to withdraw into themselves for protection and survival, thus minimizing interaction with other forms of law (Unruh, 2008).

The Darfur case also illustrates that even in cases where there is logical and functional affinity between an indigenous system and the statutory system (both functioned off of documents and precise boundaries and possessed robust institutions that interfaced well with each other and the *hakura* system was recognized in the colonial and independence era governments), the state can nevertheless act to subvert the relationship if it is not maintained in an ongoing way.

References

Abdhalla, Tajeldin. *Land Rights Confusion Hinders Darfur IDP Returns*. London, Institute for War and Peace Reporting, ACR Issue 237, 2010.

Abdul-Jalil, Musa Adam. 'Intertribal Conflicts in Darfur: Scarcity of Resources or Crises of Governance?' In *Environment and Conflict in Africa: Reflections from Darfur*, edited by Marcel Laroy, Addis Ababa: University for Peace, Africa Programme, 2009.

Abdul-Jalil, Musa Adam. 'Land Tenure, Land Use and Inter-Ethnic Conflict in Darfur'. In *Understanding the Crisis in Darfur: Listening to Sudanese Voices*, edited by Abdel Ahmed and Leif Manger. Bergen, Norway: University of Bergen, 2007.

Abdul-Jalil, Musa Adam. 'Nomad-Sedentary Relations and the Question of Land Rights in Darfur: From Complementarity to Conflict'. In *Nomad-Sedentary Relations and Failing State Institutions in Kordofan and Darfur*, edited by Richard Rottenburg. Halle, Germany: Halle-Wittenberg University, 2008.

Abdul-Jalil, Musa Adam, Azzain, Adam, and Yousuf, Adam. 'Future Prospects for Native Administration and Local Governance in Darfur'. In *War in Darfur and the Search for Peace*, edited by Alex De Waal, Boston, MA: Global Equity Initiative, Harvard University, 2007.

Abdul-Jalil, Musa Adam. 'The Dynamics of Customary Land Tenure and Natural Resource Management in Darfur'. *Land Reform, Settlement and Cooperatives*, 2 (2006) 8–23.

Abdul-Jalil, Musa Adam and Zahir, Abdal-Kareem. *Contested Land Rights and Ethnic Conflict in Mornei, West Darfur: Scarcity of Resources or Crises of Governance?* Khartoum: University of Khartoum, 2011.

Abdul-Jalil, Musa Adam and Unruh, Jon. 'Land Rights Under Stress in Darfur: A Volatile Dynamic of the Conflict'. *War and Society* 32, no. 2 (2013) 156–181.

Babiker, Mustafa. 'Resource Competition and Conflict: Herder/Farmer or Pastoralism/Agriculture?' In *African Pastoralism: Conflict, Institutions and Government*, edited by Salih, Mohamed, Dietz, Thomas, and Ahmed, Abdel. London: Pluto Press, 2001, 135–144.

Concordis, *Land Use and Tenure: A Key to Sustainable Peace in Darfur*. Cambridge: Concordis Papers, 2007.

Draft Darfur Peace Document (DDPD), *Draft Darfur Peace Document*. Doha, Qatar, 2011.

Egemi, Omer. *Land Tenure Issues in Darfur*. Nairobi: UN Habitat, 2009.

Elmekki, Abdelgalil. *DDDC Common Ground Consultations and Public Hearings.* Khartoum: Darfur – Darfur Dialogue and Consultation (DDDC), 2009.

Flint, Julie and De Waal, Alex. *Darfur: A New History of a Long War.* London: Zed Books, 2008.

Flint, Julie. *Beyond 'Janjaweed': Understanding the Militias of Darfur.* Small Arms Survey, Geneva: Graduate Institute of International and Development Studies, 2009.

Gordon, Cary. 'Recent Developments in the Land Law of the Sudan: A Legislative Analysis'. *Journal of African Law* 30, no 2 (1986) 143–174.

Government of Sudan (GOS). *The Emirate Act of 1995.* Khartoum: Ministry of Justice, 1995.

Government of Sudan (GOS). *The Investment Act.* Khartoum, Ministry of Justice, 1998.

Leroy, Marcel. *Environment and Conflict in Africa: Reflections on Darfur.* Addis Ababa: University for Peace, 2009.

O'Fahey, Rex. *The Darfur Sultanate: A History.* New York: Columbia University Press, 2008, 136.

O'Fahey, Rex and Salim, Abu. *Land in Dar Fur: Charters and Related Documents from the Dar Fur Sultanate.* Cambridge: Cambridge University Press, 2003.

Mohammed, Adam. 'The Rezaigat Camel Nomads of the Darfur Region of Western Sudan: From Co-operation to Confrontation'. *Nomadic Peoples* 8, no 2 (2004) 230–241.

Pantuliano, Sara. *The Land Question: Sudan's Peace Nemesis,* London: Overseas Development Institute, 2007.

Runger, Mechthild. *Land Law & Land Use Control in Western Sudan: The Case of Southern Darfur.* London: Ithaca Press, 1987.

Sait, Siraj and Lim, Hilary. *Land, Law, and Islam: Property and Human Rights in the Muslim World.* London: Zed Books, 2006.

Suiliman, Osman. *The Darfur Conflict: Geography or Institutions?* New York: Routledge Press, 2011.

Unruh, Jon. 'Land and Legality in the Darfur Conflict'. *African Security* 5 (2012) 105–128.

Unruh, Jon. 'Land Policy Reform, Customary Rule of Law and the Peace Process in Sierra Leone'. *African Journal of Legal Studies* 2 (2008) 94–117.

Note

1   Portions of this chapter have previously appeared in Abdul-Jalil and Unruh (2013) and Unruh (2012).

11 Indigenous rights, grey spacing and roads

The Israeli Negev Bedouin and planning in Road 31

Avinoam Meir, Batya Roded and Arnon Ben-Israel

In recent decades the disciplines of human geography, political science and planning have produced a rich literature on the issue of grey space and informality. Most discussion revolves around 'grey' neighborhoods, villages and unplanned towns as places characterized by informality and 'orderlessness'. Concomitantly, the issue of indigenous rights, property included, has also been widely discussed, including that of spatial planning for indigenous communities. Both bodies of knowledge highlight primarily these squatter places and their growth from 'below', with the underlying assumption that they are the sole geographical entities within indigenous space. In fact such a hidden assumption is not exclusive to studies of indigenous space. It leans upon the wider spatial theory of all humanity which has been criticized for overlooking the fact that space contains other types of meaningful geographical entities beyond settlements or cities (Meir and Duenias, 2008). Space needs thus to be decomposed into such entities at various scales in seeking improvement in our spatial understanding.

Roads, streets, alleys, trails, tracks and the like are, among others, such geographical entities. Yet they have so far been regarded as self-evident integral elements of space, and therefore their study has focused primarily on their functional connectivity between places. The idea that roads may carry other cultural and social meanings has broadly escaped the general scholarly discussion. In particular their rich and complex nature as places themselves was greatly overlooked. In terms of the 'white-grey' tension among disciplinary issues, they were rejected from the center stage of the geographical and social science discourse and relegated into the grey disciplinary zone.

In recent years, however, the social sciences have witnessed the growth of a new paradigm, 'the new mobility paradigm' (Sheller and Urry, 2006). This paradigm is beginning now to become home for the slowly growing research interest on roads and their *rich cultural meanings*. This implies that in decomposing space into its various geographical entities at various scales we may view a road beyond its sheer functionality; rather we should look into its essence as a rich geographical entity that is meaningful culturally and socially in and 'by itself' in 'white' and grey spaces alike. Recognition of this nature of roads through the neo-mobility paradigm shifts thus the discourse on them into the 'white' center-stage of scholarly interest.

In this chapter we wish to carry this notion into the field of planning within the contexts of indigenous property rights and greyness. We focus here on Road 31 in the northern Negev semi-arid area in Israel. This road was studied by us primarily from the perspective of a socio-cultural space shared by both its Arab-Bedouin indigenous and Jewish settler populations. The Jewish population inhabits two places at the edges of this road, but in-between there are dozens Bedouin squatter villages that are unrecognized by the state. On the one hand the state does not recognize their land ownership claims, and on the other has not offered them by far any quality resettlement solutions. Thus, while in many economic respects this Bedouin indigenous space constitutes an integral part of metropolitan Beer Sheva as the regional capital, in many other respects it meets the definition of grey space (Yiftachel and Tzfadia, 2014).

Our study originates primarily in the notion of road as a *socio-cultural place* first suggested by Ben-Israel and Meir (2013) in their study of a small local rural road within Bedouin space. This study gave birth to the present wider study of Road 31 as a *place* that is an integral major geographical entity within this space and yet was overlooked by studies on Bedouin space. While pursuing this research we encountered also the impetus for studying its planning process within the context of indigenous property rights. This derived from the fact that since 2010 the road has been undergoing a major upgrade development towards its transformation into a limited access multi-paths high-speed highway. The directives received from state planning authorities reflected the general policy towards Bedouin space in what critical planning theory regards more generally as an abstract and Newtonian view of space (Meir, 2005). Such was the manner in which these directives were implemented by the engineering firm hired by the contractor (Israel Road Company (IRC), a semi-governmental firm). Thus the planning process of the upgrade project did not include any public participation of the local Bedouin population nor consultation with them. Yet the IRC soon faced the harsh and trapping reality of Bedouin homes and petty business establishments dispersed along the upgrade route which was planned for superimposition onto them.

The ensuing conflict between the Bedouin and the IRC over their property and other rights generated dynamics that highlight the great disparities between policies and planning approaches towards peripheral indigenous groups and the grey reality of their life. It is within these two contexts that we wish to submit our major propositions for this chapter. First, a spatial policy that discriminates and excludes an indigenous minority group may backfire by producing a constraint upon the planning authorities to initiate from 'above' a grey or informal planning mechanism. Second, contrary to state intensions, this mechanism may benefit the minority/indigenous group by strengthening its grip on its land and thus further perpetuating from 'below' the greying of their space.

In order to examine these propositions we will first review the issue of informal mechanisms within formal planning in general and the role played by a grey planning mechanism within the context of settlement policy towards indigenous peoples. We then continue to the land conflict between the Bedouin and the state of Israel and state policy of non-recognition in their villages. Following this, and as a necessary condition for understanding the conflict at question, we explore the nature of Road 31 as a *place* within Bedouin space through its historical-geographical and political indigenous background. In the major part we describe the conflict that evolved around the project from the perspective of planning rights of the Bedouin. We first discuss the issue of participation, followed by Bedouin concerns for their 'right for the road', their struggle for property and other rights and the activation of a grey planning/implementation mechanism that eventually facilitated pursuance of the project. We conclude with a discussion of the significance of this process in terms of planning within grey space in general and within indigenous space in particular.

At the general background of our discussion and analysis are concepts of an ethno-national policy interlaced within economic neo-liberalism. This is manifested in a growing detachment of the state from its commitment to its citizens and its strong inclination towards planning from above. In the particular case of road planning, and further within indigenous territories, this is realized in state agency in employment of a sheer instrumental engineering approach disregarding the people or the environment (e.g., Rabinowitc and Vardy, 2010; see also Adam *et al.*, 2012; Orr, 2014; de Pina-Cabral, 1987).

Grey spacing through grey planning mechanism

Understanding state resort to a grey planning mechanism under non-recognition in indigenous rights requires first a brief discussion of two rapidly growing issues: indigenous rights, primarily property rights, in the context of planning, and grey spatialization.

The planning context of indigenous property rights

It has become commonly accepted that legal and planning systems in modern settler states consistently tend to ignore indigenous native title land claims. In light of this the discourse on indigenous groups, their rights and the need for changing their status within settler states revolves primarily around justice and its spatial manifestations. These contain distributional justice intended to amend past injustice, which in planning is practically translated into physical essences such as land and resources (Yiftachel *et al.*, 2009). In the context of the present study principles of justice in spatial planning, as suggested by Harvey (1993) and Young (1990), are particularly relevant. These include distribution of resources, benefits and costs in space and society according to real needs, compensation for past social deprivation in the form of positive discrimination, and sustainable development as an inter-generational justice. Thus realization of distributional justice in space and time is, as argued by Fraser (2000; 2003), a *necessary condition* for recognition of indigenous property rights.

These principles of culturally and socially sensitive planning contrast, however, with the origins of the idea of planning in European concepts of 'progress' which are framed within the 'rational paradigm'. Contributing precisely to the marginalization of indigenous peoples, these concepts block recognition and acceptance of other modes of knowledge towards planning issues and property rights such as spiritual modes held by the planned subjects (Small and Sheehan, 2008). In general the interactions between legal, planning and development systems, the external delimitation of adminis-trative boundaries of the planned subject groups, and the direction of capital flows are all capable of either advancing or retracting indigenous rights and thus of shaping policies toward these peoples (Sheehan, 2012). This implies, as elaborated by Lane (2006) and Lane and Hibbard (2006) that a genuine willingness of the establishment to recognize these rights is facilitated only by enabling indigenous groups' full and proactive participation in the planning process. This, however, is not always the case.

Grey and greying planning mechanism

Lack of such recognition in the rights of indigenous peoples drives them quite often to produce a 'grey space'. The concept of grey space refers to a conglo-merate of populations, areas and economic and social activities that are situated on a 'white–black' continuum. On one pole there are the 'white spaces' that is, those of full, formal, legal and secure membership. 'Black spaces' that is, those of expulsion, incrimination and destruction are at the other pole. However, for the purposes of our above two propositions we need to resort again to a con-ceptual decomposition, this time of the classic dichotomies of 'law'–'crime', 'planned'–'spontaneous' and 'belonging'–'alien' which are typical of the prevalent planning legal and political thought. In decomposing them we may surface practices employed by the state and its institutions in order to fortify or sustain its control. They may include rejection, by-passing and even suspension of the very law which they are mandated to maintain and defend. These prac-tices, which originate 'from above', encounter informal development initiatives by the people 'from below'. Under conditions of asymmetrical power relations they are responsible for the process of 'grey spacing' (Yiftachel and Tzfadia, 2014).

In other words, employing prolonged exclusionary spatial practices by the state towards a minority group that is driven into the intermediacy of greyness achieves quite the opposite: it encourages these communities to become active precisely in this very direction in the process. That is, they may generate new social movements, establish insurgent identities, and develop novel practices and tactics for survival by harnessing their grey space as a basis for self-organization and empowerment. The gap between tolerable reality and lack of legal and planning tolerance activates thus a process of 'grey spacing' during which the boundaries between the putative and the repelled are constantly at a bi-directional movement. This dynamic sustains grey spaces at 'permanent temporariness' (Yiftachel and Tzfadia, 2014). Paradoxically thus, while the state assumes a significant role in grey spacing, this process eventually undermines its own hegemony and dominance.

This is not to say that greyness and informality are exclusive to frictional realities of minorities and indigenous groups. Studies anchored in a western-democratic perspective (e.g., Allmendinger and Haughton, 2010; Fox-Rogers and Murphy, 2013; Hillier, 2000; Innes *et al.*, 2007) reveal the occasional resort of the formal planning establishment to informal mechanisms as an integral part of the planning process. In the United States, for example, this takes place when the government attempts to introduce legally-borderline changes at the local level. The advantage of this mechanism is rooted in its specific properties. These include free flow of information, creativity, shared responsibility, wider degrees of freedom, close acquaintance with the local conditions, formation of interpersonal trust, and personal commitment to the consequences. These researchers recommend therefore that maximization of the benefits for the community and facilitating openness and democratic legitimacy may be achieved by developing a holistic approach in coordination with and participation by a plurality of actors from both sides that will act in informal ways (Allmendinger and Haughton, 2010; Fox-Rogers and Murphy, 2013; Innes *et al.*, 2007).

The democratic systems in which this planning mechanism is occasionally resorted to are assumed to be relatively frictionless and balanced in terms of power relations. This situation is different under conditions of unbalanced power relations common with regard to ethnic and indigenous minorities. Yiftachel (2009) suggests that within such a system of power relations, the practice of voluntary cooperation precisely yields to greying from above as a means of control. However, this line of reasoning does not fit well with a policy of indecisiveness. Such a policy is often extant when the state is too distant and alien from one section of its population and too close and intimate with the other to an extent of merged identities. As elaborated by Bellina (2009) and Brodkin (1987), the state then finds it difficult to impose control upon the local group which on its part, as shown by Jabareen (2014), resorts to informal and extra-institutional practices.

It follows that the relationships between the state and these social groups are shaped by incapacity in creating a common social and cultural ground (Roded, 2012). This state of affairs often prevails while other processes of 'development' for 'national needs' (such as settlement or big infrastructure projects) are pursued for the benefit of the dominant majority. These processes concomitantly constitute in fact planning for the dominant group and un-planning for the excluded group, promoting thus a policy of spatial inequality. We submit therefore that this state of political power relations between the two sides, the state and the local group at question, calls for harnessing greyness at intermediate echelons of the planning establishment which, in turn, receives 'informal legitimacy' from both below and above. It is this complexity that serves as a conceptual framework for studying the case of Road 31 and the Bedouin population in the Negev within the context of indigenous rights.

Bedouin indigenous property rights and unrecognized villages

The local issues of Bedouin rights fit well, as shown by Sheehan (2012), into the more international context of indigenous property rights. As shown below, all other issues discussed under the heading of 'planning rights' emanate from this major issue. The questions of Israeli Negev Bedouin indigeneity, their property rights and their unrecognized villages date back to the establishment of the state of Israel in 1948 when around 12,000 semi-nomadic Bedouin (out of about 70,000) chose to remain in Israel after the war. Many of them were relocated by the state into a military-administered area (the *sieg*), which prevailed until 1965 and encompassed also the rest of the tribes that were allowed to remain in their traditional tribal territories. High natural increase rates (their population in 2014 has grown to about 220,000), shrinkage of traditional subsistence resources within the *sieg*, and political and administrative imperatives of the state, including land required for development of Jewish settlement in this region, all led the government in the early 1960s to decide on further relocation of the Bedouin into seven new planned towns (Meir, 1997).

It is at this juncture that the question of Bedouin property rights began to surface. In broad terms the Bedouin society is internally divided into two property-based groups: the landed class, who are the real Bedouin that have been living in their tribal territories for at least two centuries as semi-nomadic pastoralists and tillers; and the annexed landless Bedouin (fellaheen) group whose ancestors migrated from nearby areas in the Levant since the mid-19th century and became subordinate tenant farmers on Bedouin land (Ben-David, 2004). Until the late 1980s many of the latter, having no property claims, moved to the newly planned towns. Many of the former refused to evacuate their traditional tribal territories and risk loss of their property. Their places, about 45 villages (as defined by their NGO, the Regional Council for Bedouin Unrecognized Villages) constitute about 40 percent of the total present Bedouin population. They have never been recognized by the state as statutory settlements eligible for municipal services. They have retained their squatting nature as devoid of any modern infrastructure services of electric power, water supply, paved roads and environmental management capacities (Swirski and Hasson 2005; Noah,

2009; Kissinger and Karplus, 2014). Only by 2005 has the state decided to incorporate them into a non-territorial municipality which was charged solely with the provision of some services.

The primary reason for this state of affairs is rooted in the property rights conflict between the state and the landed group of Bedouin. This conflict dates back to 1858 when the Ottoman Empire legislated the Land Law over its entire imperial expanses. One clause, very critical from a Bedouin perspective, referred to *mewat* land that is, dead land that if not tilled for three years becomes imperial land. The nature of Bedouin semi-nomadic agro-pastoral spatial practices at the time, which could in principle negate the logic of this law, are detailed in a study by Meir (2009a), but in essence the outcome of the *mewat* law was to regard most Bedouin land as imperial land. At the time, and in fact until the end of the British Mandate in 1948 and further until 1958, when the State of Israel adopted the Ottoman law, the Bedouin paid little serious regard to it. The primary reason is that, typical of an indigenous group, they have always preferred their tribal customary legal system as superior to that of the state and therefore bothered little to formally register their property rights.

It was not until 1974 when for the first time they responded positively and seriously to an initiative by the State of Israel to file a request to register their property claims. However, in 1984 the *mewat* principle of the land law received a significant judicial support in a famous Supreme Court ruling that Bedouin land is *mewat* land and therefore is also a state land (*Justice Khalima in Al-Huwashlah vs. The State of Israel, Civil Appeal, 218/84*). Since then many Bedouin have been engaged in land suits against the state. In many cases they submitted expert opinions, primarily from academic circles, that were based on several major propositions: (1) As suggested by Meir (2009a, based on an expert opinion submitted in 2006), in principle Bedouin land was not necessarily *mewat* land at any particular time and place; (2) the Bedouin semi-nomadic version of a village should be regarded as similar to any other type of sedentary settlement on which the *mewat* principle was based, and; (3) significant 20th century historical evidence has been surfaced by researchers to support Bedouin claims of tilling permanently their land, sufficient enough to negate state claim that it was *mewat* land (Yiftachel *et al.*, 2012). And yet, as of now all Bedouin law suits were rejected by the court.

By 2008, following decades of struggle for recognition in their villages and for participation in their planning (Meir 2005, 2009b), the government has established a Committee for Reviewing the Settlement of the Bedouin known also as Justice Goldberg Committee. In its report (Ministry of Housing, 2008) Bedouin *historical* right to their land has for the first time received recognition. Based on this the committee recommended to the government a framework of solutions for both compensation for land that has or would become state land and recognition and development of most of their unrecognized villages. Both the Bedouin and the state were, however, highly critical of these recommendations, based by the former on their minimalism or by the latter on their 'maximalism'. Another committee was then established by the state in 2010 (following a political right-wing electoral turnover) to review again these recommendations for compensation rates and recognition levels. This Prawer Committee was accompanied with considerable and quite heated public debate over its practices and drafts. The Prawer Plan (Prime Minister Office, 2011) was highly criticized again from all political left and right wings along the same minimalism/'maximalism' lines and received little parliamentary support. By 2014 this report was shelved too, with the status quo remaining as to the questions of Bedouin indigenous property rights and recognition of their villages.

It is of significance to note here that since the late 1990s, and pursuant with a worldwide wave in this regard, the Bedouin have anchored their claims for property rights in their historical indigenous nature (Abu-Saad, 2005). Following international activism the status of the Negev Bedouin as an indigenous group was discussed by the UN in 2011 (Anaya, 2011). This UN debate, Bedouin legal and planning struggles and the Goldberg and Prawer reports, have all ignited a heated debate over the issue of Bedouin indigeneity. On the one hand a group of scholars (Frantzman *et al.*, 2012; Yahel *et al.*, 2012) have been repeatedly arguing against acceptance of this status and in support of governmental refusal to accept Bedouin claims for property rights based on their indigeneity. Another group of academics have in contrast written in support of Bedouin indigeneity (Bennett, 2005; Rangwala, 2004; Berman, 2006; Berman-Kishony, 2008; Matari, 2011; Nasasra, 2012; Karplus and Meir, 2013, 2014a, b; Yiftachel, 2009, 2013b; Yiftachel *et al.*, 2014). The significance of this debate for the current chapter is that, as shown below, paradoxically some of Road 31-related spatial practices of the Bedouin, which are rooted in their indigenous characteristics, were recognized by the planners themselves in the grey planning process.

Road 31 and the Bedouin

In this chapter we focus *inter alia* on the particular problem of Bedouin property rights. This analysis is based as noted on a wider research project that examined Road 31 as a geographical entity that is hypothesized to con-stitute a social and cultural place for the Bedouin and the Jewish population. We refer primarily to the section between Shoket Junction and the Jewish city of Arad (about 32 kilometers long, see Figure 11.1).

Our analysis is based on in-depth field interviews during 2012-13 with members of the Bedouin and Jewish populations for whom Road 31 is of direct residential or commuting relevance. We also interviewed expert, professional and administrative figures involved with various aspects of Bedouin community in general and Road 31 in specific. In addition, numerous published and unpublished documents, plans, objections, minutes of various committees and media reports were gathered. These sources were

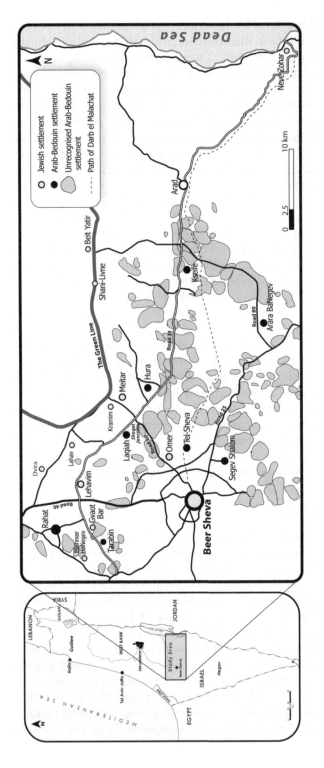

Figure 11.1 Road 31 and Bedouin and Jewish settlements in the northern Negev

then reviewed for extracting themes and notions that are related to the major purpose of analyzing the case of grey space planning of Road 31 vis-à-vis Bedouin property and other rights.

Major historical and indigenous perspectives of Road 31 as place

Bedouin tribal and clan boundaries were shaped in the late 19th century (al-Aref, 1934; Ben-David, 2004) and have since served the Bedouin internally as a spatial-political infrastructure. That is, hierarchical spatial segregation, based socio-politically on the structure of clans, tribes, sub-tribes and extended families (*hamula*), as well as ethnically between Bedouin and fellaheen, is a Bedouin territorial practice of paramount spatial significance (Meir, 1997). These divisions are not formal and are not recognized by the state for any practical matters.

Roads, central geographical entities within the spatial syntax, have naturally assumed a significant role in delineating this informal indigenous territoriality and spatial divisions at all scales. Such is the case with the historical route of Road 31 and its surroundings (Figure 11.1). Ever since the arrival of the semi-nomadic Bedouin in this area, dated back as noted to the early 19th century (and perhaps earlier, see Amara and Yiftachel, 2014; Yiftachel *et al.*, 2012), a major section of its present route which originated in the Dead Sea served them for transporting salt extracted there to regional marketplaces. This commodity, which supplemented their agro-pastoral livelihood, has given that part of the road its ancient Arabic name of Darb-el-Malachat (Road of the Salt). Its path from the present location of Kseifa avoided the hilly area to the northwest and followed the sites of major regional water wells on the plains southwestwards. The road thus served as a backbone for the major inter-tribal and intra-tribal territorial subdivisions (Atzmon, 2013). It served also as a spatial node for many interpersonal daily and periodical commercial and social encounters by members of the various Bedouin groups. The road became thus a central desert geographical entity in internal Bedouin affairs locally and regionally.

Many of the Bedouin tribes of this specific area belong to those which were allowed by the state to remain in their historical tribal territories, while others were relocated there after 1948. This setting constitutes the spatial-historical infrastructure of the various Bedouin communities in this and other areas in the Negev known presently as the 'unrecognized Bedouin villages'. The Jewish town of Arad was established in 1961 as part of the national project of developing and settling the Negev with Jewish populations. The need to connect it to the rest of Israel in the shortest path possible necessitated merging the eastern section of the road, now serving also the industrial and tourism compound of the eastern Negev, with the newly-constructed western section (between Kseifa and Shoket Junction) to become in 1962 the present Road 31. The old indigenous Bedouin road was thus gradually transformed since then into a modern all-Israeli road shared by both Jewish and Bedouin local and external users. Its old southwestward section going to Beer Sheva was deserted due primarily to the evacuation of Bedouin tribes during the construction of a military airbase in this flat terrain in 1981 following the Camp David Accords with Egypt.

As in many roads constructed by the state in the Negev, many local Bedouin families gravitated closer to the new route of Road 31 within their traditional and customary territorial subdivisions to enjoy its various benefits (Ben-David, 2004). Some non-local Bedouin of fellaheen origin, that migrated to this area before 1948 or were relocated there by the state afterwards, also purchased land there from the original Bedouin owners and under the Bedouin customary law. This process has contributed significantly to a considerable increase of Bedouin real estate values along Road 31 (Atzmon, 2013). The two Bedouin planned towns in this area, Hura and Kseifa, were established during the 1980s and were inhabited primarily by the population of the local tribes of both Bedouin and fellaheen origins.

In time dozens of trails and tracks were developed locally and spontaneously by the various Bedouin groups to connect them and their livestock to the old route of the road. Many others were added by them after 1962 to connect to the new route of modern Road 31. The introduction of the automobile transformed many of these trails into dirt roads with presently about 70 dirt entry points to the main road. Still, these roads have been retaining their indigenous traditional nature as reflective of the territorial sub-divisions and socio-spatial syntax. This is a highly significant socio-cultural and political issue among the Bedouin at most spatial scales. Members of a certain group cannot make free use of any of these roads or their entry/exit points along the main road without receiving prior consent of the local groups or families who control and maintain them. Within this conflict-ridden tribal Bedouin Muslim society that is controlled by strict honor and patrilocal codes, exclusivity of their use is meant to provide physical protection and security and to respect the privacy of their women. From a Bedouin indigenous perspective these local dirt roads and their entry points to the main road (see Figure 11.2) became an integral part of their regional indigenous road system, leaning on Road 31 as a backbone. As in many indigenous cultures (e.g., Ingold and Vergunst, 2008; Gooch, 2008; Lye, 2004), they constitute secure and intimate geographical entities and socio-cultural places that are an integral part of their homes. They are external to the official state-constructed road system however, or, in other words, they are grey roads and grey intersections as are many other geographical entities in this area.

The cultural nature of these small and local roads is significant for understanding the role of Road 31 itself as a socio-cultural place. From a Bedouin perspective, Road 31 has no independent life without these local roads and vice versa. Typical of many indigenous groups, residential mobility among the Bedouin is almost non-existent (Ben-Israel, 2009). This implies most likely that Bedouin individuals live in their birth places for the entirety of

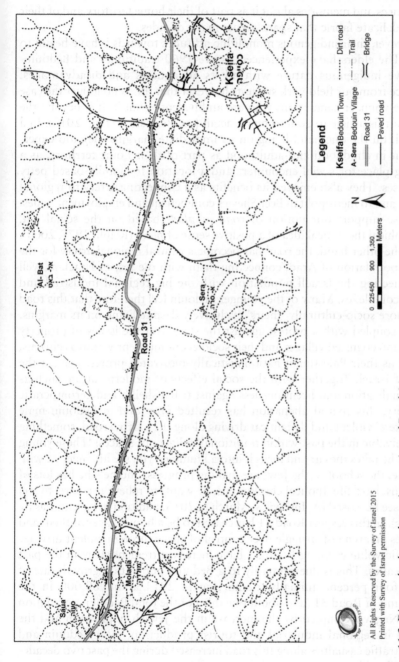

Figure 11.2 Dirt roads along the major portion of Road 31.

Source: Compiled from National GIS Data, Survey of Israel.

their lives. The implication is that Road 31 in its various traditional and modern phases has been integral to their lives regardless of age and generation. They accumulate individual and collective positive and negative experiences and memories about it as part of their home territory and of their spatial delicate fabric that spans across many decades.

However, their indigenous monolithic attitudes towards it have begun to crack. The elders have experienced its pre-1960 traditional and Bedouin-exclusive indigenous nature with all its advantages and disadvantages. Evidence from our fieldwork suggests however that this is no longer the case with the younger generations who are ambivalent about it. It is beyond the scope of this article to go into much detail (see Ben-Israel *et al.*, 2013). In a nutshell, on the one hand living on its immediate margins they too experienced it in childhood and adulthood as part of their home territory, as a meeting place for social encounters and a location for family-based petty businesses. They also enjoyed its benefits as a connecting artery to regional schools and to metropolitan Beer Sheva's commercial and employment nodes. All these support our notion of *road as place* based on the social and geographical theoretical idea of a positive sense of place (Relph, 1977, 2000).

On the other hand, the road has become a central regional artery for the Jewish population of Arad, connecting them with the rest of Israel, as well as connecting the Israeli population with the big regional industrial and tourist complexes. Many of the younger Bedouin feel therefore that this road is no more socio-culturally 'theirs' exclusively despite living on its margins. This is coupled with a protest against the state over the issues of property rights, unrecognized villages and their socio-economic deprivation as citizens, as well as their Palestinian nationalistically-motivated protest against the State of Israel. Together with the social effects of modernization, such as individualization and licentiousness against tribal sheikh and gerontocratic authority, this spatial alienation has resulted *inter alia* in Bedouin male youngsters' violent and defiant car driving along the narrow road, something inconceivable in the past within traditional indigenous spaces: 'These young guys … he takes the car and turns it into a Hummer, you see his anger … with the state, the school … the Jews are making progress, and he – he has lots of problems, hard life, [police] checkpoints, he wants to relieve pressure, to feel people see he exists' (A, Interview, March 6, 2013; addition in parenthesis by authors). In this respect Road 31 has ceased to be a home place for them and becomes an arena of struggle over control of space through violent driving.

Traffic volumes along Road 31 have increased tremendously in the past two decades. This is due primarily to a Bedouin population growth rate of about four percent annually, numbering in 2014 about 60,000 in the hinterland of Road 31 (and about one third of the total Bedouin population in the Negev). Coupled by the increase in the Jewish population and the growth in regional industrial and tourist production, fatal Bedouin and Jewish traffic casualties along this road increased during the past two decades at considerable rates, ushering in the upgrade project.

Planning the upgrade project

Despite being earmarked in the 2001 National Master Plan, implementation of the upgrade project received low priority until 2008 when these traffic circumstances made it urgent. While the immediate motivation was to reduce traffic fatalities, its implementation was framed within a wider context. The official reasoning by the District Planning Committee (DPC) was a road '...connecting a significant number of settlements and serving the northern Negev and the entire country' (DPC, 2010). Yet, an interview with the then mayor of Arad, who was the principal civil entrepreneur behind the project, revealed that the main motivation was to bring Arad and its approximately 24,000 inhabitants, located in the remote national periphery, as well as the industrial and tourist compounds of the eastern Negev, closer and safer to central Israel and thus abate their peripherality and socio-economic marginality (Bar-Lev, 2012). The Bedouin population of this area received no regard by him.

In order to implement the project, its detailed planning commenced in 2008 by the IRC which hired a private engineering firm as sub-contractor. The nature of the upgrade project, as revealed in a review of the upgrade plan (D/11/03/267) and various other internal unpublished documents of the IRC, is that of a high-speed and limited access highway, with two lanes in each direction, safety fences along its margins and a separation fence in the middle. It includes six semi-interchanges and 'right-right' mini-exits. Two of these are in coordination with five Bedouin villages along the road marked for state recognition but yet unplanned, the others are connected with extant junctions of Jewish and Bedouin places primarily at the edges of the road. Also planned are several passages underneath Road 31 for the benefit of the local Bedouin and their livestock, some of them capable of accommodating camels and private cars. Finally, infrastructure was prepared in several locations underneath the road to allow for future connection of unrecognized villages to the state water supply line running along the road. This is commensurate with a pending appeal by an NGO submitted in 2001 to the Supreme Court (*Appeal 3586/01 Council for Bedouin Unrecognized Villages against the Minister of Infrastructure*) for ruling that the Bedouin have a right to fresh water in their places Negev-wide regardless of the question of state recognition of them.

Road 31 and Bedouin rights

Prima facie, the specifics of the plan as outlined above indicate a planning process by the IRC as a state agent that is significantly considerate towards the Bedouin. However, we suggest that these planning specifics refer to Bedouin culture in a most superficial manner. Given the above background accounts of Bedouin indigenous property rights and territorial culture, there are several other key and critical issues from a Bedouin perspective that were overlooked by the planners. It is particularly here that the conflict between the Bedouin and the state over the general issue of rights and its derivatives is manifested most poignantly.

We frame our discussion of this conflict within the context of planning rights. This concept has in recent years been shaped up and elaborated by Alexander (2002, 2007) as an umbrella to cover various issues that relate to procedural and substantive aspects of the planning process. He suggests rightfully that the basis for planning rights is rooted in socially adopted political-normative principles defined as institutional rights. These include due process, participation, reason, human and civil rights, property rights and the public interest. Within this wide context we focus here specifically on participation, the human right to spatiality, property rights, and the right to a due process.

Public participation

The issue of participation in planning for the Negev Bedouin in general has already been studied within the contexts of democratization and insurgency (Meir, 2003, 2005, 2009a). These studies reveal that certain measures have been taken by the state in recent years to improve Bedouin access to planning resources.

These include a decision of the planning authorities to include an expert on Bedouin social affairs in planning teams and permission granted to Bedouin representatives to appear before the planning committees. These decisions represent some improvement over past practices. However, they cannot be regarded what participation discourse (see Lane, 2005) would refer to as a genuine public participation procedure, one that proactively enables the client population to play an equal and active role in the planning process from its outset.

Such was the case with Road 31 too. Following a lengthy process of two years of preparation the plan was submitted by the IRC to the DPC in early 2009. Minutes of a meeting of the DPC subcommittee for the road include no indication to the presence of representatives of the Bedouin unrecognized villages (DPC-SC, 2009; see also Yehudkin and Abu Samur, 2010). The mayor of the Bedouin town of Hura indicated in an interview that he was not invited to participate in the process and that the plan was presented to him only in its final stage (Al Nabari, 2012). Furthermore, an interview with an official in the engineering firm revealed that, while representatives of the Jewish population of Arad and other stakeholders had an informal access to the planning process from its outset, people of the unrecognized villages did not participate in the planning process because 'there are no Bedouin representatives to sit with' (F, Interview, November 22, 2012). Such a statement with regard to the Bedouin has been quite common for many years among politicians in Israel at large, indicating a superficial grasp or luck of will for a profound reach of this community. Furthermore the planning of the upgrade project by the engineering firm did not include an expert on Bedouin affairs. In an interview with such an expert, who later on had an opportunity to review the planning documents, it was revealed that most of the planning process by these firms was based on a photogrammetric survey of maps of this area without any contact with the local people (T, Interview, September 23, 2013). As put by an official in one of these firms: 'I did not come to fix the world. There was a road that needed an upgrade, we received instructions [from the IRC and DPC] for semi-interchanges, industrial zones, water conduits, etc. – simply physical planning'. (B-H, Interview, November 14, 2012; addition in parenthesis by authors).

As expected, individual members of the Bedouin community did not remain indifferent to their exclusion from the process. In an interview with a Bedouin woman residing near the road she expressed her concerns about it:

> They should have conducted a survey, to hear what's good, I don't know. At least they could interview us, just like you are doing right now. Because we know better, we experience what's happening. That's how when someone is sitting in the office and comes up with the idea to widen [the road], it's not...
>
> So, okay, I live in this country, I have my rights, what about me? I know the road needs [an upgrade], so how about them taking some care about us? The government and everyone else care for the road more then they care for us, they did not think about us and our experiences along the road.
>
> (H, A-Sh, Interview, May 15, 2013; addition in parenthesis by authors)

This sense of exclusion from the planning process is shared by another Bedouin interviewee: 'For whom, then, is this development meant for? I am almost certain I was not ranked top on a 1–10 scale [laughing]' (A, A-Sh, Interview, May 5, 2013; addition in parenthesis by authors).

It turns out thus that during the planning process neither a genuine participation of the Bedouin as a planning right took place at any spatial and administrative level, nor was a genuine effort made to overcome local obstacles such as the alleged 'lack of representatives'. It seems the planners are still trapped within the state approach to Bedouin issues whereby this population has to be grasped tribally and not individually for matters of rights (Meir, 2003). Despite a statement by the District Planning Committee (DPC, 2010) that 'a comprehensive work has been done with regard to the Bedouin with the necessary adjustments' and that the Bedouin public was allowed to participate in the process, this was made possible only in the very minimalistic manner of submitting objections which is anyway a legal procedure granted to anyone involved in any official planning process.

Spatiality and the right to the road

While the issue of public participation is widespread in the planning discourse, the issue of the right to the road needs some elaboration. The discourse on space and its production has referred, *inter alia*, to the Lefebvrian late-1960s and now widely accepted concept of the 'right to the city'. As elaborated recently (Harvey, 2008; Brenner *et al.*, 2012; McCaan, 2002), the general idea is a collective demand and action by the people that their access to urban life is transformed and renewed so that they assume power to reshape the processes of urbanization as they desire them vis-à-vis the desires of the neo-liberal state or market forces. In line with our approach that improving our spatial understanding requires decomposing major geographical entities, such as cities, into their components as meaningful geographical entities, so is the case with the right to the city. It is not only the city itself to which the people have a right but it is also those geographical entities within it at a more specific geographical scale for which the question of rights is very relevant.

The question of relevance is in itself significant and is culturally-contingent. That is, urban geographical entities, for example an industrial park, a university campus or a mall that are highly relevant for western culture, may not be as relevant for other cultures whose views of space, environment and resources are different. Accordingly, when the question of rights is at stake indigenous space needs to be decomposed too into those geographical entities that are endogenously relevant and critical for indigenous culture. In terms of rights we may generalize this into what Karplus and Meir (2010) refer to as the right of indigenous peoples to endogenous spatiality; that is, to produce space independent of external state or market forces. For example, Strack (2008) has studied rivers (including their beds, banks and water) in indigenous spaces in Canada and New Zealand within the context of their right to the river. The river and its subcomponents is what we refer to here as a geographical entity critical to their culture and not just a geomorphological object in a Euclidian space.

Extending this notion further into Road 31 as such a geographical entity, we may refer to the local dirt roads and their entry points shown above. Fencing the upgraded road was meant by the engineers to block breaking into the road by Bedouin drivers at haphazard locations, increase safety and prevent traffic fatalities. While this may sound reasonable and common for western culture space and places, for the Bedouin these entry points are not haphazardly located, and blocking them carries the risk of seriously threatening internal Bedouin social order. For example, one such local road and its entry point planned for obstruction belongs to a group that is at a blood feud with a neighboring one with whom, according to the plan, it has now to share an entry point (Interview with T., September 23, 2013). In Bedouin society this carries a great risk for serious friction and potential fatalities. This issue, along with that of public participation, was raised by two NGOs in an objection to the plan submitted jointly (Bimkom and

Regional Council of Bedouin Unrecognized Villages, 2009). It turns out that only 11 out of 70 such entry points were to receive a proper solution through the planned semi-interchanges and mini-exits, the rest receiving only very partial solution or none at all. Several other objections were submitted personally by individual families. These objections were rejected altogether by the state whose preference was based exclusively on a safety consideration (DPC, 2010).

While these local roads reflect the issue of right to the road at the micro-scale, the problem is reiterated at the meso-scale. The Bedouin town of Kseifa had a direct local road connection to Road 31 several hundred meters away. A strip of petty businesses developed along this connecting road and at the old intersection to serve both the local population and the tourist and other non-local traffic en route to the Dead Sea or Beer Sheva. Due to various engineering considerations its direct access to the upgraded road was blocked. The alternative offered by the planners was a semi-interchange for eastbound traffic about 2 kilometers west of its present connection from which a local road is to connect to town, and through another semi-interchange on Road 80 east of town over which traffic volume is very low (see Figure 11.1). Both solutions taken together would cut the visibility and exposure of these business outlets tremendously. An objection to the plan submitted by the town of Kseifa was rejected, as well as appeals to the regional Sub-Committee for Appeals and to the Supreme Court.

Thus, it is not only that the general 'right to the city' of the unrecognized villages at the macro-scale has been denied by the state (Yiftachel, 2013a). The specific planning approach of the state and its agents has ignored the unique social and cultural value of the road and its subcomponents as a live geographical entity for Bedouin endogenous spatiality. From the perspective of the state the upgraded road is to become a highway meant to connect the region nationally with the rest of the country, and is thus independent of and detached from its particular indigenous localness. This counter-comprehensive manner of the planning process is manifested in a DPC reaction to the objections: 'This is a *road plan*, it is not meant to solve other problems' (DPC, 2010, italics added). But from a Bedouin perspective, Road 31 has no independent life without these local roads and vice versa, all of which together constitute an indigenous integral *socio-spatial* system and cultural landscape. For them their easy and ready access to the road and to its hinterland through the entry/exit points is a precious socio-political resource. Blocking them by the upgrade cuts seriously into their delicate socio-spatial fabric and the cultural manner in which their space is endogenously produced. As put by a Bedouin interviewee: 'If you drive from Shoket [Junction] to Arad you don't see these villages anymore, so the upgrade actually contributes to realization of the [Prawer] Plan' (A, Interview, March 6, 2013; addition in parenthesis by authors).

Thus through the de-contextualization of the road and its objectification by the planners, the Bedouin indigenous unique right to spatiality and more specifically their right to the road have been seriously infringed. In fact the entire Bedouin cultural landscape along the road has been changed.

Property rights

From the perspective of planning rights specifically and human rights in general, this is the most important issue. The property conflict between the Bedouin and the state at the macro-scale is manifested here most sharply at the individual owner micro-scale. The upgrade plan determined building lines (that is minimal distance from road margin permitted for buildings) double or triple the size of Israeli highway standards. This was meant *inter alia* to secure a land stretch of about 200-400 meters (at cases up to about 600 meters) on both sides of the highway, partly providing for a future railway track (see also Abu-Mdegam *et al.*, 2009). This implies, as noted, that the upgrade path cuts right through Bedouin property adjacent to the road. It was estimated by the advocacy NGOs that about 500 to 600 home, farm and petty business structures risk possible demolition and eviction (Bimkom and Regional Council of Unrecognized Villages, 2009).

As in the cases of participation and right to the road, here too the planning authorities were entirely inattentive to objections submitted by both the advocating NGOs and individual Bedouin owners. The DPC regarded the issue of property rights as external to the upgrade project that needs to be settled elsewhere (DPC, 2010). From their perspective the eviction of the population was a real and unnegotiable option. This policy has put a considerable pressure on both the IRC and the affected local Bedouin households. On the one hand the IRC was pressed to meet the planning deadline and avoid financial damage. On the other hand the local Bedouin were caught within their own social codes of highly constrained residential mobility and strict tribal and sub-tribal residential segregation and rejected any option of eviction.

Caught thus within these constraints, the implementation of the project began to face various obstacles and setbacks. The local population used various tactics to impede its progress. They engaged in many violent protest events and riots; in several cases they have time and again destroyed highway fences to allow for their local exit/entry traffic through their traditional connecting points; local Bedouin residents threatened to turn Bedouin customary law against the non-local Bedouin sub-contractors who were hired for the project; they also threatened their life or caused damage to their heavy machinery for unpermitted trespassing on their local territory, whereby the subcontractors yielded quite willfully (Interview with T, September 23, 2013). All these actions were rooted in unique Bedouin spatiality and territorial rules that are legitimate in their eyes. They are similar to some of those practices adopted in many other local cases of Bedouin-state land conflict (see Koensler, 2013).

Desperate to expedite the project the IRC realized the urgent need for a breakthrough in settling the local problems of Bedouin property. In early 2011, about three years after commencement of the planning process, and for the first time, an urban planning firm was hired and became engaged in the process in addition to the engineering firm. In an interview with the general director of this firm he heavily criticized the initial approach taken by the engineering firms for ignoring the property rights and the other issues as explained above. Accepting however that demolitions and expropriation were inevitable, the most important issues for him were therefore as follows: 'Is there a just compensation for property? Can Bedouin life go on reasonably uninterrupted by the upgrade project?' (Y, Interview, January 18, 2013).

In order to meet these goals the firm decided, under embracement of IRC, to establish a special 'expropriation team'. The team was composed of a legal advisor, a real estate assessor, an expert on Bedouin society with long and profound field experience and familiarity with their affairs and an expropriation advisor. The team was tasked with a detailed survey of all Bedouin property at question, negotiate with the local families, and reach compensation agreements with individual households that would facilitate their relocation. In a lengthy and detailed interview with the Bedouin expert, he noted that the prime rule of conduct adopted by the team related to a most aggravating issue for the Bedouin following decades of failed policy – their lack of trust in any official governmental declaration of intent (Interview with T, September 23, 2013). Therefore, as he explained, the team adopted a firm commitment towards resolve in its expropriation task but its pursuance through honesty, openness, integrity and respect for indigenous Bedouin codes of dignity and honor.

Compliant with the two goals set by the planning firm, the survey included all relevant population up to 1.5 kilometers away from the road (total population about 30,000 at 18 clusters). Information was gathered on many aspects of Bedouin life and property such as tribal and sub-tribal affiliation, inter-group conflicts, permissible passage and traffic options along dirt roads and through local entry/exit points, actual traffic destinations and routes taken by local groups (including by children to schools), property types and size (residential, farming or commercial), property claims, number of heirs and public facilities (e.g., a mosque or graveyard). Also included was data on state land in this area. This survey served as a basis for estimation of costs associated with the various aspects of both compensation for property and local traffic solutions commensurate with inter-group relationships.

With regard to socio-territorial regulation of local traffic off-Road 31 and avoidance of internal conflicts, the team made an effort to identify the most problematic rural dirt roads and entry/exit points to be blocked. Based on this information it suggested an alternative solution of several rural paved roads that connect to some of the planned semi-interchanges to be constructed by the state on state land. Efforts were also made to guarantee that these roads are planned such that travel distances to and from them for any local group of households do not exceed 400 meters in order to minimize their possible exposure and thus ensure their security.

With regard to compensation for property, the team defined two groups: about 70 owners/holders of farming land along the road who live in its hinterland (total of 1,000 dunams marked for eviction); and about 100 roadside home or business owners/holders (with structures marked for demolition). Owners of the first group were offered two compensation options: receiving IS5000 (=~$1500) per dunam (1 dunam=one fourth of an acre) (based on average wheat crop for a period of ten years) and retaining their property claim; or receiving IL10,000 (=~$3,300) per dunam and yielding their property claim. The second group were offered a compensation of IS100,000 (=~$33,000) for each 100sq/m building size, with tax to be paid by the IRC and financed by the state.

However, the evacuees, being aware that state recognition of several villages was imminent, became concerned about the future consequences of the deal offered in case of their relocation to such a planned town. The team proposed therefore a solution composed of two principles: (1) each extended family should receive an equivalent of the value of a land lot in town (IS100,000), plus a certain compensation for each nuclear family within the extended family; (2) this compensation would not impinge upon the right to receive future compensation for further relocation to town nor upon a future right to receive a land lot in town upon relocation in exchange for their present property. The compensation money was thus meant by the team to serve temporarily 'for buying a new land lot or renting a home' until a future permanent solution of their unrecognized villages was agreed upon with the state (T, Interview, September 23, 2013).

The major question that came up, however, was the immediate relocation destination of the evacuees. Team members as well as the owners were well aware that from a socio-territorial perspective buying or renting a home elsewhere was a non-option. As noted, individual residential mobility between communities within Bedouin society is practically impossible. That is, there is virtually no housing market within Bedouin communities, no other solutions by the state to settle these groups have yet been offered or become matured, and migration to Jewish towns is nevertheless culturally undesired. Thus the only option available for evacuees was to relocate several hundred meters away from the road but still within family territory, or to reach a real estate arrangement with tribal kin internally. The hidden agenda of the team was that acceptance of this solution by Bedouin owners will serve also to receive state consent. Therefore they regarded this deal as something equivalent to an 'invented solution' that the Bedouin can live with.

However, this deal, coupled with the tax arrangement, raised furious objection by the authorities who realized the state will have to pay compensation twice (the second time upon future relocation to recognized planned towns). Fearing the public image of 'surrendering to the Bedouin', they condemned the deal and the conduct of the team as sheer corruption and threatened the planning firm with a law suit (T, Interview, September 23, 2013). The deal also caused considerable tension with the engineering firm over technical and financial matters (Y, Interview, January 18, 2013; T, Interview, September 23, 2013). As time went on, however, the team managed to reach deals with a majority of the owners and, loyal to its moral approach to the negotiations, it willfully fettered itself vis-à-vis the Bedouin-style word of honor it has given to them. It should be noted that initially the Bedouin on their part also hired Bedouin-origin lawyers but these were found incompetent vis-à-vis the establishment. Therefore they later hired an expert on Bedouin affairs who had walks within the establishment to represent them on an individual family basis for negotiating with the expropriation team (A, Interview, 2013). In early 2013 the state eventually realized the political and financial costs of a further delay in the project due to possible Bedouin riots and obstructions, and while gnashing, accepted this solution and legitimized it. Such was also the case with a mosque located adjacent to the road and marked for demolition, in which the state accepted the recommendation of the team to finance the establishment of a new one. Currently the upgrade project is making considerable progress with an anticipated completion by the end of 2015.

Due planning process

Finally there is the issue of how appropriate the planning process has been vis-à-vis the Bedouin as the most deprived group in Israel. From a sheer planning perspective, several stakeholders participated in the process on both sides. On the Bedouin side there were the two planning advocacy NGOs and the expert on Bedouin affairs hired by them, himself of a non-Bedouin origin, implying a Bedouin lack of self-produced professional resources. On the planners' side these are the state, which has major national interests in both the Bedouin property conflict and through the 2001 National Master Plan of Roads; the District Planning Commission, which is in charge of confronting this plan with the regional circumstances of the upgrade project; the IRC, which was charged with its planning and implementation; the engineering firm, which actually operated the planning and implementation; the urban planning firm, which was called in to untangle the local perplexity and facilitate the breakthrough in the deadlock; and the expropriation team, which made this breakthrough possible. All agents involved on behalf of the state were of a non-Bedouin origin. As shown, the closer the planning agency is to the field the more it becomes exposed and sensitive to reality and to the need to reorient its practices towards the indigenous needs of the local people. And yet, the long list reflects also the lingering nature of the process with considerable political and financial costs.

A major part of the problem of the multiplicity of players, the complexity of the process, its lingering and its consequences, rests within the relationships between the state and the indigenous Bedouin. While previous accounts of these relationships have reviewed them mostly at the macro- and meso-levels (Meir, 1999; Swirski and Hasson, 2005), the present research reveals that even at the micro-level the state has failed to attempt a genuine and profound understanding of their indigenous culture. This is reflected in the fact that the planning process began with an engineering firm whose Newtonian attitude towards Bedouin space, devoid of any consultation with the local people or the assistance of experts on their affairs, abstracted it and objectified it and its people. This is augmented with the passage of three years before the state realized the need for involving an urban planning firm with a more comprehensive approach, which in its turn realized the need to establish an expropriation team, which in its own turn decided upon conducting a comprehensive survey with the assistance of an expert on Bedouin affairs. Such a survey, if conducted before commencement of the planning process, and such an expert, if available at its onset, could quite easily and very early unearth the fact that the originally planned route of the upgrade road cuts straight across a lively Bedouin space and cultural landscape. Furthermore, the statement by the planners that 'there are no Bedouin representatives to sit with', another reflection of the failure of state planners over seven decades to grasp the true nature of contemporary Bedouin society, is overturned by the success of the expropriation team to overcome this alleged representation obstacle. Thus our analysis surfaces what Alexander (2002, 2007) would regard as a violation of the right to *due process* as part of the nexus of planning rights.

Indigenous rights, grey spacing and grey planning mechanism

There are two insights to this planning process. The first is what may be termed 'non-formal crawling recognition' that is, there are various indications of the emergence of recognition without official formal and legal status. This refers not only to state crawling recognition of the major issue in question – the villages (Meir, 2003). Based on our findings here, we suggest this notion refers also to what the literature has greatly overlooked – Bedouin indigeneity. The very fact that the state was compelled to accept the property deal and some recommendations regarding the local rural roads implies a crawling informal recognition of an important component in Bedouin spatial life that originates in their indigenous view of space.

In this respect a micro-scale greyness practice has been also permeating the refusal by the state to recognize Bedouin indigeneity. On the other hand, the degree of this permeation has been quite limited as other components of their indigeneity have been interrupted. The Bedouin's sense of Road 31 as place has diminished considerably with their growing spatial and physical detachment from direct access to it and with changes in their cultural landscape caused by the upgrade project.

The informal recognition leads to our second insight, which is the major one: the continuation of the implementation of the upgrade project was facilitated only through retained Bedouin grey status in both issues of property rights and villages. This case is different in several respects from the literature on grey mechanisms reviewed above (Allmendinger and Haughton, 2010; Innes *et al.*, 2007). First, despite the successful negotiation process, it was not conducted with maximum benefits for all the regional Bedouin population in mind. Rather, it was imposed and managed from above in order to promote the engineering project exclusively through solving the particular local property problem. Second, we regard the expropriation team as a grey planning mechanism. The negotiations were meant exclusively to achieve the immediate goal of evacuation for the benefit of the state, but in complete contradiction with state extant policy of non-recognition so that it can be retained in the long run. Third, in the long run the grey mechanism contributed significantly to worsening the position of the Bedouin and the state alike with respect to space. It did not bring the fundamental solution to the property and village regulation of conflicts any closer. Rather it distanced it by creating a precedent that enables reaching a local agreement without solving the greater residential problem of the Bedouin. They remain with the stressful residential solutions outside a recognized village or town.

We may equate post-upgrade Bedouin space with what Wall (2011) has referred to as interstices. These are areas whose legal status is left unregulated following the construction of an interchange, thus inviting informal activities. In the case of Road 31 these areas are a product of several layers of contradicting authority: the state, the IRC and socio-cultural indigenous codes of users of these specific spaces. The users reject the formal procedures as an act of expropriation and exclusion superimposed upon their indigenous culture. Their objection thus reveals the clash between the western neo-liberal technological efficiency (IRC) and local indigenous codes of cultural conduct (the Bedouin).

Thus, this grey space and the unique process analyzed here generate a new scene of regional and local power balance. From the Bedouin perspective, it provides them with an opportunity to realize their live presence within it. Furthermore, they interpret this process as an informal recognition in their rights, thus enabling them to benefit from indecisiveness of the state which is compelled now to allow them retain their status within the claimed area. They can thus continue their life uninterrupted within these unregulated areas that is, the unrecognized villages. This generates also grey consciousness in their culture that is, accepting this spatial reality as permanent, to an extent of accumulating power precisely from their weakness as a minority indigenous group and deprivation of their rights. Paradoxically thus, the implementation of the upgrade project, which is a symbol of state power, further augments this indigenous power of the Bedouin.

As for the state, grey spatialization, a product of its historical failed policy, transfers power unwillingly to the local group. Unlike a situation of 'over-sovereignty' suggested by Yiftachel and Tzfadia (2014) in the relationships between the state and the Bedouin, this grey planning mechanism indicates precisely the opposite – 'under-sovereignty' of the state. The more profound implication is that eventually the status of the local Bedouin as a weak minority has remained virtually unchanged, but the hegemony of the state as a governing entity has been undermined.

Conclusion

We submit that this state of power relations necessitated greyness at the middle and bottom levels of the planning establishment that now receives legitimacy from above (the state) and below (the Bedouin) alike. That is, the pressures of viewing Bedouin space as illegal from above, and insurgency action from below, require recruitment of the grey medium. The need to evict Bedouin without a real solution of the issues of property and unrecognized villages produces perpetuation and even deepening of grey spacing. It facilitates sustenance of the Bedouin in the unrecognized villages and empowers their *tzumud* value (Arabic for 'grip of the land'). Thus, in addition to the absence of a 'whitening' solution for Bedouin grey space, we suggest that the upgraded nature of Road 31 as a limited access highway generates spatial separation which deepens spatial segregation of Bedouin communities from Jewish space. This supports Yiftachel's (2013a) argument about processes among the Bedouin who strive for autonomous existence, where it further distantiates them from participation in the Israeli state affairs.

The process analyzed in this chapter has both positive and negative aspects. On the negative side there is a pendulum motion in two dimensions. The first dimension is between the pole of Bedouin's 'stripping' from the formal western state law (by sustaining their customary indigenous law) and that of political incapacity of the state to impose its policy upon them. The second dimension is between the pole of customary normativity of the Bedouin, which is devoid of modern formalism, and that of state modern formalism which is devoid of recognizing the normativity inherent in indigenous Bedouin unique customary spatiality (viewed by the government as chaotic and unregulated). That is, this supposedly chaotic Bedouin space can be regulated, as is nowadays occurring among many other indigenous peoples in the western nations (Roded and Tzfadia, 2012). Yet in Israel it is the state which prevents it and thus contributes to its chaotic nature.

On the positive side, it is precisely the perpetuated temporariness of greyness which, as shown, is capable of producing efficient dialogue mechanisms that may serve both sides beneficially. This insight has conceptual implications for several issues – grasping the positive aspects of grey space often portrayed negatively, the view that grey space can become an integral part of planning and, finally for grasping the unique and significant role played by micro-scale geographical entities within this greyness.

Acknowledgements

Research for this chapter was conducted during 2012–14 and supported by a grant from the Israeli Science Foundation (ISF Grant 77/12). We wish to thank all those Bedouin and Jewish interviewees for their cooperation with us, to Mr. Atef Abu-Rabiah for his help in the fieldwork, to Tal Svoray and Raya Kogan for their help in transforming the National GIS digital data into the local dirt road map, and to Roni Livnon-Bluestein for her cartographic production of the maps. We are grateful to Survey of Israel for granting us the National GIS data required for this map.

References

Abu-Mdegam, S., Hamdam, H. and Na'amna, Ch. (2009) 'The Plan for D11/03/267, Road 31, the Shoket Junction-Arad section: Sustained planning discrimination'. *Adalah Electronic Monthly* 67, December (Hebrew).

Abu-Saad, I.E. (2005) 'Forced sedentarisation, land rights and indigenous resistance: The Palestinian Bedouin in the Negev'. Masalha, N., (ed.). *Catastrophe Remembered: Palestine, Israel and the Internal Refugees.* London & NY: Zed Books, 113–141.

Adam, M.-C., Kneeshaw, D. and Beckley, T.M. (2012) 'Forestry and road development: Direct and indirect impacts from an Aboriginal perspective'. *Ecology and Society* 17(4): 1. http://dx.doi.org/10.5751/ES-04976-170401 Accessed June 23, 2013.

Al-Aref. A. (1937) *The History of Beer Sheva and its Tribes: The Bedouin in the Beer Sheva District.* Jerusalem: Ariel (Hebrew).

Alexander, E.R. (2002) 'Planning rights: Toward normative criteria for evaluating plans'. *International Planning Studies* 7(3): 191–212.

Alexander, E.R. (2007) 'Planning rights in theory and practice: The Case of Israel'. *International Planning Studies.* 12(1): 3–19.

Allmendinger, P. and Haughton, G. (2010) 'Spatial planning, devolution, and new planning spaces'. *Environment and planning. C, Government & Policy, 28*(5): 803–818.

Al Nabari, A. (February, 10, 2012), Personal interview.

Amara, A. and Yiftachel, O. (2014) *Confrontation in the Negev: Israel Land Policies and the Indigenous Bedouin-Arabs.* Berlin: The Rosa Luxemburg Foundation. www.rosalux.co.il/confrontation_in_the_negev_eng Accessed October 16, 2014.

Anaya, J. (2011) 'Promotion and protection of all human rights, civil, political, economic, social and cultural rights, including the right to development'. *Human Rights Council Eighteenth Session Agenda item 3.* 22 August 2011. www2.ohchr. org/english/issues/indigenous/rapporteur/docs/A-HRC-18-35-Add-1.pdf Accessed January 12, 2014.

Atzmon, E. (2013) 'The policy of settling the Bedouin in the Negev, 1948–2012'. Pedatzur, R., (ed.). *The Bedouin in the Negev-A Strategic Challenge,* Netanya: The S. Daniel Abraham Center for Strategic Dialogue, Netanya Academic College, 50–64 (Hebrew).

Bar-Lev, G. (December 4, 2012), Personal interview.

Bellina, S. (2009) 'The legitimacy of the state in fragile situations'. *Report for the OECD DAC International Network on Conflict and Fragility.* Norad and French Ministry of Foreign and European Affairs. www.norad.no/en/Tools+and+ publications/Publications/Publication+page?key=134243.

Ben-David, Y. (2004) *The Bedouin in Israel – Social and Land Perspectives.* Jerusalem: Jerusalem Institute for Israel Studies and the Institute for Research on Land Use Policy (Hebrew).

Ben-Israel, A. (2009) *Bedouin Formation of Place: Space and Landscape Construction by Urbanized Pastoral-Nomads*, Ph.D. Dissertation, Beer-Sheva: Department of Geography and Environmental Development, Ben-Gurion University of the Negev (Hebrew).

Ben-Israel, A. and Meir, A. (2013) 'Placializing roads – Tarig Atir (Road 316) and Bedouin reconstruction of space'. Karplus, Y. and Meir, A., (eds). *The Production of Bedouin Space in the Negev*. Beer Sheva: Negev Center for Regional Development, Ben-Gurion University of the Negev, 192–226 (Hebrew).

Ben Israel, A., Roded, B. and Meir, A. (2013) 'Road as place and as absolute space: Highway 31 between encounter and conflict'. *The Israeli Geographical Association, Annual Meeting*, Ramat Gan (Hebrew).

Bennett, M. (2005) 'Indigeneity as self-determination'. *Indigenous Livejournal 4*, 71–115.

Berman, G.S. (2006) 'Social services and indigenous populations in remote areas'. *International Social Work 49*(1): 97–106.

Berman-Kishony, T. (2008) 'Bedouin urbanization legal policies in Israel and Jordan: Similar goals, contrasting strategies'. *Transnational Law & Contemporary Problems 17*(2): 393–412.

Bimkom and Regional Council for Unrecognized Villages (2009) *Objection to Plan 267/03/11 – Road 31 Section Shoket Junction-Arad*, Jerusalem (Hebrew).

Brenner, N., Marcuse, P. and Mayer, M. (eds). (2012) *Cities for People Not for Profit: Critical Urban Theory & the Right to the City*. New York: Routledge.

Brodkin, E.Z. (1987) 'Policy politics: If we can't govern can we manage?' *Political Science Quarterly 102*(4): 571–587.

District Planning Commission, Sub-Committee (DPC, SC) (2009) Minutes of District Planning Commission-Sub Committee for Principle Issues May 5, 2009, Beer Sheva (Hebrew).

District Planning Commission, Sub-Committee (DPC, SC) (2010) Minutes of District Planning Commission-Sub Committee for Appeals, March 22, 2010, Beer Sheva (Hebrew).

Fox-Rogers, L. and Murphy, E. (2013) 'Informal strategies of power in the local planning system'. *Planning Theory*, 1473095213492512.

Frantzman, S., Yahel, H. and Kark, R. (2012) 'Contested indigeneity: The development of an indigenous discourse on the Bedouin of the Negev, Israel'. *Israel Studies*, 17(1): 78–105.

Fraser, N. (2000) 'Rethinking recognition'. *New Left Review 3*(3): 107–120.

Fraser, N. (2003) 'Social justice in the age of identity politics: Redistribution, recognition, and participation'. Fraser, N. and Honnet, A. (eds). *Redistribution or Recognition? A Political-philosophical Exchange*. London: Verso, 7–109.

Gooch, P. (2008) 'Feet following hooves'. Ingol, T. and Vergunst, J.L. (eds). *Ways of Walking, Ethnography and Practice on foot*. Aldershot: Ashgate, 67–80.

Harvey, D. (1993) 'Class relations, social justice and the politics of difference'. Keith, M. and Pile, S. (eds). *Place and the Politics of Identity*. London: Routledge, 41–66.

Harvey, D. (2008) 'The right to the city'. *New Left Review 53*, 23–40.

Hillier, J. (2000) 'Going round the back? Complex networks and informal action in local planning processes'. *Environment and Planning A 32*, 33–54.

Ingold, T. and Vergunst, J.L. (2008) 'Introduction'. Ingold, T. and Vergunst, J.L. (eds). *Ways of Walking, Ethnography and Practice on foot*. Aldershot: Ashgate, 1–20.

Innes, J.E., Connick, S. and Booher, D. (2007) 'Informality as a Planning Strategy'. *Journal of the American Planning Association* 73(2): 195–210.

Jabareen, Y. (2014) '"Do it yourself" as an informal mode of space production: conceptualizing informality'. *Journal of Urbanism: International Research on Placemaking and Urban Sustainability* 7(4), 414–428.

Karplus, Y. and Meir, A. (2010) 'The right for endogenic spatiality: The case of indigenous peoples'. A discussion paper presented in Minerva Conference for Human Rights in Israel, Neve Ilan. (Hebrew)

Karplus, Y. and Meir, A. (2013) 'The production of space: A neglected aspect perspective in pastoral research'. *Environment and Planning D: Society and Space, 31*, 23–42.

Karplus, Y. and Meir, A. (2014a) 'From congruent to non-congruent spaces: Dynamics of Bedouin production of space in Israel'. *Geoforum 52*, 180–19.

Karplus, Y. and Meir, A. (2014b) 'Past and present in the discourse of Naqab/Negev Bedouin geography and space'. Nasasra, M., Richter-Devroe, S., Abu-Rabia-Queder, S. and Ratcliffe, R. (eds). *The Naqab Bedouin and Colonialism: New Perspectives*. Oxon: Routledge, 68–89.

Kissinger, M. and Karplus, Y. (2014) 'IPAT and the analysis of local human–environment impact processes: The case of indigenous Bedouin towns in Israel'. *Environment, Development and Sustainability*, DOI 10.1007/s10668-014-9540-y, published online, 29 April 2014.

Koensler, A. (2013) 'Frictions as opportunity: Mobilizing for Arab-Bedouin ethnic rights in Israel'. *Ethnic and Racial Studies* 36(11): 1808–1828.

Lane, M.B. (2005) 'Public participation in planning: an intellectual history'. *Australian Geographer* 36(3): 283–299.

Lane, M.B. (2006) 'The role of planning in achieving indigenous land justice and community goals'. *Land Use Policy* 23, 385–394.

Lane, M.B. and Hibard, M. (2006) 'Doing it for themselves: transformative planning by indigenous peoples'. *Journal of Planning Education and Research* 25, 172–184.

Lye, T.-P. (2004) *Changing Pathways: Forest Degradation and the Batek of Pahang, Malaysia*. Lanham, MD: Lexington Books.

Matari, S.S. (2011) 'Mediation to resolve the Bedouin-Israeli government dispute for the Negev Desert'. *Fordham International Law Journal* 34(4): 1089–1130.

McCaan, U.J. (2002) 'Space, citizenship, and the right to the city: A brief overview'. *GeoJournal 58*, 77–79.

Meir, A. (1997) *As Nomadism Ends: the Israeli Bedouin of the Negev*. Boulder: Westview Press.

Meir, A. (1999) 'Local government among marginalized ex-nomads: The Israeli Bedouin and the State'. IJussila, H., Majoral, R. and Mutambirwa, C.C. (eds). *Marginality in Space-Past Present and Future*. Aldershot: Ashgate, 101–119.

Meir, A. (2003) *From Planning Advocacy to Independent Planning: The Negev Bedouin on the Path to Democratization in Planning*. Beer Sheva: The Negev Center for Regional Development, Ben-Gurion University of the Negev (Hebrew).

Meir, A. (2005) 'Bedouin, the Israeli state and insurgent planning: Globalization, localization or glocalization?' *Cities* 22(3): 201–215.

Meir, A. (2009a) 'Contemporary state discourse and historical pastoral spatiality: Contradictions in the land conflict between the Israeli Bedouin and the state'. *Ethnic and Racial Studies* 32(5): 823–843.

Meir, A. (2009b) 'What public, whose interest: The Negev Bedouin and the roots of planning from below'. *Geography Research Forum 29*, 103–132.

Meir, A. and Duenias, J. (2008) 'University, community, and shaping regional identity: A case study in Southern Israel'. *Journal of World Universities Forum 1*(3): 35–45.

Ministry of Housing (2008) 'Report of the Justice Goldberg Committee for regulating Bedouin settlement in the Negev'. Jerusalem (Hebrew).

Nasasra, M. (2012) 'The ongoing Judaisation of the Naqab and the struggle for recognising the indigenous rights of the Arab Bedouin people'. *Settler Colonial Studies 2*(1): 81–107.

Noach, Ch. (2009) *There and Not There – Unrecognized Bedouin Villages of the Negev.* Haifa: Pardes (Hebrew).

Orr, D.M.R. (2014) 'Regulating mobility in the Peruvian Andes: Road safety, social hierarchies and governmentality in Cusco's rural provinces'. *Ethnos: Journal of Anthropology*, 1–24.

de Pina-Cabral, J. (1987) 'Paved roads and enchanted mooresses: The perception of the past among the peasant population of the Alto Minho'. *Man*, 715–735.

Prime Minister Office (2011) 'A plan for regulating Bedouin settlement in the Negev'. Jerusalem (Hebrew).

Rabinowitc, D. and Vardi, A. (2010) 'Driving forces: Cross-Israel highway and the privatization of public infrastructures in Israel'. Jerusalem: Van Leer Institute (Hebrew).

Rangwala, T.S. (2004) 'Inadequate housing, Israel, and the Bedouin of the Negev'. *Osgoode Hall Law Journal 42*(3): 415–472.

Relph, T. (1977) 'Humanism, phenomenology, and geography'. *Annals of the Association of American Geographers 67*(1): 177–183.

Relph, E. (2000) 'Author's response: *Place and Placelessness* in a New Context [Classics in Human Geography Revisited, *Place and Placelessness*]'. *Progress in Human Geography 24*(4): 613–619.

Roded, B. (2012) Planning in the face of indecision: a case study of the Negev. *Planning 9*(1): 141–164 (Hebrew).

Roded, B. and Tzfadia, E. (2012) 'Indigenous land rights recognition: A comparative observation of the Arab-Bedouins in the Negev'. *The Public Space 7*, 66–99 (Hebrew).

Sheehan, J. (2012) 'Applying an Australian native title framework to Bedouin property'. Amara A., Abu-Saad, I. and Yiftachel, O. (eds). *Indigenous (In)Justice: Human Rights Law and Bedouin Arabs in the Naqab/Negev.* Cambridge, MA: Harvard University Press, 228–253.

Scheller, M. and Urry, J. (2006) 'The new mobilities paradigm'. *Environment and Planning A 38*, 207–226.

Small, G. and Sheehan, J. (2008) 'The metaphysics of indigenous ownership: Why indigenous ownership is incomparable to western conceptions of property value'. Simmons, R.A., Makmgren, R.M. and Small, G. (eds). *Indigenous Peoples and Real Estate Valuation.* New York: Springer, 103–119.

Strack, M.S. (2008) *Rebel Rivers: An investigation into the River Rights of Indigenous People of Canada and New Zealand* (PhD). University of Otago, Dunedin, New Zealand.

Swirski, Sh. and Hasson, A. (2005) *Transparent Citizens: State Policy Toward the Negev Bedouin.* Tel Aviv: Adva Center (Hebrew).

Wall, E. (2011) 'Infrastructural form, interstitial spaces and informal acts'. IHauck, T. Keller, R. and Kleinekort, V. (eds). *Infrastructural Urbanism Addressing the In-between*. Berlin: DOM Publishers, 145–157.

Yahel, H., Kark, R. and Frantzman, S. (2012) 'Fabricating Palestinian history: Are the Negev Bedouin an indigenous people?' *Middle East Quarterly*, Summer, 1–14.

Yehudkin, S. and Abu-Samur, S. (2010) 'National Plan 31/A/21 Plan for Highway 6 South – an expert opinion, Bimkom Association and the Regional Council for unrecognized villages'. www.bimkom.org/lawActivity_objectionView.asp?objectionId=4 (Hebrew) (Retrieved April 2010).

Yiftachel, O. (2009) 'Towards recognition of Bedouin villages? Planning metropolitan Beer Sheva in the face of the Goldberg Committee'. *Tichnun* 6(1): 165–184 (Hebrew).

Yiftachel, O. (2013a) 'Critical theory and "grey space": The Bedouin in the Beer Sheva region'. Karplus, Y. and Meir, A. (eds). *The Construction of Bedouin Space in the Negev*, Beer Sheva, Negev Center for Regional Development, 225–251 (Hebrew).

Yiftachel, O. (2013b) 'The unrecognized Bedouin space: The development of a strategic issue'. Pdatzur, R. (ed.). *The Bedouin in Israel: Strategic issues*. Netanya: The Academic College of Netanya, Daniel Center for Strategic Dialogue, 8–17 (Hebrew).

Yiftachel, O., Goldhaber, R. and Nuriel, R. (2009) 'Urban justice and recognition: Affirmation and hostility in Beer Sheva'. Marcuse, P., Connolly, J., Now, J., Ouvo, I., Potter, C. Steil, J. (eds). *Searching for the Just City*. London: Routledge, 120–143.

Yiftachel, O., Kedar, A. and Amara, A. (2012) 'A new perspective on the 'dead Negev rule': Property rights in Bedouin space'. *Law and Governance* 14(1–2): 7–147 (Hebrew).

Yiftachel, O., Kedar S. and Amara, A. (2014) 'Indigenous challenge to a legal doctrine: Bedouin land and planning rights in Israel/Palestine'. International Conference of the Planning Law and Planning Rights Association (PLPR), Technion, Haifa.

Yiftachel, O. and Tzfadia, E. (2014) 'The grey city of tomorrow'. Fenster, T. and Shlomo, A. (eds). *Cities of tomorrow: Planning, justice and sustainability*. Tel Aviv: Hakibbutz Hameuchad, 176–192 (Hebrew).

Young, I.M. (1990) *Justice and the Politics of Difference*. Princeton, NJ: Princeton University Press.

12 Conclusion

Land, indigenous peoples, and the resolution of conflict

Alan C. Tidwell and Barry Scott Zellen

As chronicled in the preceding chapters, indigenous peoples find themselves in an asymmetrical struggle with the state over property rights. In both historical and contemporary terms, this struggle has been characterized by comparatively weak capacity on the part of the indigenous peoples when compared to the full spectrum of state powers and resources. Contributors to this volume have all underscored the myriad of ways in which these asymmetrical conflicts have played out. In most cases the story is one in which indigenous peoples have been unable to adequately protect their rights or promote their interests due to the actions of the state. But in a few encouraging instances – Australia, New Zealand, Canada and the United States, for example – indigenous peoples have been able to eke out substantial protections of rights and interests, but only with considerable effort and cost, sometimes after decades of protracted, and very often expensive, negotiations.

These are more often than not exceptions in the global historical experience of indigenous peoples, for whom the arrival of the state has been nothing short of an existential challenge. In virtually every instance, indigenous peoples find themselves the victims of violence – physical, structural and cultural – as they pursue their interests and struggle to have their rights recognized. Indigenous peoples and the state have often clashed violently over property rights. The violence of this clash is sometimes physical, often structural, and almost always cultural. Throughout this volume, our authors have highlighted the numerous ways in which that clash takes place. Physical, structural and cultural forms of violence have all been used by the state to erode the capacity of indigenous peoples to defend themselves over time.

Physical violence has featured as a common experience amongst indigenous peoples since at least as far back as 1492.[1] Direct military attacks on indigenous communities, resulting in the loss of land, features in the history of the United States, Canada, Australia and New Zealand, but are mostly features from the 17th through 19th century, and less characteristic of contemporary relations between indigenous peoples and these formerly British colonies which in the 20th and 21st centuries have embraced a decidedly nonviolent path toward restoring native rights, and reversing earlier state policies of assimilation, land conquest and cultural oppression.

Elsewhere, however, the direct use of physical violence against indigenous peoples by the state is not something from a bygone era. In places where physical violence is still used, indigenous peoples find any negotiation with the state problematic. The violent conflicts in Darfur (as described by Jon Unruh in 'Indigenous Land Rights and Conflict in Darfur: The Case of the Fur Tribe') and Paraguay (as described by Cheryl Duckworth in 'President Lugo and the Indigenous Communities of Paraguay') underscore the reality of physical violence, as do periodic recurrences of violence in Canada, where blockades and armed protests continue to punctuate an otherwise nonviolent trajectory of reconciliation between state and indigenous peoples. Of course, as the Darfur example demonstrates, violent conflict can be brought about when the state favors one set of indigenous property rights against another. In Canada, the great strides forward toward re-empowerment and the restoration of indigenous rights by the Inuit differs from the experience of many of the non-Inuit indigenous peoples to their south, as Barry Scott Zellen describes in his chapter, 'From Counter-Mapping to Co-Management: The Inuit, the State and the Quest for Collaborative Arctic Sovereignty', and it comes as no surprise that it has been among these inland peoples that we see the continued simmering of violence that manifests itself in occasional outbreaks of armed confrontation in such contrast to the pacified Far North.

Just as striking a contrast can be seen when comparing progress on indigenous land rights in Canada, as described by Ken Coates and Greg Poelzer in their chapter, 'Re-Imagining Indigenous Space: The Law, Constitution and the Evolution of Aboriginal Property and Resource Rights in Canada', with conditions among natives in Russia's far northern territories on the other side of the Arctic – even the relatively positive case of the Sakha Republic in the Russian Far East, as described by Marjorie Mandelstam Balzer in her chapter ('Indigeneity, Land and Activism in Siberia').

Even when physical violence is absent, however, indigenous peoples must struggle with the structural violence imposed upon them. Structural violence refers to those social structures that limit a person's life chances – the potential of what a person could be is limited by structural inequalities. 'The violence is built into the structure and shows up as unequal power and consequently as unequal life chances'. (Galtung 1969:171) The loss of land and ensuing poverty, isolation, and lack of clear political and property rights hobble the negotiation capacity of indigenous peoples. Structural violence complicates any negotiation with the state. Indigenous peoples find themselves at a disadvantage at the negotiation table because they must seek the state's acquiescence allowing some sort of equivalence between the two parties.

Indigenous peoples universally experience cultural violence. The values, mores, and beliefs of indigenous peoples stand in juxtaposition to those values, mores and beliefs inherent to the modern state. Indigenous peoples may imbue land with cultural significance well beyond the commodity value of land, as discussed in Spike Boydell's chapter on 'The 'Pacific Way':

222 Alan C. Tidwell and Barry Scott Zellen

Customary Land Use, Indigenous Values and Globalization in the South Pacific', which describes how indigenous peoples of the South Pacific value their lands based upon principles of customary land tenure quite distinct from the modern state, which embeds concepts of land title in neoclassical economic theory. This is, much as Debra Wilson has observed among New Zealand's indigenous Maoris in her chapter, 'Satisfying Honour? The Role of the Waitangi Tribunal in Addressing Land-Related Treaty Grievances in New Zealand', which chronicles the recent transformation in indigenous relations with the state as the state's policies toward indigenous peoples have warmed, becoming more inclusive and less oppressive than earlier in history, with a recent – and increasing – recognition of the Treaty of Waitangi as New Zealand's founding document.

Similarly, Saleem H. Ali and Julia Keenan chronicle the emergence of a new environmental alignment between indigenous and non-indigenous peoples whose shared commitment to environmental stewardship presents much potential for what began as a sometimes 'awkward alliance' to evolve into a new pillar for indigenous peoples' relations with the state and the preservation of the ecological security of their homelands ('Awkward Alliances: Is environmentalism a bonding agent between indigenous and rural settler politics in America and Australia?'). They examine how the development of large extractive industrial projects has led to new alliances between indigenous groups and non-indigenous ranchers, groups which had previously not shared much in common. Something similar has been unfolding half a world away in the Tonle Sap Lake in Cambodia's interior, a hotly contested space marked by complex issues of resource governance where the biggest challenges to human and ecological security for the indigenous river- and water-based peoples – the 'neak tonle' – are primarily exogenous, relating to long-term land-cover change, water diversions, hydropower development, and climate change that will affect the duration, timing and reliability of wet and dry seasons, and the regulatory flood-pulse of the Mekong Basin, as described by Carl Grundy-Warr and Mak Sithirith in their chapter ('Threats and Challenges to the 'Floating Lives' of the Tonle Sap').

Cultural violence is more difficult for non-indigenous peoples to see, however. Physical violence is obvious, though often denied by the state. Structural violence, when one bothers to look, is often apparent. One may wonder, in 'blissful' ignorance, why indigenous peoples experience poverty when surrounded by a wealth of natural resources, and while residing within states that are blessed with high living standards and per capita incomes. A moment's thought, however, would shine a light on the inequitable structures that make poverty endemic. Cultural violence, on the other hand, is subtler. Cultural practices, languages, and histories vanish under state pressure. A striking example of cultural violence comes from Russia where Balzer observes claiming indigenous identity remains subject to bureaucratic tests and restrictions, never mind the views of the indigenous person. The same contest of cultural identity is played out around the world in both oppressive states and those deemed 'free'. One of the results of cultural violence is to diminish the voice of indigenous peoples. A diminished voice makes negotiation difficult. It is hard to explain one's needs and wants when the audience won't listen.

Periodically, however, indigenous peoples and the state find some common ground over property rights. The effect of that common ground is to temper the severity of the physical, structural and cultural violence. Sovereignty privileges the negotiating position of the state giving the Leviathan the upper hand. How that privilege is used, for good or ill, is determined by the relative power difference between the indigenous peoples and the state, as well as by the force of public opinion and the extent to which the state observes the rights of its citizens. Even in the most benign negotiations indigenous peoples find outcomes that are subsumed under the sovereignty and control of the state. More often than not, however, indigenous peoples struggle to win even the most meager of outcomes, and negotiate with a state that is far from committed to fair and just agreements.

Indigenous peoples have been comparatively more successful in their negotiations with the state when they find their voice to mobilize resources, followers and support. It should not be surprising that the places where indigenous peoples fair the best are those in which public opinion plays a central role in politics. The ultimate protection of indigenous rights may well be a constitutional one. In Canada and Australia discussions over amending their written constitutions, and increasingly recognizing and constitutionally protecting the unique status of indigenous peoples, mark the pinnacle in giving voice to their concerns, as noted by Coates and Poelzer, Zellen, Ali and Keenan, and Wilson in their respective chapters. In New Zealand accepting the Treaty of Waitangi's role as a foundational document would be equally important, as Wilson observes in her chapter. Of course, totalitarian, oligarchic or otherwise anti-democratic states are not particularly well known for their improved relations with indigenous populations. In these states, indigenous voices like so many other marginalized peoples, goes unheard and no public opinion can form to help support indigenous rights.

While finding an indigenous voice is critically important in negotiations with the state, some matters fall outside of the scope of formal negotiations and require much improvisation and initiative by state officials. Sovereignty, for example, is not typically on the table. Only when the state views indigenous autonomy to be in the state's interest is it acceded to, as Zellen described in his chapter examining the historic case of Nunavut. Barely occupying its own far northern territories, Ottawa relies upon Nunavut to help cement state sovereignty by offering the Inuit autonomy – only a sovereign state can bestow autonomy but only the indigenous peoples can bestow legitimacy upon the sovereign in unsettled frontier regions. Canada has thus, in a sense, shared the land with the Inuit. In a similar way some indigenous groups have shared land with other indigenous groups. The Arab pastoralist indigenous groups of northern Darfur would often migrate to lands claimed by others.

Unlike the Canadian example, shared land has erupted into competition and violence in Sudan. Managing such shared land is a complex matter, as described by Unruh in his chapter. But change is possible, and ongoing. After inter-ethnic violence erupted during the 2007 presidential elections, which was rooted to a large degree in land disputes, Kenya adopted a new constitution, its first national land policy, and a series of land laws that provide a solid legal foundation through which indigenous rights could at last be recognized and protected, for the very first time in the region. In their chapter, 'Long Road to Justice: Addressing Indigenous Land Claims in Kenya', Darren Kew and Abra Lyman consider the case of the Maasai and Ogiek, and how Kenya's national and regional legal landscapes have changed in recent years – creating a new opportunity for these, and other similar conflicts across the region, to be amicably resolved.

Sometimes resolving such issues takes place in the absence of constitutional change of the sort experienced in Kenya in recent years. In Israel, progress continues to be made, as described by Avinoam Meir, Batya Roded and Arnon Ben-Israel in their chapter, 'Indigenous Rights, Grey Spacing and Roads: The Israeli Negev Bedouin and Planning Road 31', which considers the evolution of Israel's relationship with its Bedouin minority, which has manifested what the authors described as a 'non-formal crawling recognition' that show indications of an emergent recognition without either official formal and legal status.

Customary and native title certainly exists in the minds of indigenous peoples, but it often does not exist in either the laws or minds of those who govern states, and this is the challenge indigenous peoples have faced around the world, often at different times in history, depending on the particular indigenous rights policies and historical experiences of their state. The failure to effectively address shared title has often been the result of both a willful disregard, and an enduring historic myopia shaped by generations of state expansion onto native lands that only recently has awakened to the persistence and endurance of indigenous land rights and to a new spirit of multiculturalism that can strengthen the foundations of sovereignty itself.

The negotiation between the state and indigenous peoples is not often one where the parties sit around a table and hammer out an agreement based upon a mutuality of recognition and respect. More often than not, it is a negotiation characterized by a profound asymmetry of power, and the continuing collision of state power with traditional land use and occupancy in remote frontier regions. Historically, the state has set the rules for negotiation, determining the scope and nature of the negotiation, but increasingly, native leaders and activists have shown a tremendous tenacity and resilience, pushing to expand the scope and nature of what is possible – and it appears that native values are now enjoying a global ascendency as more and more states embrace their indigenous peoples and traditions with a newfound vigor that was notably absent during colonial times.

While indigenous peoples may desire the right to be masters of their own destiny, the state has until recent times had other plans – and it has taken a great deal of patience, energy, and innovation by native peoples around the world to persuade the state that indigenous interests and values are not incompatible with the sovereign prerogative of the state, but in fact are an essential part of effective and inclusive sovereignty – a lesson that many states now appear to recognize around the world, from the farthest north to the global south.

Reference

Galtung, J. (1969) 'Violence, Peace and Peace Research', *Journal of Peace Research*, 6:171.

Note

1   For Asia, a similar moment occurred even further back, in 334 BC, when Alexander 'the Great' crossed the Hellespont, throwing his spear into Asian territory proclaiming that he thus accepted Asia as his 'spear-won territory'.

Index